Apple® FORTRAN

Dr. George H. Blackwood is a retired Navy pilot and a former college professor with bachelor's, master's, education specialist, and D.D.S. degrees. He now devotes full time to writing.

Brian D. Blackwood has studied computer science and engineering at Michigan State Univesity, and has a B.S. degree in computer science from Lamar University. He is presently employed as a programmer at a large data processing center that services banks and financial institutions.

Apple® FORTRAN

(Detailed Language Instructions
Specifically for the Apple® Computer)

by Brian D. Blackwood and
George H. Blackwood

Howard W. Sams & Co., Inc.
4300 WEST 62ND ST. INDIANAPOLIS, INDIANA 46268 USA

FIRST EDITION
FIRST PRINTING — 1982

International Standard Book Number: 0-672-21911-5
Library of Congress Catalog Card Number: 81-86556

Edited by: *C. W. Moody*
Illustrated by: *R. E. Lund* and *Wm. D. Basham*

Printed in the United States of America.

Preface

This book is written for the beginning programmer using the FORTRAN language on the Apple computer. Specific details are given for the use of each keyword, column relationship of the FORTRAN language, program statements, edit descriptors, and block statements. The book gives a brief history of computers, the development of the FORTRAN language, an introduction to the Pascal operating system, and the use of FORTRAN on single- and multiple-disk drive systems.

Each new topic is presented in clear and concise details. There are numerous programs that use these details so all aspects of the language are presented. The details of the language are broken down to the simplest form, and from this form the details are incorporated into the programs. The programs range from the elementary level, to demonstrate how the specific details of the language are used, to an advanced level useful in the business and engineering world.

There are numerous illustrations that demonstrate the specific parts of the language. The text and illustrations are coordinated to make the learning process as easy as possible. Should there be a difference of interpretation between the text and an illustration, the information in the illustration is the best authority. The interpretation of text and semantics can vary when approached from different points of view. The interpretation of an illustration may give a better understanding than does the text.

Originally, FORTRAN was developed for use by the scientific and engineering professions. Business is now using FORTRAN more because the language has so many features that are useful in solving business problems. FORTRAN certainly has the necessary computational features for handling business problems, and it also has formatting flexibility to produce business reports. There are numerous tested and cataloged function and subroutine subprograms available.

This book deals primarily with the FORTRAN language and is not intended as a programming manual. The flowcharts of some programs are given to introduce the logic of programming, but the problem-solving aspect of programming is not emphasized.

The problem-solving aspect of programming involves five points — (1) the problem must be completely understood, (2) the problem can be solved by the programmer using a pencil and paper, (3) the different conditions and cases relating to the problem must be completely understood, (4) sufficient checks should be built into the program to prevent input data that is out of the legal range, and (5) the solution by the program must produce the correct results.

There is a story about the student who was complaining to his computer science professor about a failing grade on a program. The student said the program was beautifully written, well documented, and the printout was correctly formatted — only the output was incorrect. The professor replied, "I can get the wrong answer without writing a program."

BRIAN D. BLACKWOOD
GEORGE H. BLACKWOOD

Contents

CHAPTER 1
Introduction to Apple FORTRAN

The first electronic computers were developed around 1945 and 1946. The language used by these computers was in the binary (base-2) number system, and programs were very difficult to code and debug. In the period of 1951 to 1958, the UNIVAC computer was introduced and was programmed in machine language, which was assembled into binary. The machine language was easier to program because it used the hexadecimal (base-16) number system. In the period of 1958 to 1964, the batch-processing computers were introduced and they were programmed in assembly language. Assembly language is coded in mnemonics that resemble English words. Each higher level of language made communication between the computer and the programmer clearer and more understandable.

In 1954, John W. Backus at IBM began development of a FORTRAN compiler. The compiler translates FORTRAN source code into machine object code. FORTRAN and the FORTRAN compiler were further developed until the data-communications computers began using FORTRAN as a higher-level language for engineering and scientific purposes. FORTRAN was used with keypunched cards as the primary source of input to the computer.

The acronym *FORTRAN* stands for *FOR*mula *TRAN*slator. FORTRAN is a high-level problem-oriented language that can easily represent mathematical formulas. FORTRAN has great problem-solving capabilities for engineering and science, and the output is related to the problem. The output is not as "pretty" as it is when using other languages.

When the information-handling computers and the executive-aid computers were introduced, the computer terminal was used for input and output. With the use of the computer terminal as the primary source of input and output, keypunched cards were no longer necessary to input programs and data. FORTRAN was adapted for use with the terminal.

Apple FORTRAN is a subset, or dialect, of ANSI (American National Standards Institute) Standard FORTRAN, and is called Apple FORTRAN 77.

Although keypunched cards are not used with a terminal, FORTRAN programs are coded according to the columns on Hollerith (or IBM) cards. Each segment of the program statement must begin and end in the proper card column. For this reason, the relationship between Hollerith cards and the computer terminal is very important and will be referenced frequently.

Since cards are not used for the program or the input of data into the program, the data input into terminal-generated programs is entirely different.

There are three ways to input data into a terminal-generated program — (1) the data is placed in data statements within the program, (2) the data can be input from the keyboard into a compiled and linked program and produce output while the program is being executed, and (3) the data can be input from files on magnetic disks to produce output while the program is running.

The greatest change from using FORTRAN with keypunched cards and FORTRAN on a terminal is with the READ and DATA statements. The other aspects of FORTRAN on cards and FORTRAN on the terminal of the Apple microcomputer are very similar.

Integer BASIC and Applesoft use an interpreter to convert program statements into machine code during the live execution of the program. The program statements are translated by subroutines contained in read-only memory (ROM) into machine-code instructions. The interpreted statements are immediately used to run the program and to process data and information.

FORTRAN uses a compiler to convert source (initial) coded statements into machine-language object (final) code. The compiled source statements are called object code, and the object code is read and acted on by the computer.

For a source program to run, the computer must first translate each source-code language statement into its machine-code equivalent. The computer must also incorporate into the object program any library subroutines requested by the programmer and required by the computer. In addition, the program must be supplied with interconnecting links between different parts of the program.

A compiled program runs faster than an interpreted program; however, errors are more difficult to change and correct on a compiled program.

Each FORTRAN compiler is written for a specific computer and must convert the source-code program into object code for the specific computer. FORTRAN source programs are generally independent of the computer on which they will run, as long as the syntax between the language and the compiler is compatible. Many of the FORTRAN programs in this book were originally written to be run on a Honeywell 6000, and only a few changes were needed to make the programs execute on the Apple computer.

Source statements are written by the programmer to be converted to machine code by the compiler and linked to the system library so the program can execute.

Each FORTRAN statement is classified as executable or nonexecutable. An executable statement generates machine-code instructions that are executed by the computer. Nonexecutable statements are those statements that specify instructions to the compiler, and do not generate machine code or comments.

SOURCE STATEMENTS

There are seven types of source statements used in FORTRAN.

Executable Statements

1. *Input/Output Statements* — These statements are used to control input and output devices and to transfer data and information between memory and input and output devices. READ and WRITE statements are examples of executable input and output statements.

2. *Assignment Statements* — Assignment statements assign a value to a storage location. The equals sign (=) following a variable assigns the value on the right side of the equals sign to the variable on the left side. The equals sign is used to provide the formulas needed for solution of problems, but has a different computer evaluation than in the mathematical usage.

3. *Logical and Control Statements* — These statements are used to control the order of execution of the program statements, and to terminate the execution of the program. Such statements include ELSE, ELSEIF, IF, GOTO, STOP, END, DO, and CONTINUE.

4. *Subprogram Statements* — These statements are used to execute subprograms, FUNCTION and SUBROUTINE, and to return from the subprograms. Such statements include CALL and RETURN.

Nonexecutable Statements

5. *FORMAT Statements* — These statements are used to shape the input and output statements, and control the location, form, and type in which data appears in the input and output. The keyword FORMAT appears at the beginning of each statement.

6. *Specification Statements* — These statements provide the FORTRAN compiler with information that is needed when the program is compiled. Specification statements initialize storage location to specified values, describe the limits of certain storage locations, establish array address locations, and supply other data and information about the program. Keywords include COMMON, DATA, DIMENSION, EQUIVALENCE, INTEGER, LOGICAL, and REAL.

7. *Subprogram Statements* — These statements include the FUNCTION and SUBROUTINE statements.

Fig. 1-1 is a FORTRAN program to show some of the types of executable and nonexecutable source statements.

A FORTRAN program consists of a series of FORTRAN statements (Figs. 1-1 and 1-2). FORTRAN statements are comprised of different elements that must conform to a consistent pattern for the program to be compiled and

```
C234567                                        Comment statement         (1)
      PROGRAM SUM3                             Program statement         (1)
      DIMENSION SCORE (5)                      Specification statement   (1)
      DATA SCORE/89.,75.,100.,69.,47./         Data input into program
      SUM = 0.                                 Assignment statement      (2)
      DO 20 J = 1,5                            Control statement         (2)
      SUM = SUM + SCORE(J)                     Assignment statement      (2)
 20   CONTINUE                                 Control statement         (2)
      WRITE (0,50) SUM                         Output statement          (2)
 50   FORMAT (1X,//,' SUM = ',F10.0//)         FORMAT statement          (1)
      AVG = SUM/5.                             Assignment statement      (2)
      WRITE (0,60) AVG                         Output statement          (2)
 60   FORMAT (1X,' AVERAGE = ',F10.2,//)       FORMAT statement          (1)
      STOP                                     Control statement         (2)
      END                                      Specification statement   (1)
```

(1) Nonexecutable statement
(2) Executable statement

Fig. 1-1. FORTRAN statements.

executed. Any element that does not conform to the language standard causes a compile error, or run-time error.

Fig. 1-2A shows how data is placed into a FORTRAN variable. The keyword DATA is the beginning of the statement and is followed by the array variable (SCORE). A slash separator indicates that the values between the beginning and ending slashes are related to the array (SCORE), and conform to the dimension statement, DIMENSION SCORE (5). The numbers are reals, as indicated by the decimal following each number. Each real is separated by a comma (carriage return) to indicate the end of the value, and the last slash indicates the end of the list.

Fig. 1-2B shows an assignment statement. The values of the array SCORE are to be summed and assigned to the variable SUM. To make sure the first value in the address location SUM is zero, the variable SUM is initialized to zero.

The statement in Fig. 1-2C is the head of a loop control statement. The values in the loop must be integers and must relate to an integer loop variable. The value 20 in the DO loop statement relates to statement number 20, CONTINUE, which is the foot of the loop control statement (Fig. 1-2D).

Fig. 1-2E is a statement that outputs the value held in the address location AVG. This WRITE statement is written to the CRT (0 is the CRT), and uses the statement numbered 60 to format the output.

Fig. 1-2F is a FORMAT statement that prints AVERAGE = on the screen, and the AVG value is placed in a floating point (F) field that has 10 places in the total field width, and 2 places (F10.2) after the decimal point.

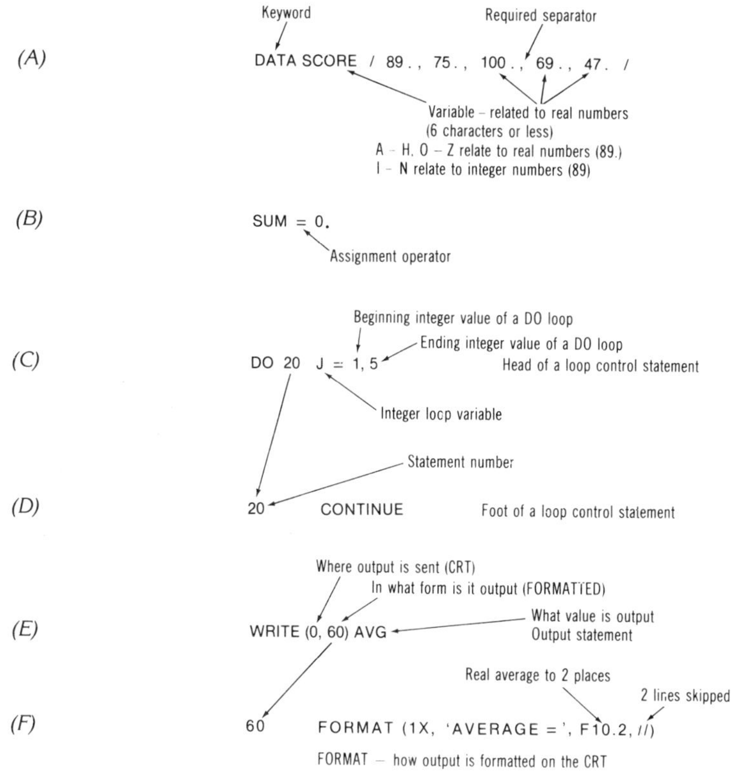

Fig. 1-2. FORTRAN source statements.

ELEMENTS OF THE FORTRAN LANGUAGE

The following elements are used to construct FORTRAN program source statements:

1. Character set — a set of characters forming the FORTRAN language, and a subset of FORTRAN 77. The FORTRAN character set is the same as the *ASCII* (*A*merican *S*tandard *C*ode for *I*nformation *I*nterchange) character set (Table 1-1). The character set is generally thought of as the 26 upper-case alphabetic characters, the 10 numeric characters, and 11 special characters.
2. Keywords, or FORTRAN words (Table 1-2), denote specific actions or operations to be performed by the computer during the execution of the FORTRAN statement. In Apple FORTRAN, keywords can also be used as variables, or identifiers, as long as they do not exceed six characters in length. Some FORTRAN keywords exceed the six-character rule — BACKSPACE, CHARACTER, DIMENSION, ENDFILE, EQUIVALENCE, EXTERNAL, FUNCTION, IMPLICIT, LOGICAL, PROGRAM, and SUBROUTINE. A keyword must be spelled

Table 1-1. ASCII Character Codes

Code		Char	Code		Char	Code		Char	Code		Char
Dec	Hex		Dec	Hex		Dec	Hex		Dec	Hex	
0	00	NUL	32	20	SP	64	40	@	96	60	`
1	01	SOH	33	21	!	65	41	A	97	61	a
2	02	STX	34	22	''	66	42	B	98	62	b
3	03	ETX	35	23	#	67	43	C	99	63	c
4	04	EOT	36	24	$	68	44	D	100	64	d
5	05	ENQ	37	25	%	69	45	E	101	65	e
6	06	ACK	38	26	&	70	46	F	102	66	f
7	07	BEL	39	27	'	71	47	G	103	67	g
8	08	BS	40	28	(	72	48	H	104	68	h
9	09	HT	41	29	)	73	49	I	105	69	i
10	0A	LF	42	2A	*	74	4A	J	106	6A	j
11	0B	VT	43	2B	+	75	4B	K	107	6B	k
12	0C	FF	44	2C	,	76	4C	L	108	6C	l
13	0D	CR	45	2D	-	77	4D	M	109	6D	m
14	0E	SO	46	2E	.	78	4E	N	110	6E	n
15	0F	SI	47	2F	/	79	4F	O	111	6F	o
16	10	DLE	48	30	0	80	50	P	112	70	p
17	11	DC1	49	31	1	81	51	Q	113	71	q
18	12	DC2	50	32	2	82	52	R	114	72	r
19	13	DC3	51	33	3	83	53	S	115	73	s
20	14	DC4	52	34	4	84	54	T	116	74	t
21	15	NAK	53	35	5	85	55	U	117	75	u
22	16	SYN	54	36	6	86	56	V	118	76	v
23	17	ETB	55	37	7	87	57	W	119	77	w
24	18	CAN	56	38	8	88	58	X	120	78	x
25	19	EM	57	39	9	89	59	Y	121	79	y
26	1A	SUB	58	3A	:	90	5A	Z	122	7A	z
27	1B	ESC	59	3B	;	91	5B	[	123	7B	{
28	1C	FS	60	3C	<	92	5C	\	124	7C	¦
29	1D	GS	61	3D	=	93	5D	]	125	7D	}
30	1E	RS	62	3E	>	94	5E	∧	126	7E	~
31	1F	US	63	3F	?	95	5F	_	127	7F	DEL

exactly as in Table 1-2 or a syntax error will be generated and the program will not execute. Blanks within keywords do not cause compile errors. Some keywords are more readable with imbedded blanks, such as ELSE IF, GO TO, and END FILE.

3. Constants, or numbers, are items of data that remain unchanged within the program. A numeric constant may be signed (+ or −) or unsigned. If no sign is used, the number is assigned a positive value by the computer. There are two types of constants used in FORTRAN — *integer constants* and *real constants.*

   A. An integer constant (Table 1-3) is a whole number and does not contain a decimal point. The integer constant must be in the range of −32768 to +32767 for the Apple computer. The positive sign

Table 1-2. Apple FORTRAN Keywords

ASSIGN	BACKSPACE	CALL
CHARACTER	COMMON	CONTINUE
DATA	DIMENSION	DO
ELSE	ELSE IF	END
END IF	ENDFILE	EQUIVALENCE
EXTERNAL	FORMAT	FUNCTION
GOTO	IF	IMPLICIT
INTEGER	INTRINSIC	LOGICAL
OPEN	PAUSE	PROGRAM
READ	REAL	RETURN
REWIND	SAVE	STOP
SUBROUTINE	WRITE	

is optional for the positive integer constant, but the negative sign is mandatory for the negative integer constant. The zero requires no sign as it is not referred to as either positive or negative.

Integer constants (Table 1-3) are referred to as *fixed-point* numbers. The unwritten decimal point is to the right of the last number of the constant. Integer constants are used as counting numbers to be used to set aside memory locations when dimensioning arrays, and in loops. Since integer constants are fixed-point numbers used in counting, no fractional values are produced when adding, subtracting, multiplying, dividing, or raising integers to a power. In mathematical operations, integers are truncated (fractional digits are supressed or dropped) toward the zero value. Positive integers are truncated down toward zero, and negative integers are truncated up toward zero. An integer constant always implies there is no fractional part of a number associated with the number.

B. Real constants (Table 1-3) are numbers that contain a decimal point, in deference to integer constants that do not contain a decimal point. Real constants are the whole numbers and decimal fractions used in daily living. Real constants are called *floating-point* numbers since the decimal point can be moved to give greater accuracy or precision. The real constants are used when measuring the size of objects, or distances from one point to another.

4. A variable is a symbolic reference to an address location that holds a specific value. In FORTRAN, a variable name (Table 1-4) is composed of up to six characters. The first character must be an alphabetic character, and the other five characters may be alphabetic or numeric characters. No special characters may be used within the variable name. A variable name over six characters long will cause compile-time error message #14, IDENTIFIER TOO LONG, to be printed on the CRT. Variables may be used as symbolic names to aid the program-

Table 1-3. Integer and Real Constants

Legal Integer Constants Range (−32768 to +32767)		Legal Real Constants Range (−1.7 E+38 to 5.8 E−39) (−5.8 E−39 to 1.7 E+38)	
478		478.31	
0		0.00	
+10		+10.00	
−100		−100.00	
32766		7.8 E 21	
Illegal Integer Constants		**Illegal Real Constants**	
3.1416	Contains a decimal point	31416	Contains no decimal point
33851	Exceeds largest value	1.7 E+51	Exceeds largest value
100−	Sign must precede	100.+	Sign must precede
100,000	Contains a special character	100,000.	Contains a special character

mer. HOURS is a symbolic name that has meaning when computing total pay in a program statement:

```
TOTPAY = HOURS * RATEOP
```

In some languages that allow only two characters per variable, it is difficult to keep track of what a variable name means, or to what it refers.

FORTRAN has two types of variables — *integer variables* and *real variables.*

A. Integer variables (Table 1-4) begin with the letters I through N and should relate to the integer constants (I = 5). A convenient way to remember the I through N rule is to relate to the first two letters in the word INteger to I–N. The use of integer variable names and real constants (I = 5.), called mixed mode, is to be avoided in most cases. One method to avoid the mixed mode and to use symbolic names is to begin the symbolic names with an integer character, and use integer constants in the computation:

   ```
   ITOTPY = JHOURS * KRATE
   ```

   Every different legal combination of alphabetic and numeric characters represents a different integer variable to the compiler. JHOUR and JHOURS are two different integer variables.

B. Real variables (Table 1-4) begin with the letters A through H and O through Z. They represent floating-point numbers, which include a fractional value. The fractional part of the real number may be a zero, but the capability is there to contain the fractional part of the number. Special care must be taken to avoid the mixed mode between real variables and integer constants, as this will cause compile (logical) errors, and the program will probably not execute. If the program does execute, run-time computational errors will occur.

```
TOTPAY = RATE * HOURS
TOTPAY = 5.90 * 40.0
```

Every different legal combination of alphabetic and numeric characters is a different real variable. RATE and RATES are two different real variables.

Table 1-4. FORTRAN Variable Names

Legal Integer Variables (Integer variables are denoted by the letters "I" through "N")	Legal Real Variables (Real variables are denoted by the letters "A" through "H" and "O" through "Z")
INT123 JSUM KRATE L123 M N2	COST DAYS HOURS PRICE R530 X
Illegal Integer Variables	**Illegal Real Variables**
INTEGER — 7 Characters J*SUM — Special character K,RATE — Special character SUM — Real variable 9L123 — Begins with a numeric character	ASSIGNMENT — 10 Characters B-SUM — Special character X+RATE — Special character MONEY — Integer variable 8ZEBRA — Begins with a numeric character

C. When a variable is used in a program, that variable is assigned a memory location that can hold a value. Memory locations are similar to mailboxes in the postoffice. Each mailbox that is rented has a person's name assigned to that mailbox. As different people rent the mailbox, the variable name is changed. In Fig. 1-1, SUM was assigned a memory location. The value assigned to this memory location was zero, because the value of the first five test scores were to be summed and placed in the address location. If the initial value had been anything but zero, the final summation would be incorrect. Table 1-5 shows the six changes in the address location whose name is SUM. The first example shows SUM initialized to zero, and the last example shows the SUM address location when the five scores have been summed. Table 1-5 also shows the five test grades stored in the DIMENSION SCORE (5) memory locations.

5. An identifier is a label given to a program, subprogram, function, or array. Identifiers (Table 1-6) are composed of a maximum of six alphanumeric characters in length, and must begin with an alphabetic character. An identifier beginning with a numeric or special character

Table 1-5. Address Locations for SUM and SCORE

	SUM*	SCORE†
1	0.	89.
2	89.	75.
3	164.	100.
4	264.	69.
5	333.	47.
6	380.	

*SUM has only one address location, and as each number is summed the value is stored in the address location assigned to SUM.

†SCORE has five address locations.

will cause a compile-time error when the program is compiled. The identifiers associated with CALL, FUNCTION, PROGRAM, and SUBROUTINE do not invoke the integer (I–N) or real (A–H, O–Z) rule. The identifiers associated with these keywords are not related to the integer constant, integer variable, real constant, and real variable rule.

The identifiers associated with arrays do invoke the integer and real rule; however, the real identifier operates in the mixed mode. The real array identifier, DIMENSION ARRAY (5), uses an integer constant to establish the memory locations. The real array identifier uses an integer variable, ARRAY (J), as the subscript when processing in a loop.

Table 1-6. Identifiers

Legal Identifiers	Illegal Identifiers
PROGRAM MINMAX CALL S583 Y = FUNCT(X,Y) FUNCTION (A,B)	PROGRAM MINMAX3 — 7 Characters CALL 45 SORT — Numbers precede Y = FUN,FUN(X,Y) — Special character FUNCTION (A,B — No closing parenthesis
(Program, function, and subroutine identifiers do not follow the integer (I–N) or real (A–H, O–Z) rule)	
Legal Array Integer Identifiers	**Legal Array Real Identifiers**
INCOME (5) MONEY (10, 20)	ARRAY (5) DOUBAR (10, 20)
Illegal Array Integer Identifiers	**Illegal Array Real Identifiers**
INCOME10X (5) — 9 Characters MON,EY (10, 20) — Special character ARRAY (5) — Real identifier	ARRAY45 (5) — 7 Characters DOU-AR (10, 20) — Special character INCOME (5) — Integer identifier
(Array identifiers do follow the integer and real rule)	

6. An operator is a character which designates a different operation. An operator defines the action to be taken on the operand to obtain a result.

   In FORTRAN, there are four types of operators — (1) arithmetic operators, (2) assignment or replacement operators, (3) relational operators, and (4) logical operators.

   A. Arithmetic operators (Table 1-7) are represented by symbols that are commonly used in algebraic equations. In algebra the symbols are optional, but in converting algebraic expressions to FORTRAN code the symbols are mandatory. If the symbols are not used, a compile-time error will occur. The only arithmetic operator (Table 1-7) that might be unfamiliar is the double multiplication symbol for exponentiation.

```
EXPONT = 4.**2
```

   In algebra, exponentiation is represented as a superscript of a number. In the BASIC language, exponentiation is represented as an up arrow (↑), a tilde (~), or a "house top" (∧).

   The arithmetic operators may be used with constants, variables, integers, or reals.

```
JSUM = KPRINC + INTRST
JSUM = 400 - 200
SUM = PRINCP * XINST
SUM = 400.00/200.00
```

   Precedence is the order in which operations occur. The precedence (Table 1-7) of arithmetic operators used in FORTRAN is (1) exponentiation, (2) multiplication and division from left to right as the formula is processed by the computer, and (3) addition and subtraction from left to right as the formula is processed by the computer.

   In many arithmetic operations, numbers must be added and/or subtracted before they are multiplied and/or divided. When a number must be added and/or subtracted before it is multiplied and/or divided, precedence must be overcome, or changed.

   The method to overcome precedence is to use parentheses around the operation that is to be performed first (Table 1-8).

   B. An assignment operator is an equals sign. It is used to assign (store) the resulting value on the right side of an algebraic expression to the variable on the left side of the equals sign.

```
SUM = 0.
SUM = SUM + SCORE (J)
```

   The assignment operator (=) should not be confused with the algebraic definition of "equals." In algebra, the value on the right side of the equals sign is the same as the value on the left side of

Table 1-7. Arithmetic Operators and Their Precedence of Action

Symbol	Name	Precedence
**	Exponentiation	1st
–	Unary Minus Sign (Algebraic negation of a value.)	2nd
* and /	Multiplication and Division	3rd (Equal precedence from left to right.)
+ and –	Addition and Subtraction	4th (Equal precedence from left to right.)
( )	Parentheses	Precedence can be overcome by the use of parentheses. The action within the parentheses takes 1st precedence over any other action.

Table 1-8. Parentheses to Alter Precedence

LENGTH = XSIDE (20)
WIDTH = XSIDE – 5

Incorrect answer without parentheses:

AREA = XSIDE * XSIDE – 5
AREA = 395

Correct answer with parentheses:

AREA = XSIDE * (XSIDE – 5)
AREA = 300

1st. Five (5) is subtracted from XSIDE because of the parentheses.
2nd. XSIDE is multiplied from (XSIDE – 5).
3rd. The total value of 300 is assigned to the variable AREA.

the equals sign. In computers, the value on the right side of the equals sign is assigned, stored, or transferred to the variable on the left side of the equals sign. To phrase it another way, the value in the variable on the left side of the equals sign is replaced by the value on the right side of the equals sign. Assignment operators and replacement operators are used synonymously.

C. Relational operators are operators that are used to compare values of two arithmetic expressions, or two alphanumeric character expressions (Table 1-9).

When relational operators are used to compare two values, the result is either true (1) or false (0). The relational operators are used in decision statements to test conditions that occur within a program.

Table 1-9. Relational Operators

Relational Operator	Comparison A to B	Expression
.LT.	less than	IF (A .LT. B) GOTO 10
.LE.	less than or equal to	IF (A .LE. B) A = B
.EQ.	equal to	IF (A .EQ. B) RETURN
.NE.	not equal to	IF (A .NE. B) STOP
.GT.	greater than	IF (A .GT. B) B = A
.GE.	greater than or equal to	IF (A .GE. B) KOUNT = KOUNT + 1

```
      A = 10.
      B = 5.
      IF (A .GE. B) STOP
      B = B - A
      WRITE (0,50) B
   50 FORMAT (1X,'B = ',F5.0)
```

In the program example, the IF statement tests to determine if A is greater than or equal to B. If A is greater than or equal to B, the program stops. If A is less than B, the program defaults to subtract A from B and writes the value of B.

Relational operators will be discussed in greater detail with decision statements.

D. Logical operators are expressions that compare two or more conditions by using relational operators (Table 1-10). The uses of logical operators in the logical IF statements are complex operations. The logical operator makes programming easier and more flexible.

Table 1-10. Logical Operators

Logical Operator	Precedence	Comparison
.NOT.	1st	IF (.NOT. K .EQ. 2) GOTO 99
.AND.	2nd	IF (A .GT. B .AND. C .LE. D) STOP
.OR.	3rd	IF (A .LE. B .OR. C .GT. D) RETURN

IF (.NOT. K .EQ. 2) GOTO 99 (NOT reverses the logic.)

IF (A .GT. B .AND. C .LE. D) STOP (For the statement to be logically true, both conditions must be true. If either condition is false, the statement is false.)

IF (A .LE. B .OR. C .GT. D) RETURN (If either condition is true, the statement is true. Logically, for the statement to be false, both conditions must be false.)

Table 1-11 shows the order of precedence of the arithmetic, relational, and logical operators.

Table 1-11. Precedence of Operators

Operator	Precedence
Arithmetic	1st
Relational	2nd
Logical	3rd

THIS CHAPTER IS A REFERENCE LIBRARY

This chapter contains a great deal of information relating to FORTRAN programming. It was written to be a quick reference to the peripheral details of FORTRAN. Many times, the details necessary to understanding a certain relationship are scattered throughout a book. I hope the concentrated library will aid in your understanding of the language.

CHAPTER 2
Essential Rules of FORTRAN

FORTRAN is a column-oriented language. As originally developed, FORTRAN was punched into 80-column Hollerith (IBM) cards. These cards were encoded with program and data statements by means of a keypunch machine. The holes, punched in the card, represented alphanumeric data and special characters, and were punched in specific columns on the card. When FORTRAN was developed to be used with computer terminals, the column relationship between punched cards and the CRT was retained. The FORTRAN program must be typed from the keyboard onto the CRT using a specific column format for the program to be properly compiled.

SCREEN COLUMNS FOR INPUTTING FORTRAN

The 80-column Hollerith card (Fig. 2-1) and CRT utilize the first 72 columns on the card for program information, as follows:

Column 1	Comment only.
Columns 1–5	Statement number.
Column 6	Continuation.
Columns 7–72	FORTRAN statement.
Columns 73–80	Ignored by the computer.

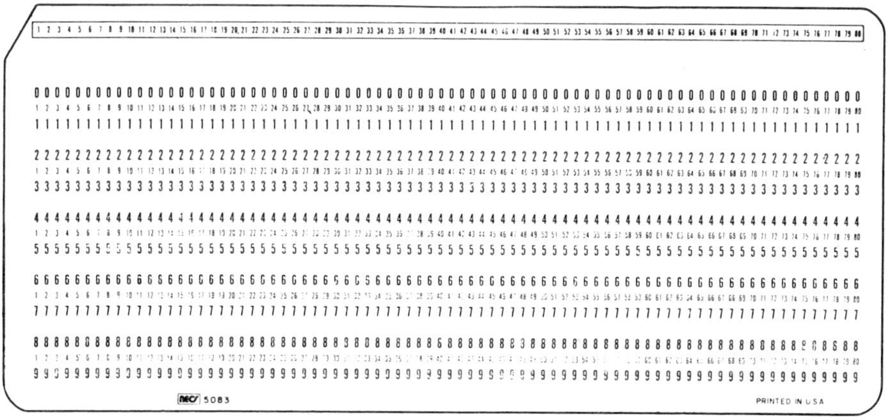

Fig. 2-1. A Hollerith (IBM) card.

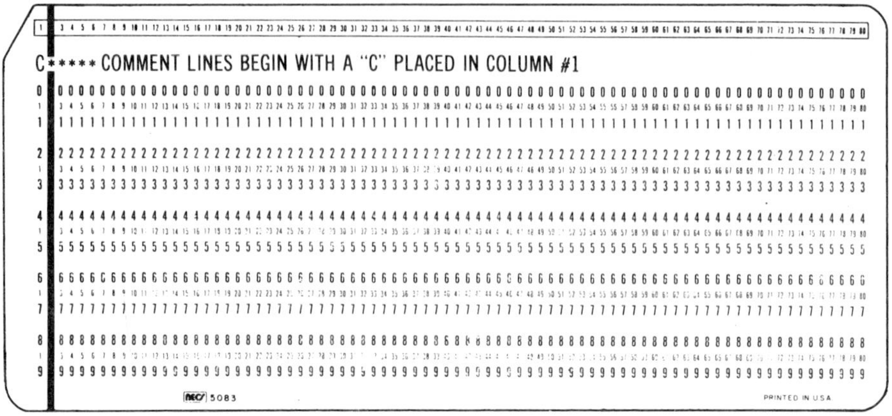

Fig. 2-2. Comment lines.

A comment line (Fig. 2-2) in Apple FORTRAN explains details of the program, or sets up the columns on the screen for easier programming. An upper-case "C," a lower-case "c," or an asterisk in column 1 on the screen designates a comment line. Comment lines must be followed immediately by other comment lines or program lines. Comment lines do not have continuation lines; only executable statements have continuation lines. Comment information is coded in columns 2 through 80 on the screen. There are no limits to the number of comment lines in a program. Comment lines should be used freely to document the problem and solution to the problem. Some computer authorities suggest one line of comment for each two lines of code. Even though symbolic variables are used in FORTRAN, programs need complete documentation for easy and long-term understanding.

Comment lines are not processed by the FORTRAN compiler. The comment lines are simply printed in the text file. Any special character may be included in a comment line. Comment lines may be placed anywhere in the program, except between continuation lines.

One way to align the column count on the screen is to use the comment line, C234567. This comment line may be inserted within the program to line up the elements of the program in the proper column (Fig. 2-3).

A statement number, or statement label, is a sequence of from one to five integer digits that occupy columns 1 through 5 on the CRT (Fig. 2-4). The statement label may be placed anywhere in columns 1 through 5. It is common to left-justify statement labels (begin in column 1), but it is more readable to right-justify them (end in column 5). The statement label serves as a label or tag with which to refer to a program statement. Not all FORTRAN statements have statement numbers. Only those statements that have a relationship with another statement need a statement number. Each Applesoft statement needs a line number (statement number), but relatively few

```
C*****FORTRAN PROGRAM TO SELECT THE MAX AND MIN NUMBERS
C*****FROM A LIST OF NUMBERS
C234567
      PROGRAM MINMAX
      DIMENSION X( 5 )
      DATA X( 1 ),X( 2 ),X( 3 ),X( 4 ),X( 5 )/5.,-5.,10.,3.,2./
      LIMIT = 5
      XMAX = X( 1 )
      XMIN = X( 1 )
      DO 20 J = 2, LIMIT
      IF ( X( J ) .GE. XMAX ) XMAX = X( J )
      IF ( X( J ) .LE. XMIN ) XMIN = X( J )
 20   CONTINUE
      WRITE ( 0, 100 ) XMAX, XMIN
100   FORMAT ( 1X,'THE LARGEST IS ',F5.0,
     *' AND SMALLEST IS ',F5.0 )
      STOP
      END
```

Fig. 2-3. Aligning the column count in a FORTRAN program by using the comment line, C234567.

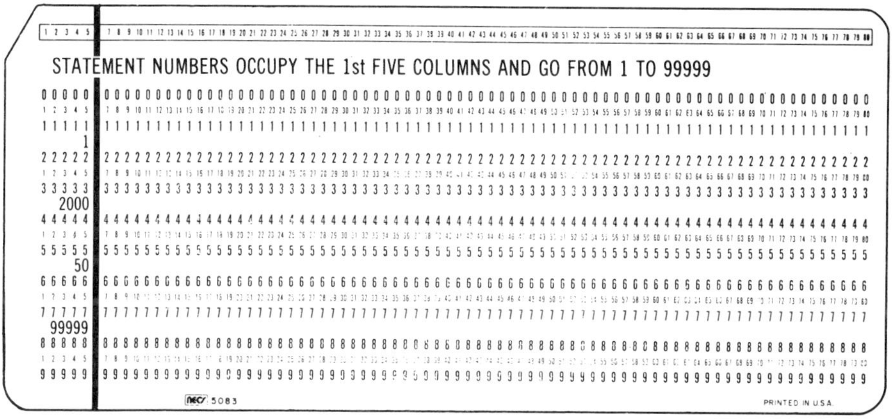

Fig. 2-4. Statement numbers.

FORTRAN statements have a statement number. However, all FORTRAN statements may have a statement number.

In FORTRAN, the main program and each subprogram is a separate entity. No two statement labels in the main program may be assigned the same number, or a compile error of ERROR IN LABEL will occur. The same statement label may be used once in the main program, and once in each subprogram, with no compile error.

Column 6 is reserved for the continuation of an executable statement (Fig. 2-5). Since FORTRAN statements may exceed 72 columns in length, a provision must be made to indicate that the succeeding lines are a continuation of the FORTRAN statement, and not a new statement.

A continuation line is any line that is not a comment line or a computer directive line. A continuation statement contains any character in column 6 (a blank may not be used), and there may be nine continuation lines per program statement. Statement labels are forbidden in continuation lines.

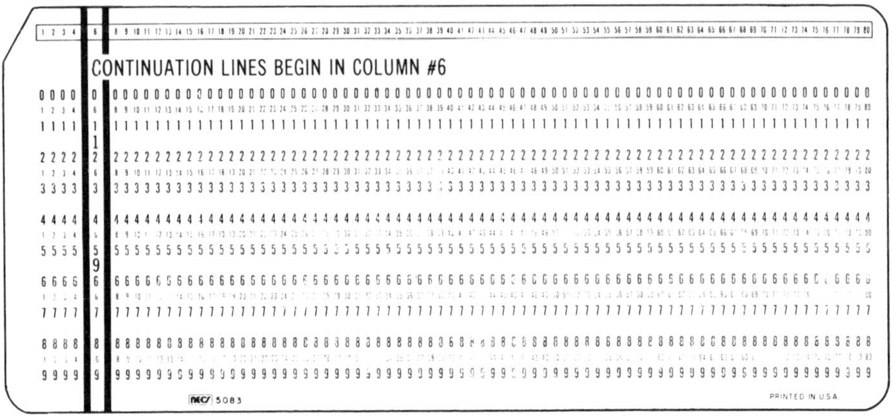

Fig. 2-5. Continuation lines.

An initial program line has a statement label in columns 1 through 5, a blank or zero in column 6, and FORTRAN text in columns 7 through 72.

The FORTRAN statement is placed in columns 7 through 72 (Fig. 2-6). The FORTRAN statement must not begin before column 7, but it can begin after column 7 with no compile error. The FORTRAN statement consists of an initial line, and may be followed by nine continuation lines. Blanks within the statement line are ignored.

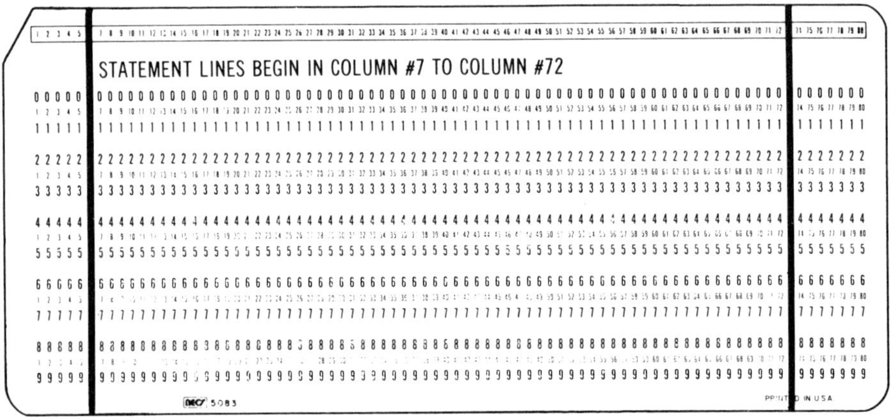

Fig. 2-6. Statement lines.

Columns 73 through 80 (Fig. 2-7) are used as program identification, or a line sequence number. These columns are ignored by the Apple FORTRAN compiler, and are of little use with a microcomputer using a terminal. When cards are used as input, columns 73 through 80 are important. Programs with 2000 cards in a deck need a program identification and a card sequence number. In a data processing center with many card decks and

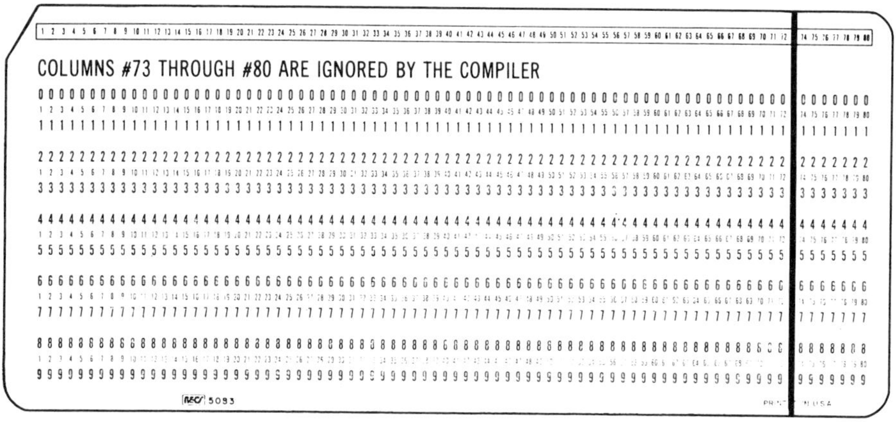

Fig. 2-7. Columns 73 through 80.

many programs, identification and card sequence are needed to keep order during hectic times. When 2000 cards are dropped and randomly scattered on the floor, the program identification and card sequence become very important.

The different parts of the FORTRAN statement must be in the proper beginning and ending column. This indicates a very ordered structure for the statements. This ordered structure also applies to the program itself. Each part of the program must be in the proper order, or the program will not execute.

FORTRAN PROGRAM STRUCTURE

The program structure (Fig. 2-8) contains the FORTRAN keywords in their proper order. Even though the keywords are not defined or explained at this point, they are presented to give the complete picture of the program structure.

I. Comment lines may be placed anywhere in the program, and follow the rule that a capital "C," a lower-case "c," or an asterisk, must be placed in column 1.

II. The program name, function name, or subroutine name, if present, must appear as the first line of the program unit (not including the comment line). The program name, or program identifier, is optional, but the function name, or identifier, and subroutine name, or identifier, are mandatory.

III. The FORMAT statement must appear after the program identifier, function subprogram, or subroutine subprogram statement, but after fulfilling this requirement, may appear anywhere in the program. Original procedure was to place all FORMAT statements at the beginning of the program so they could be debugged more

I. Comment lines can be placed anywhere in the program.
PROGRAM AND SUBPROGRAM STATEMENTS
II. Program Function Subroutine
III. Format statements must be placed after the program, function, and subroutine statements, but can be placed anywhere else in the program.
IV. Implicit statements
A. Implicit integer (I–N)
B. Implicit real (A–H, O–Z)
C. Implicit logical
D. Implicit character
V. Specification statements
A. Dimension
B. Common
C. External
D. Save
E. Intrinsic
F. Equivalence
VI. Data statements
VII. Functions
A. External
1. Integer function
2. Real function
3. Logical function
B. Intrinsic and transcendental
C. Statement function
D. Assignment statements
VIII. Executable statements
IX. Return and end statements

Fig. 2-8. FORTRAN program structure.

easily. This procedure is still common, but the FORMAT statements are often placed below the associated READ or WRITE statement.

IV. IMPLICIT statements allow the programmer to override the integer or real rule for determining variables and arrays by specifying that names beginning with certain letters be of a certain type of variable. The IMPLICIT statement must be the first statement in the program or subprogram unit. In Chapter 1, integer and real variables were allocated specific letters of the alphabet. The IMPLICIT statement enables the programmer to override the integer-real rule.

The IMPLICIT statement should be used judiciously, and sparingly. A program that has the normal integer and real variables changed by an IMPLICIT statement is more difficult to debug. The mind sets a lock on using I–N for integers and A–H, O–Z for reals, and a change in this pattern is difficult for the mind's eye to detect.

IMPLICIT can be used with the keywords INTEGER, LOGICAL, REAL, and CHARACTER.

```
IMPLICIT INTEGER (A–D, H)
IMPLICIT LOGICAL
IMPLICIT REAL (I–N)
IMPLICIT CHARACTER
```

V. Specification statements initialize storage locations with specified values, establish arrays, and supply other pertinent data about variables and conditions for the program. They control the type, size, initial value, and placement of variables within the program. The keywords used in specification statements are DIMENSION, COMMON, EXTERNAL, SAVE, INTRINSIC, and EQUIVALENCE.

VI. DATA statements tell the FORTRAN compiler to place certain values at the indicated variables when the program is compiled. When these data values are compiled with the program, they are more difficult to change than when the DATA statement is used with Applesoft. In FORTRAN, the program must be rewritten with the data values changed in the text version. The text must be compiled into code, and the code must be linked before the program can be executed.

VII. Functions (different from FUNCTION subprograms) may be constructed by the user, such as (1) statement functions, SUM(X,Y,Z) = X + Y + Z, or (2) they may be intrinsic functions, SIN (X), built into the computer.

A. If they are constructed functions, they may be either one-line constructed functions, FUNCT (A,B) = A**2 + B, or multiline functions that may compute the value of an unknown using several variables.

1. EXTERNAL is the FORTRAN word that permits the symbolic name in the subprogram to be passed as a parameter. EXTERNAL specifies to the compiler that the symbolic name is that of the subprogram, and not a variable, when it is passed as an argument in a parameter list.

2. Functions may be designated as either integer or real, in order to override the A–H, O–Z real variable rule, or the I–N integer variable rule. The function may also be designated as a logical function.

```
INTEGER FUNCTION ARRAY(J)
REAL FUNCTION MIN(K)
LOGICAL FUNCTION X, Y, Z
```

B. Intrinsic functions are functions that are built into the computer. In Apple FORTRAN, intrinsic functions are separated into two groups — (1) pure intrinsic functions and (2) transcendental functions. Transcendental functions are functions that return only real results.

Functions are called different names in different books, so the name must be defined explicitly. Some books refer to functions as external (in deference to the FORTRAN word EXTERNAL) and internal. Some books refer to Apple intrinsic functions as library functions used in business and scientific programs, and refer to Apple transcendental functions as a library of trigonometric functions. *Intrinsic functions are those functions built into the Apple computer and are nonmathematical, except for the square-root function. Transcendental functions deal with mathematical functions.*

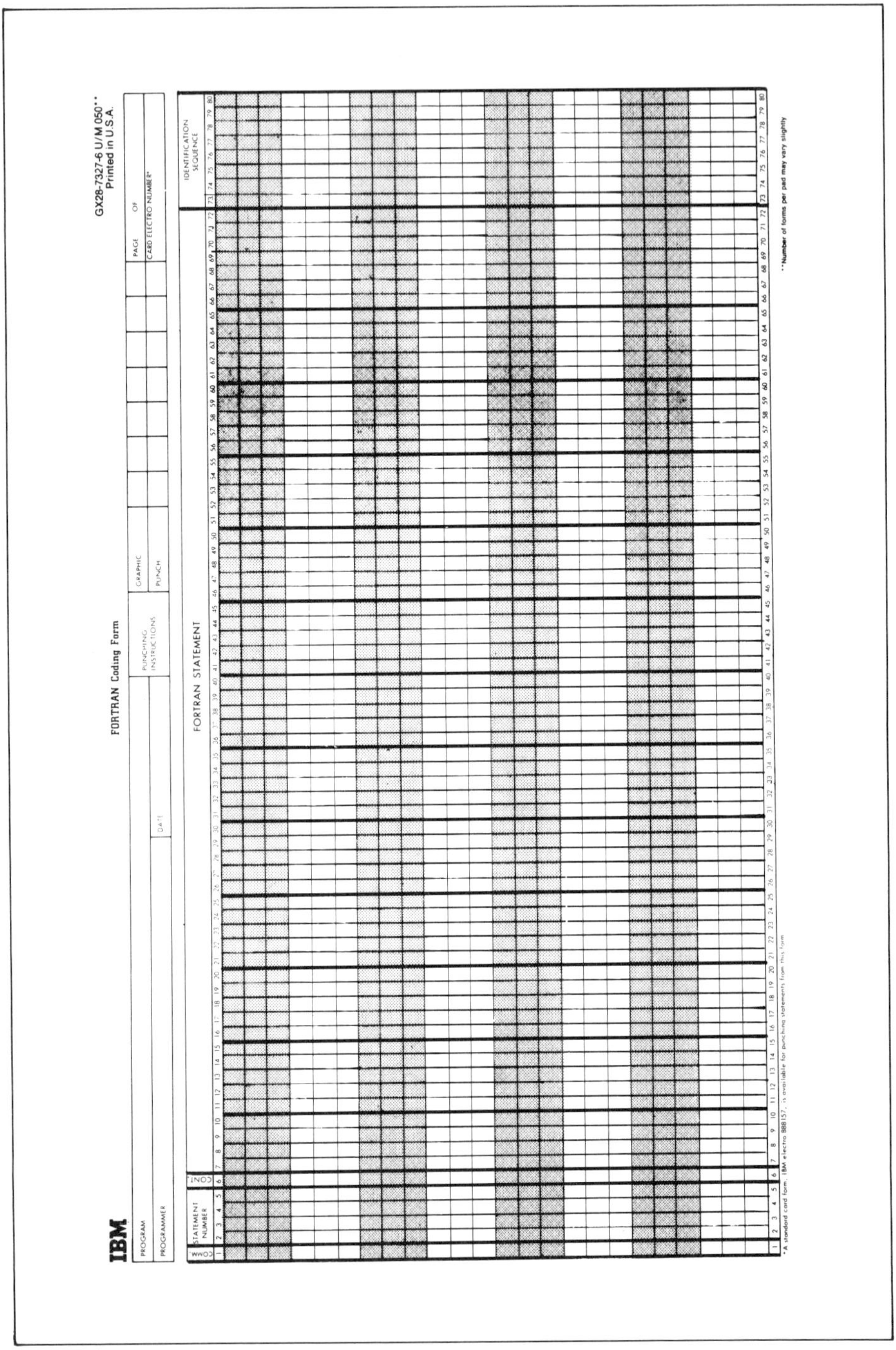

Fig. 2-9. FORTRAN coding form.

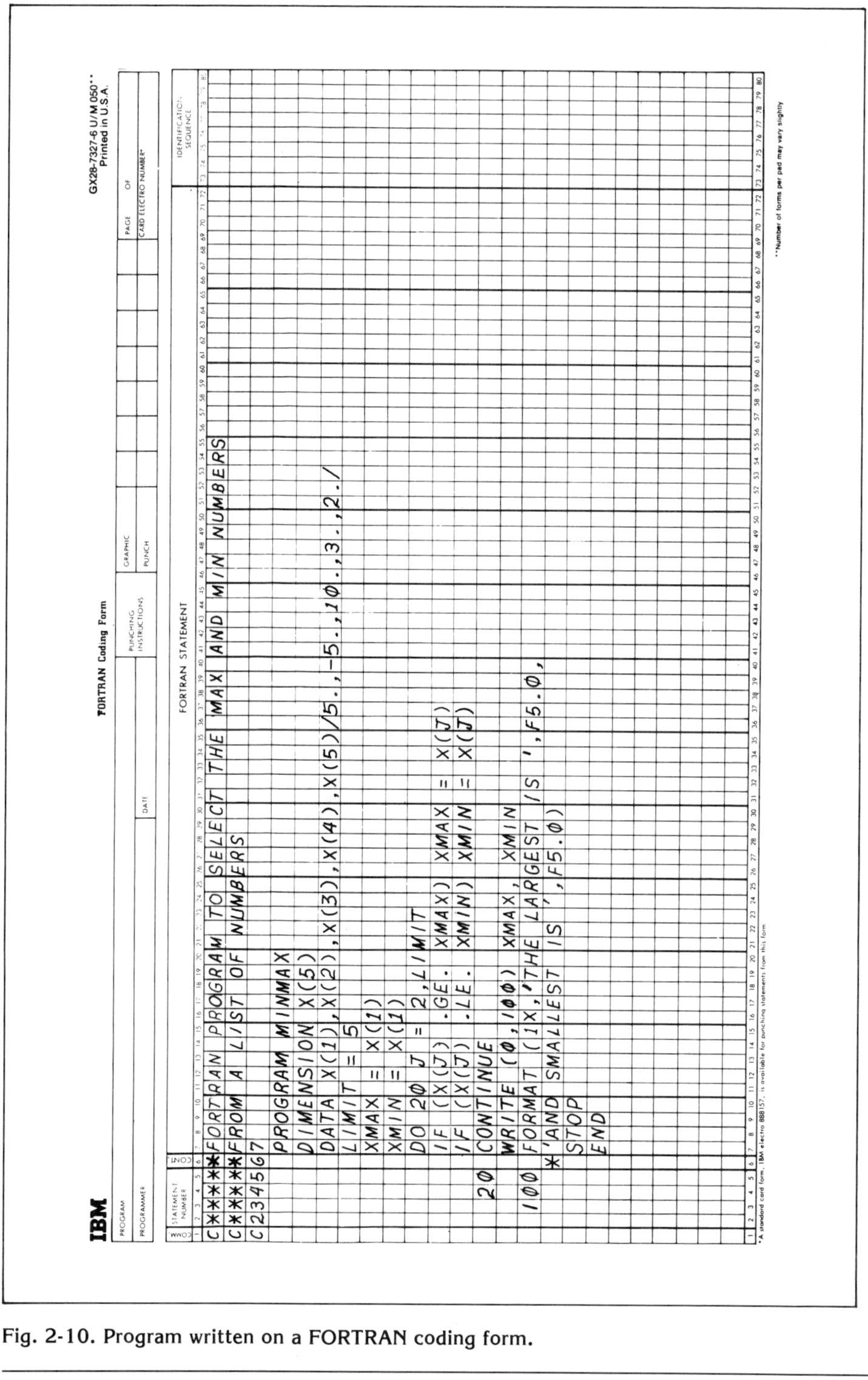


```
C****FORTRAN PROGRAM TO SELECT THE MAX AND MIN NUMBERS
C****FROM A LIST OF NUMBERS
C234567
      PROGRAM MINMAX
      DIMENSION X(5)
      DATA X(1),X(2),X(3),X(4),X(5)/5.,-5.,10.,3.,2./
      LIMIT = 5
      XMAX = X(1)
      XMIN = X(1)
      DO 20 J = 2,LIMIT
      IF (X(J) .GE. XMAX) XMAX = X(J)
      IF (X(J) .LE. XMIN) XMIN = X(J)
   20 CONTINUE
      WRITE (0,100) XMAX, XMIN
  100 FORMAT (1X,'THE LARGEST IS ',F5.0,
     *'AND SMALLEST IS ',F5.0)
      STOP
      END
```

Fig. 2-10. Program written on a FORTRAN coding form.

VIII. Executable statements are those statements that generate machine-code instructions that are executed by the compiler.

IX. The last class of statements in the program or subprogram group is RETURN and END. Each subprogram must have a RETURN and END statement. The main program must have an END statement. Some compilers require a STOP statement before an END statement in the main program, and many programs in this book have the optional STOP statement.

FORTRAN CODING

A FORTRAN program is generally coded on a special coding form (Fig. 2-9) that has the columns for each part of the statement laid out in the correct numerical position. Each column in the coding sheet represents the same relative position on the screen.

The FORTRAN program presented in Fig. 2-10 selects the largest and smallest value from a list of five real values. The program style demonstrates the use of correct programming procedures and statement configuration.

In coding FORTRAN, only capital letters are used. Special care should be taken to print each character legibly on the coding sheet so the program can be typed accurately from the keyboard. The old joke about not being able to read your own handwriting can waste time and cause aggravation. Certain letters are difficult to distinguish if not carefully written, such as zero (0) and "oh" (o), and "B" and eight (8). It is recommended that the distinction between similar characters be very clear, so you and the compiler have a common understanding of terminology.

Spaces may be included in FORTRAN statements to enhance readability. The compiler ignores spaces in FORTRAN statements, and reads the statement as if no blanks are present, except in literals and Hollerith editing. For readability, a FORTRAN statement should look like this:

```
IF (X(J) .GE. XMAX) XMAX = X(J)
```

The FORTRAN compiler would read the statement like this:

```
IF(X(J).GE.XMAX)XMAX=X(J)
```

Blanks or spaces should be used in any place in the program statement to increase readability. The more readable a program is to the human eye, the easier it is to debug. There are few programs written that do not contain bugs. The closer programs resemble text, the more likely the typing mistakes can be recognized and corrected.

CHAPTER 3
Input and Output

When the FORTRAN language uses cards for input, the READ statement is the only means for data to be entered in the program. In Applesoft and FORTRAN, the READ-DATA combination is one of the three methods to enter data into the program. In FORTRAN, the READ statement is a very important part of data entry. When FORTRAN was adapted to the Apple computer, the READ statement lost some of its importance in the relationship of data to the program.

In Apple FORTRAN, the READ statement is used to read data from an external source, such as disk or keyboard. When data is placed directly in the source code program, a DATA statement is used but no READ statement is necessary. When the DATA statement is compiled into the object code program, the data cannot be changed without changing the program.

To explain input/output in the FORTRAN/Pascal configuration, a slight digression must be made. In the READ statement, the parentheses following the READ contain two integers, READ (0,50). The first integer, 0, relates to the input/output device, and the second integer, 50, relates to the FORMAT statement.

Pascal has a command level, FILER, and the filer has a command level in which Volumes is a command. When V(olume) is pressed at the filer level, the volumes on-line (Fig. 3-1) appear on the screen.

```
VOLS ON-LINE:
1.   CONSOLE:   (Keyboard)
2.   SYSTEM:    (CRT)
3.
4. # FORT 2:    (Disk drive #1 - Interface card is in I/O slot #6)
5. # FORT 1:    (Disk drive #2)
6.   PRINTER:   (Printer interface card is in I/O slot #1)
ROOT VOLUME IS - FORT 2:
PREFIX IS      - FORT 2:
```

This is the required configuration with the printer interface card in I/O slot #1, and the dual disk drive interface card in I/O slot #6.

READ (0, 910) X - READ ZERO (or asterisk) is designated to read from the keyboard. WRITE (0,920) X - WRITE ZERO (or asterisk) is designated to write to the CRT. Zero does not correspond to the volumes-on-line designation (1 for the console or keyboard, and 2 for the system or CRT), but zero or asterisk is the designator to READ from the keyboard, or WRITE to the CRT.

Fig. 3-1. Volumes on-line.

The volumes-on-line designator for the keyboard (console) is one (1), and the designator for the CRT (system) is two (2). However, the operations designator for both the keyboard and the CRT is zero (0) or an asterisk (*).

```
READ (0,900) X
WRITE (0, 920) KOUNT, SUM, AVG
```

The zero, or asterisk, designator is available in any part of the program, or subprograms. This is also true of any file-number designator.

INPUT

READ Statements

The first use of READ is to input from the keyboard. A combination of statements must be used (Figs. 3-2, and 3-3). The first statement in Fig. 3-2, "WRITE (0, 900) 'ENTER A REAL:'," causes the literal 'ENTER A REAL:' to be printed on the CRT, so the program user knows what is expected. The second statement in Fig. 3-2, "900 FORMAT (A$)," sets up the continuous character editing (A$) so the end of the record is left open for more input. When the end of the record is left open by the A$, it allows the user to enter data on the same line.

```
(1st)          WRITE (0, 900) 'ENTER A REAL:'
(2nd)      900 FORMAT (A$)
(3rd)          READ (0,910) X
(4th)      910 FORMAT (BN, F7.2)
```

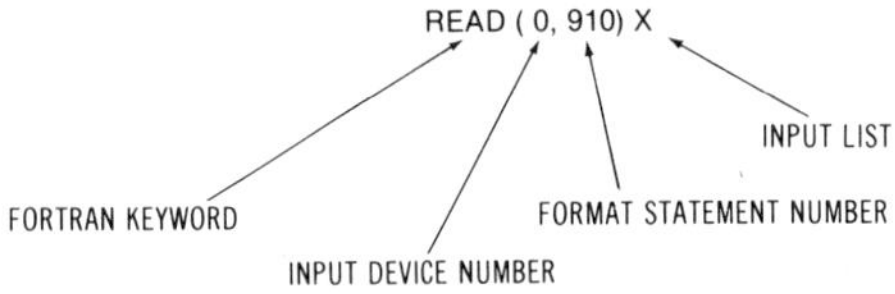

Fig. 3-2. Statements to input data from the keyboard.

The third statement in Fig. 3-2, "READ (0,910)X," reads the input from the keyboard using the zero designator for input. The fourth statement in Fig. 3-2, "910 FORMAT (BN,F7.2)," is the FORMAT statement for "READ (0,910) X." BN is the edit descriptor that causes blanks within the field (F7.2) to be ignored. BN is primarily used for integers and is placed in this example to introduce a concept. The "F" (floating-point) edit descriptor sets aside seven columns in one field for the real to be input.

The second use of the READ statement for input from the keyboard is with an implied DO loop (Fig. 3-4). The array is dimensioned (DIMENSION X(3)). Line one (1) formats the 30 columns, 10 at a time, on the CRT to represent the 10 columns into which the reals are placed. After three reals have been input below the 30 columns on the screen, RETURN is pressed and the three reals are output to the CRT.

```
&C**** THIS PROGRAM DEMONSTRATES THE USE
C**** OF ZERO TO READ FROM THE KEYBOARD
C**** AND ZERO TO WRITE TO THE CRT
C234567
      PROGRAM WRITE2
      OPEN (6, FILE = 'PRINTER:')
      SUM = 0
      KOUNT = 0
   10 WRITE (0,900) 'ENTER A REAL: '
      WRITE (6,900) 'ENTER A REAL: '
  900 FORMAT (A$)
      READ (0,910) X
      CALL CHECK (X)
      WRITE (6,910) X
  910 FORMAT (BN, F7.2)
      IF (X .LE. 0.00) GOTO 20
      KOUNT = KOUNT + 1
      SUM = SUM + X
      GOTO 10
   20 AVG = SUM/KOUNT
      WRITE (0,920) KOUNT, SUM, AVG
      WRITE (6,920) KOUNT, SUM, AVG
  920 FORMAT (///,'NUMBERS ENTERED = ',
     *I3,' SUM = ',F10.2,' AND AVG = ',
     2F7.2)
      STOP
      END
      SUBROUTINE CHECK (X)
      IF (X .LE. 9999.99) RETURN
      WRITE (0,930)
  930 FORMAT (///,'REAL IS TOO LARGE')
      WRITE (0,940)
  940 FORMAT ('ENTER A NUMBER BELOW 10000')
      STOP
      END


ENTER A REAL:  100.00
ENTER A REAL:  200.00
ENTER A REAL:  300.00
ENTER A REAL:  400.00
ENTER A REAL:     .00


NUMBERS ENTERED =   4 SUM =     1000.00 AND AVG =   250.00
```

Fig. 3-3. Program to demonstrate the use of zero to read from the keyboard and write to the CRT.

```
&C**** PROGRAM TO READ FROM KEYBOARD
C**** WITHOUT USING THE A$ MODE
C234567
      PROGRAM RDCRT
      DIMENSION X(3)
      WRITE (0,1)
    1 FORMAT (3(10H!--------*))
      READ (0,5) (X(J), J = 1,3)
    5 FORMAT (3(F10.2))
      WRITE (0,10)
   10 FORMAT (//,3(10H!--------*),/)
      WRITE (0,20) (X(K), K = 1,3)
   20 FORMAT (3(F10.2))
      STOP
      END
```

Fig. 3-4. Program to read from the keyboard using an implied DO loop (not using the A$ mode).

```
&C**** PROGRAM TO DEMONSTRATE READ FROM DISK
C**** A FILE THAT HAS BEEN CREATED
C**** ON DISK
C234567
      PROGRAM RDDISK
      OPEN(14,FILE='#5:WRITE',ACCESS='SEQUENTIAL',
     *STATUS='OLD')
      DO 20 I = 1,100,10
      X = I
      READ (14,1) I, X, Y
      WRITE (0,1) I, X, Y
 20   CONTINUE
  1   FORMAT (I6,3X,F7.2,3X,F8.2)
      CLOSE(14,STATUS='KEEP')
      STOP
      END
```

Fig. 3-5. Program to read a sequential file from disk.

```
C**** PROGRAM TO DEMONSTRATE WRITE TO DISK
C**** PROGRAM WRITES FILE TO DISK
C234567
      PROGRAM WRDISK
      OPEN(14,FILE='#5:WRITE',ACCESS='SEQUENTIAL',
     *STATUS='NEW')
      DO 10 I = 1,100,10
      X = I
      WRITE (14,1) I, X, X*X
 10   CONTINUE
  1   FORMAT (I6,3X,F7.2,3X,F8.2)
      CLOSE(14,STATUS='KEEP')
      STOP
      END
```

Fig. 3-6. Program to write a sequential file to disk.

The third use of the READ statement is to read a file on disk (Fig. 3-5). The file name is "#5:WRITE" and was created by the program in Fig. 3-6. The file created on disk (Fig. 3-7) is a file of the integers, reals, and reals times reals from one to 100 in steps of 10 increments each.

```
  1      1.00        1.00
 11     11.00      121.00
 21     21.00      441.00
 31     31.00      961.00
 41     41.00     1681.00
 51     51.00     2601.00
 61     61.00     3721.00
 71     71.00     5041.00
 81     81.00     6561.00
 91     91.00     8281.00
```

Fig. 3-7. File created by the program in Fig. 3-6.

The file must be opened by the statement, "OPEN(14, FILE = '#5: WRITE', ACCESS = 'SEQUENTIAL', STATUS = 'OLD')." The DO loop reads the file in the same manner as it was created. READ (14, 1) I, X, Y, reads the file from the disk. The READ statement will not accept expressions such as X*X, so the variable "Y" is used to read in the "X*X" expression. The statement "WRITE (0, 1) I, X, Y," writes the file on the screen as it is read. The file is closed by the statement "CLOSE(14,STATUS = 'KEEP')." Files should always be closed after they are read.

The file is opened as device #14 in the OPEN statement. The file should be a number from 13 to 255. The Apple peripheral slots (Table 3-1) can use the integers zero (0) through 12 for devices, should the computer system be fully loaded and each input/output slot filled.

Table 3-1. Peripheral Input/Output Slots

Input/ Output Slot	Device Assigned to the Slot Number	Use
0	Apple language card.	Stores P-code interpreter and I/O system.
1	Printer, communications, serial, or parallel interface card.	Printer or #6:
2	Modem, Apple to Apple communication, communications, serial, or parallel interface card.	REMIN: or #7: REMOUT: or #8:
3	External CRT, communications, serial, or parallel interface card.	
4	Additional disk drives, interface card.	Drive #1 is #9: Drive #2 is #10:
5	Additional disk drives, interface card.	Drive #1 is #11: Drive #2 is #12:
6	Required first disk drive interface card in this slot. Second disk drive.	Drive #1 is #4: or referenced by disk name. Boot drive. Disk #2 is #5: or referenced by disk name.
7	Must not contain a disk drive.	

Slot #0 required for the language card.
Slot #1 required for the printer.
Slot #6 required for the first disk drive interface card.

The file name, "#5:WRITE," is also significant. In FORTRAN, the disk devices are accessed by using the specific disk name followed by a colon (GDISK:), or the disk drive number followed by a colon (#5:). In this example, the sequential file, "WRITE," was on a disk in disk drive number 5, so the file and disk drive number had to be accessed by FILE = '#5:WRITE'.

The third type of data input is written directly into the program using the FORTRAN keyword DATA. The first example of data written into the program (Fig. 3-8) shows three real variables, A, B, C, and three integer variables, I, J, K, in the DATA statement. A slash (/) after the last variable indicates the end of the list. The first three items in the data list are reals, to match the three real variables, and the last three items in the data list are integers, to match the last three integer variables. A slash designates the end of data. The program is executed to show how the integers and reals are output according to the FORMAT statement. The FORMAT statement places two spaces (2X) between each number, so the unevenness of spacing is caused by the fields in F10.0, F10.2, and I3 not being filled by the values.

```
C****  PROGRAM TO DEMONSTRATE DATA INPUT
C****  WITH REAL AND INTEGER VARIABLES
C234567
      PROGRAM VADATA
      DATA A,B,C,I,J,K/10.,20.,100.,10,
     *20, 100 /
      OPEN (6,FILE='PRINTER:' )
      WRITE (0,50) A,B,C,I,J,K
      WRITE (6,50) A,B,C,I,J,K
   50 FORMAT (//,F10.0,2X,F10.2,2X,
     *F10.4,2X,I3,2X,I3,2X,I3)
      STOP
      END


       10.        20.00      100.0000    10    20   100
```

Fig. 3-8. Program to read and write data with real and integer variables.

Fig. 3-9 shows a list of five reals in a data statement. The reals are related to the real array "A." The DATA statement sets up the memory locations by designating each memory location in the array. A slash edit descriptor indicates the end of the array list and the end of the constant list.

```
C****  PROGRAM TO DEMONSTRATE WRITING AN
C****  ARRAY USING ONLY THE DIMENSION
C****  STATEMENT AND NO DO LOOP
C234567
      PROGRAM W1
      DIMENSION A(5)
      DATA A(1),A(2),A(3),A(4),A(5)/
     *5.,10.,15.,20.,20./
      WRITE (0,50) A
   50 FORMAT (//,5F10.2,//)
      STOP
      END
```

Fig. 3-9. Program to read and write variable data using only the array variable.

Second Method of Data Input

A second method of data input (Fig. 3-10) places the constants in the array. In this case, only the array variable "A" is used in the DATA statement, and the subscripts are omitted. The real constants are placed in the address locations reserved by the specification statement DIMENSION A(5). The run of Fig. 3-10 uses a format of F10.2, so each of the reals in the DATA statement is rounded to two places and written into 10 columns by the floating-point edit descriptor.

Fig. 3-11 is an example of a DATA statement with a double subscripted real array. The constants in the DATA statement are related to the double subscripted variable by its position in the list. For example, D(1,1) contains the value 2.0, etc. The reals are printed on the screen and the printer, using the FORMAT statement with statement labeled #50. This straightforward

```
C**** PROGRAM TO DEMONSTRATE DATA INPUT
C**** INTO A SINGLE SUBSCRIPTED ARRAY
C**** AND WRITING THE DATA USING AN
C**** IMPLIED DO LOOP
C234567
      PROGRAM A1DATA
      DIMENSION A(5)
      DATA A/100.5,210.12,300.123,400.1234,
     *500.12345/
      OPEN (6,FILE='PRINTER:')
      WRITE (0,50) (A(J),J = 1,5)
      WRITE (6,50) (A(J),J = 1,5)
   50 FORMAT (//,5F10.2,//)
      STOP
      END


    100.50    210.12    300.12    400.12    500.12
```

Fig. 3-10. Program to demonstrate data input into a single subscripted array, and writing the data using an implied DO loop.

```
C**** PROGRAM TO DEMONSTRATE DATA IN A
C**** DOUBLE SUBSCRIPTED ARRAY
C234567
      PROGRAM DBDATA
      DIMENSION D(2,3)
      DATA D(1,1),D(1,2),D(1,3),D(2,1),
     *D(2,2),D(2,3)/2.,4.,6.,8.,10.,12./
      OPEN (6,FILE='PRINTER:')
      DO 20 J = 1,2
      WRITE (0,50) (D(J,K),K = 1,3)
      WRITE (6,50) (D(J,K),K = 1,3)
   20 CONTINUE
   50 FORMAT (/,3F10.0,/)
      STOP
      END


        2.        4.        6.

        8.       10.       12.
```

Fig. 3-11. Program to input and output data in a double subscripted array.

placement of reals into the reserved address locations is caused by the specification statement, DIMENSION D(2,3).

The DATA statement in Fig. 3-12 uses only "D" as the input variable, and the data was placed in ascending order from 1 to 6. When the program was executed, the data was output 1., 3., 5., 2., 4., 6., instead of 1., 2., 3., in the first row, and 4., 5., 6., in the second row. In this mode, using only "D" as the array designator, the data is read into memory vertically instead of horizontally. The program had to be changed so the "J" outer loop increments more rapidly than the "K" inner loop. This caused the program

```
C**** PROGRAM TO DEMONSTRATE DATA IN A
C**** DOUBLE SUBSCRIPTED ARRAY
C234567
      PROGRAM D1DATA
      DIMENSION D(2,3)
      DATA D/1., 2., 3.,
     *     4., 5., 6./
      OPEN (6,FILE='PRINTER:')
      DO 20 J = 1,3
      WRITE (0,50) (D(J,K),K = 1,2)
      WRITE (6,50) (D(J,K),K = 1,2)
   20 CONTINUE
   50 FORMAT (/,3F10.0,/)
      STOP
      END

         1.        3.

         2.        4.

         3.        5.
```

```
   1.     3.     5.
   2.     4.     6.
```

When the program above was changed to:
DO 20 J = 1, 2
WRITE (0,50) (D(J,K),K = 1,3
this output was produced.

Fig. 3-12. Program to input and output data in a double subscripted array using only the subscript variable (the output was incorrect).

to print out in a 3 × 2 matrix form, and the output was incorrect because it outputted 1., 2., 3., 3., 4., 5.. This input and output was completely unexpected, and emphasizes the need to debug programs.

Open a File

The OPEN statement is necessary to create (write) files, read files, and to activate peripheral devices. Fig. 3-3 shows the statement, OPEN(6,FILE = 'PRINTER:'). The printer is #6 in the volumes on line. To use the printer in WRITE statements when a program is executed, the printer must be activated. The FILE = statement requires that the file activated be enclosed in single quotes (apostrophe). The legal format for the printer is 'PRINTER:'.

Fig. 3-6 shows the correct OPEN statement for opening (and writing) a sequential file. In this case, the integer 14 is an arbitrary number between 13 and 255. The file is named WRITE and is on disk drive #5:, thus FILE='#5:WRITE' accesses the correct file. The access mode has two modes — sequential or direct (random).

In Fig. 3-6, the file to be created is a sequential file, thus ACCESS='SEQUENTIAL',. The file is being created, thus STATUS='NEW'. The STATUS= has two options — 'NEW' or 'OLD'. If the ACCESS= had been 'DIRECT', a RECL= of a specific length would be specified with an integer (RECL=60).

Fig. 3-5 contains an OPEN statement to open a file to be read. The file was created by the program in Fig. 3-6, and the file is shown in Fig. 3-7. The only difference in the open statement, STATUS='OLD', is that the file had been created previously.

With the Apple system there are only two options on which to use the OPEN statement — the printer and the disk drives.

Close the File

The CLOSE statement (Figs. 3-5 and 3-6) is used to close files. The integer number, 14, relates to the integer in the OPEN statement. The STATUS= has two options — 'DELETE' the file or 'KEEP' the file. In Figs. 3-5 and 3-6, the option 'KEEP' was used because the file was to be used in another example, Fig. 3-7.

OUTPUT

In conjunction with the OPEN statement, the WRITE statement (Fig. 3-6) is used to create a file on disk. In the example in Fig. 3-6, the "WRITE (14,", references the "OPEN (14,". The 14 is an integer that references a file number designator on which the file is to be opened, and the OPEN and WRITE statements must use the same device designator to create the file. The integer one (1) in parentheses relates to the FORMAT statement of information in the file. The input/output list contains the variables into which the values in the file are placed. If a direct, or random-access, file is to be created, the record number must be designated in the WRITE statement:

```
WRITE (14,FILE = '#5:WRITE',REC = 1) I, X, X*X
```

In FORTRAN, the record number begins with record #1, and not with record #0. The OPEN statement contains the record length argument, RECL=60, so the WRITE statement contains the record number argument. These two statements are tied together to give the length of each record in the file and the beginning record so the operating system can keep track of the records placed in the file. Examples of WRITE statements are shown in Fig. 3-13.

WRITE (0,10) with no input list (Fig. 3-4) is used for writing headings, or literal data. The output list, or literal constant, is contained in the FORMAT statement.

```
   WRITE (0,10)
10 FORMAT (3(10H!--------*))
```

In this example, 30 columns are designated on the CRT. Each column begins with an exclamation mark and ends with an asterisk. This 30-column heading is printed on the CRT to prompt the user that there are to be three real numbers input into three floating-point fields of 10 columns each. The "H" edit descriptor stands for Hollerith, and equates to the apostrophe editing.

```
   WRITE (6, 50)
50 FORMAT (//,'PAY REPORT',//)
```

In this example, PAY REPORT would be printed as a heading using

(1)	WRITE (0,10)	(FIG. 3-4)
(2)	WRITE (0, 50) A, B, C, I, J, K	(FIG. 3-8)
(3)	WRITE (14, 1) I, X , X*X	(FIG. 3-6)
(4)	WRITE (6, 50) (A(J), J = 1,5)	(FIG. 3-10)
(5)	WRITE (0, 50) (D(J,K), K = 1,2)	(FIG. 3-12)

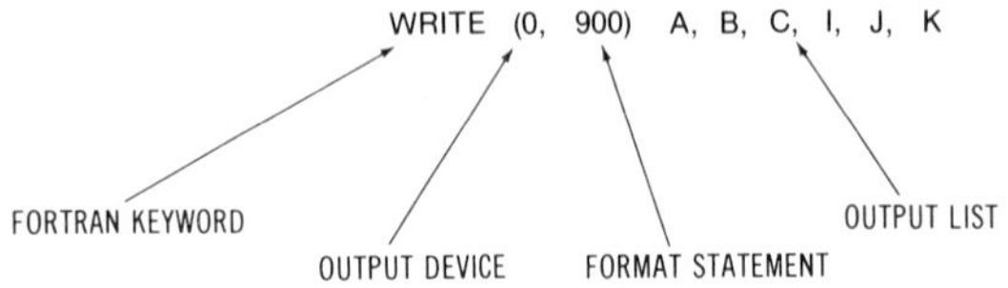

1. WRITE statement with no output list that writes headings and explanations.
2. WRITE statement with output list.
3. WRITE statement that creates a sequential file on a disk.
4. WRITE statement that outputs to the printer five real values in an array list.
5. WRITE statement that outputs six values to the screen and uses an outer DO loop (DO J = 1,3) in conjunction with the implied DO loop in the WRITE statement.

Fig. 3-13. Examples of WRITE statements.

apostrophe editing. The slash editors cause two lines to be skipped before the heading is printed and two more lines to be skipped after the heading is printed.

```
   WRITE (0, 50), A, B, C, I, J, K
50 FORMAT (//,F10.0,2X,F10.2,2X,
  *F10.4,2X,I3,2X,I3,2X,I3)
```

This combination of statements causes three reals, A, B, C, and three integers, I, J, K, to be output. The FORMAT statement skips two lines, outputs the real "A" in a 10-column floating-point field with zero decimal places. It skips two spaces (2X) and outputs the real "B" in a field of 10 columns with two decimal places. It skips two spaces, and outputs the real "C" in a field of 10 columns with four decimal places. The integers "I," "J," and "K" are output in fields of three columns each, and two spaces are skipped between each integer.

```
   DIMENSION A (5)
   OPEN (6, FILE='PRINTER:')
   WRITE (6, 50) (A(J),J=1,5)
50 FORMAT (//,5F10.2,//)
```

This combination of statements (Fig. 3-10) causes the printer to be activated, and the data in array "A" is output on the printer using an implied DO loop. The FORMAT statement causes two lines to be skipped; the five values in the DATA statement are printed on one line in 10-column floating-point format with two decimal places. Two lines are skipped after the data is printed.

```
      DIMENSION D (2,3)
      DO 20 J = 1,2
      WRITE (0,50) (D(J,K), K = 1,3)
   20 CONTINUE
   50 FORMAT (/,3F10.0,/)
```

This combination of statements (Fig. 3-11) causes the data in the double subscripted array "D" to be printed in a 3 × 2 matrix. The FORMAT statement causes a line to be skipped and three reals are printed in a 10-column floating-point field with no decimal places. The implied DO loop causes 2., 4., 6. to be printed on the CRT on the first line. The DO loop increments a second time and causes the implied DO loop to print 8., 10., 12. two lines below the original line. The ending slash causes a line to be skipped, and on the second increment of the DO loop, the beginning slash causes another line to be skipped between the two lines of print.

FORMATTING

FORMAT is the keyword that identifies a FORMAT statement. The FORMAT statement is related to READ and WRITE statements to describe the location and type of data to be input or output. A FORMAT statement must always have a statement number. This statement number is the same as the second integer in the parentheses following the READ or WRITE keyword, so the FORMAT statement can be properly referenced. A FORMAT statement can be used by more than one READ or WRITE statement. Information can be read from the keyboard or disk, and information can be dually written to the CRT and the printer (Fig. 3-8). In most cases, there is a single FORMAT statement associated with a READ or WRITE statement. The FORMAT statement must be placed after the program or subprogram statement, but can be placed anywhere else in the program. Generally, the FORMAT statement is placed after the associated READ or WRITE statement.

Each input/output statement has a related FORMAT statement and an input/output list (the output list for writing headings is implied).

Rules of the FORMAT Statement

The rules for using the FORMAT statement are as follows:

1. The FORMAT statements are not executed. Their function is to supply information concerning the input/output data to the program. FORMAT statements should be referenced only by a READ or WRITE statement.
2. The FORMAT statement is placed after the PROGRAM, FUNCTION, or SUBROUTINE statements, but may be placed anywhere else in the program.

3. The FORMAT statement defines the print field to the input/output medium. The maximum usable CRT space is 80 columns, and printer space ranges to 132 columns.
4. It is not necessary to fill the remaining positions in an input/output field with blanks. The remaining blank spaces are left unfilled.
5. All FORMAT statements in the main program are available only to the main program. Each subprogram must contain its own FORMAT statements.

The rules pertaining to the input/output list following a READ or WRITE statement are as follows:

1. The input/output list can contain any type of variable name.
2. The READ statement must not include any constants or arithmetic expressions, but the WRITE statement may contain constants or arithmetic expressions.
3. Each name in the input/output list must be separated by a comma.
4. Each name in the input/output list is transmitted to or from memory on a one-to-one basis.
5. Each name in the input/output list is transmitted on a one-to-one basis to the FORMAT statement except for apostrophe, Hollerith, or space (X) editors.
6. The names in the input/output list must be consistent with the left to right order of the data items in the FORMAT statement, in number type, format, edit descriptor, and size for proper output.

READ-FORMAT Statements

The READ statement (Figs. 3-3 and 3-4) is used as an input mode from the keyboard or disk. The FORMAT statement is used in conjunction with the READ statement to input an integer, a real, exponentiation, or scientific notation, either as a single entity (F10.2) or as a multiple entity (3(F10.2)). When data is entered directly into the program in a DATA statement, no READ and READ-FORMAT statements are necessary.

WRITE-FORMAT Statements

A FORMAT statement is generally written for each WRITE statement. When the same FORMAT statement is to be used to WRITE to CRT, disk, and/or printer, the FORMAT statement is the same and the device integer in the WRITE statement is changed.

```
WRITE (0,110) I — To CRT
WRITE (6,110) I — To Printer
WRITE (14,110) I — To Disk
```

TYPES OF EDITING TO CONTROL INPUT AND OUTPUT

Descriptor editing, or formatting, will be discussed according to the listing in Table 3-2, where possible. At times, the input and output characteristics of the descriptor editors are different, and this will be noted in the discussion. At times, two descriptors, like apostrophe and Hollerith editing, will be discussed as a single item.

Table 3-2. Edit Descriptors

Edit Type	Used for Input	Used for Output
Apostrophe	No	Yes
A*w*	Yes	Yes
BN	Yes	No
BZ	Yes	Yes
*n*E*w*.*d*	Yes	Yes
*n*E*w*.*d*E*e*	Yes	Yes
*n*F*w*.*d*	Yes	Yes
*n*H	No	Yes
*n*I*w*	Yes	Yes
L*w*	Yes	Yes
*k*P	Yes	Yes
*n*X	Yes	Yes
/ (slash)	Yes	Yes
$	Yes	Yes

d—An unsigned positive integer constant that specifies the number of decimal places in the real.
n—An unsigned positive integer constant that is a multiplier that causes the edit descriptor to be used the same number of times as the integer.
k—A positively or negatively signed integer constant. A positive integer moves the decimal point to the right an equal number of places as the positive integer. A negative integer moves the decimal to the left an equal number of places as the negative integer.
w—An unsigned positive integer that reserves the number of fields equal to the value of the integer.

Apostrophe or Hollerith Editors

Apostrophe (') or Hollerith (H) editors (Fig. 3-14) are used to write headings, or literal data. Since the literal is a constant that is formed, and not stored as a variable in memory, there is no input/output list associated with the WRITE statement.

```
WRITE (0,100)
WRITE (6,100)
```

The apostrophe or Hollerith editors are for output only. A variable name must never be associated with an apostrophe or Hollerith format code.

The printer used for this exercise was set to 64 columns, so the centering was based on column 32 as the center of the page. If a single line of heading

```
C**** PROGRAM TO DEMONSTRATE USING THE
C**** WRITE STATEMENT TO OUTPUT MULTIPLE
C**** LINE HEADINGS
C234567
      PROGRAM W2
      DIMENSION A(5)
      DATA A(1),A(2),A(3),A(4),A(5)/
     *5.,10.,15.,20.,25./
      OPEN (6,FILE='PRINTER:')
      WRITE (0,100)
      WRITE (6,100)
  100 FORMAT (///,22X,'OUTPUT FOR ARRAY DATA',
     *//,3X,8HCOLUMN 1,5X,8HCOLUMN 2,5X,
     *8HCOLUMN 3,5X,8HCOLUMN 4,5X,
     *8HCOLUMN 5,/)
      WRITE (0,150) A
      WRITE (6,150) A
  150 FORMAT (1X,5(F10.2,3X),//)
      STOP
      END
```

```
                      OUTPUT FOR ARRAY DATA

   COLUMN 1     COLUMN 2     COLUMN 3     COLUMN 4     COLUMN 5

       5.00        10.00        15.00        20.00        25.00
```

Fig. 3-14. Program to demonstrate apostrophe and Hollerith editing.

was to be printed and centered on a page (Fig. 3-14), the WRITE and FORMAT statements would be as follows:

```
      WRITE (0,100)
  100 FORMAT (22X,'OUTPUT FOR ARRAY DATA')
or
  100 FORMAT (22X,21HOUTPUT FOR ARRAY DATA)
```

The literal contains 21 characters, and the center of the page is column 32. To center the heading, 22 spaces (22X) are skipped, so the first letter of the heading is printed in column 23.

The Hollerith code must be specified to the exact number of characters, including spaces. If the number of characters in the literal are too few or too many, in relation to the Hollerith editor, a syntax error will occur. The apostrophe editor is easier to use because all the characters to be printed are between the two apostrophes. Spaces are significant in apostrophe or Hollerith editing and are output as specified.

In ANSI Standard FORTRAN, editors that control printer output are specified by Hollerith editors. In Apple FORTRAN 77, there are no Hollerith editors that control the printer output. In Apple FORTRAN, the slash (/) edit descriptor terminates the end of a line of input variables, a line of input constants, and is used to skip lines during printer output. Any other printer controls, such as page feed, end of page feed, or end of page spacing, must be controlled by the dual in-line purpose (DIP) switches.

In Fig. 3-14, two heading lines are to be output. These lines use the slash editor to close out the first line, and skip one line. When there is more than one field in a format statement, the fields are separated by commas.

```
      WRITE (0,100)
100   FORMAT (///,22X,'OUTPUT FOR ARRAY DATA',
     *//,3X,8HCOLUMN 1, 5X, 8HCOLUMN 2,5X,
     *8HCOLUMN 3,5X,8HCOLUMN 4,5X,
     *8HCOLUMN 5,/)
```

Using FORMAT line 100, the literal constants are printed over the corresponding columns (Fig. 3-14) of the output values to identify the output results. Report and column headings are printed on every report to clarify the meaning of the information for the user.

Headings are frequently used to define the output information for the user. The following example demonstrates a method to place literal headings with output data on the same line:

```
      WRITE (0,620) KOUNT, SUM, AVG
      WRITE (6,620) KOUNT, SUM, AVG
620   FORMAT (///,'NUMBERS ENTERED = ',
     *I3,'SUM = ',F10.2,' AND AVG = ',
     *2F7.2)
```

In Fig. 3-3, a program was written to demonstrate the use of zero to READ from the keyboard and to WRITE to the CRT. An unknown number of real numbers was input, their values were summed, and then averaged. For user clarification, the literal headings and numeric output were combined into one line of output. No blank spaces (*n*X) were used in this format because the spaces were controlled by the use of the fields in the numeric output, the space between the apostrophe editors, and the literal. In literals with both apostrophe and "H" editing, spaces are significant. A sufficient number of columns should be reserved for any result, either positive or negative. If the value is too large for the given field, the field will be overprinted with asterisks. In Fig. 3-3, the output line looks ragged because of the uneven spacing. This is because the FORMAT statements allow a value up to 9999.99 to be input and a floating-point field of 10 columns to be output.

Alphanumeric Edit Descriptor

The "A" alphanumeric edit descriptor (Fig. 3-15) is used for both input and output. Alphanumeric is used to describe data which may be alphabetic, numeric, special characters, or a combination of these types. Alphanumeric data is treated as a literal, or string, and must not be used in mathematical computations. The literal, or string, is enclosed between two apostrophes to designate the "A" data. When used in a DATA statement, the alphanumeric characters are enclosed between two apostrophes. The possessive case requires that two single apostrophes be used. A special condition causes the compiler to convert the two apostrophes to a single apostrophe, and continue building the literal. Inventory items that use both alphabetic and numeric characters are typical of data types that require the "A" edit descriptor.

Any character, except the apostrophe, can be used with the "A" format code. The general form to reserve memory space for the alphanumeric code is with the FORTRAN word, CHARACTER.

CHARACTER*20 NAME — A20
CHARACTER*20 N(5) — A20

The program in Fig. 3-15 was written to demonstrate the relationship between CHARACTER*20 and A20. The CHARACTER*20 NAME causes 20 bytes, 20 characters, to be reserved in memory for the input of the list NAME. The data statement contains the variable NAME, and the character string between the two apostrophes. The slash editors indicate the end of the variable list, and the end of the constant list. The printer file in volumes-on-line #6 is opened, and the literal, GEORGE BLACKWOOD, is printed on the CRT and the printer. The A20 in the FORMAT statement relates to the 20 characters reserved by CHARACTER*20 NAME. Since the literal contains only 16 characters, it is left-justified, and four blanks fill the remaining four columns that are reserved. This blank padding and left-justification is represented by Xs in Fig. 3-18, so that the 16 characters will be filled. If no character multiplier is written, the default value is one. The maximum multiplier is 255.

```
C**** PROGRAM TO DEMONSTRATE A METHOD TO
C**** OUTPUT A NAME
C234567
      PROGRAM N1
      CHARACTER*20 NAME
      DATA NAME/'GEORGE BLACKWOOD'/
      OPEN (6,FILE='PRINTER:')
      WRITE (0,100) NAME
      WRITE (6,100) NAME
  100 FORMAT (//,10X,A20,//)
      STOP
      END



          GEORGE BLACKWOOD
```

Fig. 3-15. Program to demonstrate the "A" edit descriptor.

The program in Fig. 3-16 was written to demonstrate the effect of a literal that is longer than the memory area reserved by the CHARACTER multiplier. The string, GEORGE BLACKWOOD, is 16 characters long, and the memory reserved is 10 characters, CHARACTER*10 NAME. When the program is compiled, it causes compile time error #78 in the line which con-

```
FORTRAN Compiler II.1  [1.1]
     0.        0 C**** PROGRAM TO DEMONSTRATE WHAT HAPPENS
     1.        0 C**** WHEN THE CHARACTER MULTIPLIER IS LESS
     2.        0 C**** THAN THE LENGTH OF THE STRING
     3.        0 C234567
     4.        0       PROGRAM LNAME
     5.        0       CHARACTER*10 NAME
     6.        0       DATA NAME/'GEORGE BLACKWOOD'/
***** Error number: 78 in line: 6
     7.       16       OPEN (6,FILE='PRINTER:')
     8.       36       WRITE (0,100) NAME
     9.       64       WRITE (6,100) NAME
    10.       92   100 FORMAT (//,10X,A20,//)
    11.       92       STOP
    12.       99       END

LNAME   PROGRAM
NAME    CHAR* 10       3
```

Fig. 3-16. Compiled program to demonstrate the result when the CHARACTER multiplier is less than the number of characters in the literal.

tains the literal data. Compile error #78 is "TYPE CONFLICT IN DATA STATEMENT." A literal longer than the character multiplier causes an error when the program is compiled.

The program in Fig. 3-17 was written to demonstrate the output of a list of names using implied DO loops.

```
&C**** PROGRAM TO DEMONSTRATE A METHOD TO
C**** OUTPUT A LIST OF NAMES USING AN
C**** IMPLIED DO LOOP
C234567
      PROGRAM N2
      CHARACTER*20 N(5)
      DATA N(1),N(2),N(3),N(4),N(5)/
     *'GEORGE BLACKWOOD','MARY SMITH',
     *'SUE JONES',
     *'MARY HO','BILL JONES'/
      OPEN (6,FILE='PRINTER:')
      WRITE (0,100) (N(J),J = 1,5)
      WRITE (6,100) (N(J),J = 1,5)
  100 FORMAT (10X,A20)
      STOP
      END


          GEORGE BLACKWOOD
          MARY SMITH
          SUE JONES
          MARY HO
          BILL JONES
```

Fig. 3-17. Program to output a list of names using implied DO loops and the "A" edit descriptor.

CHARACTER*20 N(5) reserves memory for 20 characters for each of five names to be printed. CHARACTER*20 N(5) also serves as a DIMENSION statement. If DIMENSION N(5) and CHARACTER*20 N(5) are used in the same program, compile error #30, "ARRAY DIMENSIONED MORE THAN ONCE," is printed. In this example, each array element is written into a DATA statement to demonstrate one of the methods to input alphanumeric data. The list is output one name to the line since 20 characters per line were reserved.

The program in Fig. 3-18 was written to incorporate apostrophe and Hollerith editing, "A" editing, creation of multiple line headings, floating-point editing, and slash editing. The program computes regular and overtime wages, and generates a usable report.

The specification statement is DIMENSION N(5), to reserve memory for the five names in the list. The CHARACTER*16 N references this reserved memory. The data is input with a single array variable to show a second type of data input. The "T" heading is input at the end of a literal in FORMAT line 500, and the A17 references the CHARACTER*17 T. The WRITE statement without an output list prints the second line of the heading. The lines are separated by two slashes at the end of FORMAT line 500.

When the headings have been printed, the program defaults to a DO loop, and the computations are completed and stored in arrays. When the computations are completed, the results are printed out by using a second DO loop. Each line is written out using a WRITE statement, and all the arrays are printed on one line. When all five lines have been printed, the program ends.

BN Edit Descriptor

BN (blank) interpretation is used for input only, and causes blanks in the input field to be ignored by the format controller. The BN edit descriptor is used in Fig. 3-3 to cause blanks to be ignored. In Fig. 3-3, the BN edit descriptor was not really necessary. When reals are input, the blanks are ignored because of the way FORTRAN is configured. When a real is input into an "F" edit descriptor, the real is output in the same column relationship if the "F" fields are the same, and the leading and trailing blanks in the column are ignored. The number of decimal places in the "F"edit descriptor are filled with zeros where it is necessary to complete the field.

The program in Fig. 3-19 was written to demonstrate how blanks are handled with integers without the BN edit descriptor. Integers were input and output in a field with 10 columns (I10). Leading blanks were output as blanks. Input trailing blanks were output as zeros. If a positive integer was input beginning in column 5, or a negative integer was input beginning in column 4, run-time error #651, "INTEGER OVERFLOW ON INPUT," was generated. The Apple does not allow a positive integer greater than 32767, or a negative integer less than −32768, to be legally input.

If the positive integer one (1) is input in column 5 (100,000), run-time error #651 is generated because the leading and trailing blanks are significant. If the negative integer one (−1) is input in column #4 (−100,000),

```
C**** PROGRAM TO DEMONSTRATE "A" EDIT DESCRIPTOR,
C**** APOSTROPHE EDITOR, CHARACTER CONTROL,
C**** AND CHARACTERS WRITTEN INTO A DATA STATEMENT
C234567
      PROGRAM AEDIT
      DIMENSION N(5),PARATE(5),TOTHRS(5),OTHRS(5),
     * OTPAY(5),PAY(5)
      CHARACTER*17 T
      CHARACTER*16 N
      DATA T/'JONES TOOL WORKS'/
      DATA N/'JOHN SMITHXXXXXX','JIMMY CARTERXXXX',
     *'STEWART EWINSERD','HELEN ZEBRONSKI',
     *'MARY HOXXXXXXXXX'/
      DATA PARATE/10.50,3.25,3.25,16.25,14.75/
      DATA TOTHRS/40.,10.,10.,60.,60./
      OPEN (6,FILE='PRINTER:')
  500 FORMAT (///,17X,'REPORT FOR ',A17,//)
  510 FORMAT (7X,16HMACHINIST'S NAME,3X,
     *8HPAY RATE,3X,11HTOTAL HOURS,5X,3HPAY,/)
  520 FORMAT (7X,A16,4X,F5.2,7X,F5.0,7X,F7.2)
      WRITE (0,500) T
      WRITE (6,500) T
      WRITE (0,510)
      WRITE (6,510)
      DO 30 J = 1,5
      IF (TOTHRS(J) .GT. 40.) GOTO 20
      PAY(J) = PARATE(J) * TOTHRS(J)
      GOTO 30
   20 PAY(J) = PARATE(J) * TOTHRS(J)
      OTHRS(J) = TOTHRS(J) - 40.
      OTPAY(J) = OTHRS(J) * PARATE(J) * 1.5
      PAY(J) = PAY(J) + OTPAY(J)
   30 CONTINUE
      DO 40 K = 1,5
      WRITE (0,520) N(K),PARATE(K),TOTHRS(K),
     *PAY(K)
      WRITE (6,520) N(K),PARATE(K),TOTHRS(K),
     *PAY(K)
   40 CONTINUE
      END




                 REPORT FOR JONES TOOL WORKS


       MACHINIST'S NAME   PAY RATE   TOTAL HOURS     PAY

       JOHN SMITHXXXXXX    10.50         40.        420.00
       JIMMY CARTERXXXX     3.25         10.         32.50
       STEWART EWINSERD     3.25         10.         32.50
       HELEN ZEBRONSKI     16.25         60.       1462.50
       MARY HOXXXXXXXXX    14.75         60.       1327.50
```

Fig. 3-18. Program to output a payroll report using apostrophe and Hollerith editing, "A" editing, creation of multiple line headings, floating-point editing, and slash editing.

run-time error #651 stops the program. When the positive integer one (1) is input in column 7, the output value is 1000.

When the BN edit descriptor is included in the FORMAT statement, integers between +32767 and −32768 can be input beginning in column 1 in a 10-column "I" edit descriptor field, and the output is legal.

```
C**** PROGRAM TO SHOW HOW BLANKS ARE HANDLED
C**** IN AN INTEGER INPUT IN TEN COLUMNS
C234567
      PROGRAM INT10
      DIMENSION I(3)
      OPEN (6,FILE='PRINTER:')
      WRITE (0,1)
      WRITE (6,1)
    1 FORMAT (3(10H!--------*))
      READ (0,5) (I(J), J = 1,3)
      WRITE (6,5) (I(J), J = 1,3)
    5 FORMAT (3(I10))
      WRITE (0,10)
      WRITE (6,10)
   10 FORMAT (//,3(10H!--------*),/)
      WRITE (0,20) (I(K), K = 1,3)
      WRITE (6,20) (I(K), K = 1,3)
   20 FORMAT (3(I10))
      STOP
      END


!--------*!--------*!--------*
     32767    -32768     10000

!--------*!--------*!--------*

     32767    -32768     10000



!--------*!--------*!--------*
         1        10      1000

!--------*!--------*!--------*

         1        10      1000



!--------*!--------*!--------*
100000000

 **** FORTRAN RUNTIME ERROR #651 ****
      S# 7    P# 1    I# 90
```

MAXIMUM VALUE FOR AN INTEGER IS 32767, MINIMUM VALUE FOR AN INTEGER IS −32768

Fig. 3-19. Program to demonstrate how blanks are handled with integers without the BN edit descriptor.

BZ Edit Descriptor

The BZ edit descriptor is the FORMAT specification, and is set at the beginning of each line of code where the BN edit descriptor is not set. The BZ edit descriptor is set for input and output. In Fig. 3-19, the BZ edit descriptor is set by default, and causes leading blanks to be significant and trailing blanks to be printed as zeros.

The program in Fig. 3-20 was written to demonstrate the "I," "F," "E," "E*e*," and "P" edit descriptors. Each edit descriptor was dimensioned in an array with five reserved memory locations. The data was input as integer and real. The output was in I10, F10.2, E10.2, E10.2E3, and 2PE10.2E3. The data was output in fields of 10 columns each so the comparison between FORMAT statements and columns could be easily seen.

```
*** PROGRAM TO DEMONSTRATE FORMATTING
*** OF INTEGERS, REALS, EXPONENTIATION,SCIENTIFIC
*** NOTATION, AND P-CODE
34567
    PROGRAM W3
    DIMENSION I(5),F(5),E(5)
    DATA I/12,123,-1234,12345,32767/
    DATA F/12.,12.3,12.34,-12.235,12345678910./
    DATA E/12.345,12.3456,-12.345,-12.3456,.00001/
    OPEN (6,FILE='PRINTER:')
    WRITE (0,100)
    WRITE (6,100)
100 FORMAT (///,3X,'OUTPUT OF FORMATTED DATA ',
   *'IN THIS ORDER: INTEGERS, REALS,',/,
   *7X,'EXPONENTIATION, SCIENTIFIC NOTATION ',
   *'AND P-CODE',///,
   *3X,8HCOLUMN 1,5X,8HCOLUMN 2,5X,8HCOLUMN 3,
   *5X,8HCOLUMN 4,5X,8HCOLUMN 5,/)
    WRITE (0,110) I
    WRITE (6,110) I
    WRITE (0,120) F
    WRITE (6,120) F
    WRITE (0,130) E
    WRITE (6,130) E
    WRITE (0,140) E
    WRITE (6,140) E
    WRITE (0,150) E
    WRITE (6,150) E
110 FORMAT (1X,5(I10,3X))
120 FORMAT (1X,5(F10.2,3X))
130 FORMAT (1X,5(E10.2,3X))
140 FORMAT (1X,5(E10.2E3,2X))
150 FORMAT (1X,5(2PE10.2E3,3X))
    STOP
    END
```

```
 OUTPUT OF FORMATTED DATA IN THIS ORDER: INTEGERS, REALS,
       EXPONENTIATION, SCIENTIFIC NOTATION AND P-CODE


 COLUMN 1      COLUMN 2      COLUMN 3      COLUMN 4      COLUMN 5

       12           123         -1234         12345         32767
    12.00         12.30         12.34        -12.23    **********
  .12E+02       .12E+02      -.12E+02      -.12E+02       .10E-04
.12E+002      .12E+002     -.12E+002     -.12E+002      .10E-004
12.3E+000     12.3E+000    -12.3E+000    -12.3E+000     10.0E-006
```

Fig. 3-20. Program to demonstrate the "I," "F," "E," "E*e*," and "P" edit descriptors.

Integer Edit Descriptor

The "I" edit descriptor, used for both input and output, is used for transmitting integer data fields only. The edit descriptor used in the FORMAT statement consists of the capital letter "I," followed by an integer constant that represents the number of columns in the data field. The general form of a single "I" edit descriptor is

I*w*
I1
I2
I8
I10

to a maximum of I255. If the "I" edit descriptor is to be repeated, a positive integer precedes the capital letter "I."

*r*I*w*
2I5
4I6
10I3

The "I" edit descriptor was discussed in relation to the BN and BZ edit descriptors.

On input, leading blanks are ignored. Embedded and trailing blanks are interpreted as zeros. If an integer greater than 32767 or less than −32768 is input, it will cause a run time error. The value input must be accommodated by the edit field size. If the integer is preceded by a sign, an extra column must be reserved in the field size.

Value Input	I Edit Descriptor
456	I3
+456	I4
−456	I4
32767	I5
−32768	I6
123456	I6 (out of bounds)

On output, the "*w*" represents the number of positions in the input field. The plus sign is not printed on output. However, an extra space should be included in the field size if the output should be negative. The output field is right-justified, and if the field is greater than the integer value, blanks will be inserted in the leading field columns.

Value In Memory	I Descriptor	Output
456	I3	456
+456	I4	+456
−456	I4	−456
32767	I5	32767
−32768	I6	−32768
1234456	I6 (out of bounds)	

Floating-Point Edit Descriptor

The "F" (floating-point) edit descriptor is used for input and output. The edit descriptor used in the FORMAT statement consists of the capital letter "F," followed by an integer constant, decimal point, and another integer constant. This represents the number of columns and decimal places in the data field. The total number of decimal places and the decimal point must be counted in the total number of places in the data field. The following examples are based on the number 99.1111111:

```
Fw.d
F3.0  99.
F4.1  99.1
F5.2  99.11
F6.3  99.111
```

The "F" edit descriptor also has a repetition factor that is represented by an "*r*" prefix.

```
rFw.d
3F3.0
5F4.1
10F5.2
2F6.3
```

When the "F" edit descriptor is used for input, a field position must be reserved for the sign of the real. If the number of input real decimal positions is greater than the "F" edit descriptor decimal indicator, the "F" edit descriptor controls the actual number of decimal positions.

Value Input	F Edit Descriptor
12.3	F4.1
12.34	F5.2
12.345	F6.3
12.3456	F7.4

On output, the "F" edit descriptor will print a real, followed by as many decimal positions as given in the "*d*" parameter. The output will be right-justified. A column width must be provided for a plus or minus sign preceding the real. If insufficient field positions are provided, asterisks will be printed in all field positions. If excessive field positions are reserved in the "F" edit descriptor, the leading positions will be filled with blanks. If there are excessive decimal positions in the input real, the output is rounded.

Value In Memory	F Descriptor	Output
12.	F5.2	12.00
12.123	F5.2	12.12
123.4567	F8.4	123.4567
123.4567	F10.2	xxxx123.46
123.4567	F3.0	xxx

Exponential Edit Descriptor

The "E" (exponential floating-point code) edit descriptor is used for input and output, and for transmitting numeric fields represented by scientific notation. The edit descriptor used in the FORMAT statement consists of the capital letter "E," followed by a positive integer and a decimal point, followed by a second positive integer.

E*w*.*d*
E5.2
E7.2
E10.3

This represents the "E" edit descriptor followed by a specific number of reserved columns for the real, and the fractional part of the real.

The "E" edit descriptor also has a repetition factor, as have the "I" and "F" edit descriptors. All rules that apply to the "F" edit descriptor apply to the "E" edit descriptor, and the "E" format can be used either with integers or reals. The "E" edit descriptors can read values in scientific notation (4.5E+2), real (45.578), and integer (456). The field of the "E" edit descriptor must be increased by four columns over a similar "F" value to accommodate the E+02. If the field of columns is too small to accommodate the value in memory of the "E" format, the field will be filled with asterisks.

The program in Fig. 3-21 was written to demonstrate the output (Fig. 3-22) by "E" format on positive and negative reals. In Figs. 3-21 and 3-22, the real 45.678 exactly accommodates the fields reserved by E10.5. In the third line of the output in Fig. 3-22, using the real 45.678, and an "E" format of E9.5, the field is deficient by one column. This causes the field to be over-printed with asterisks. If the real is negative, another column must be re-

```
C**** PROGRAM TO DEMONSTRATE OUTPUT USING
C**** THE "E" EDIT DESCRIPTOR FOR SCIENTIFIC
C**** NOTATION
C234567
      PROGRAM W4
      DATA E1/45.678/
      DATA E2/45.678/
      DATA E3/45.678/
      DATA E4/45.678/
      DATA E5/-45.678/
      DATA E6/-45.678/
      DATA E7/-45.678/
      DATA E8/.0001/
      OPEN (6,FILE='PRINTER:')
      WRITE (0,100)
      WRITE (6,100)
      WRITE (0,110) E1
      WRITE (6,110) E1
      WRITE (0,120) E2
      WRITE (6,120) E2
      WRITE (0,130) E3
      WRITE (6,130) E3
      WRITE (0,140) E4
      WRITE (6,140) E4
      WRITE (0,150) E5
      WRITE (6,150) E5
      WRITE (0,160) E6
      WRITE (6,160) E6
      WRITE (0,170) E7
      WRITE (6,170) E7
      WRITE (0,180) E8
      WRITE (6,180) E8
  100 FORMAT (//,'VALUE IN MEMORY',5X,'FORMAT FIELD',5X,
     *'OUTPUT FIELD',/)
  110 FORMAT (5X,'45.678',12X,'E10.5',9X,E10.5)
  120 FORMAT (5X,'45.678',12X,'E10.4',9X,E10.4)
  130 FORMAT (5X,'45.678',12X,'E9.5',9X,E9.5)
  140 FORMAT (5X,'45.678',12X,'E10.3',9X,E10.3)
  150 FORMAT (4X,'-45.678',12X,'E10.6',9X,E10.6)
  160 FORMAT (4X,'-45.678',12X,'E12.4',9X,E12.4)
  170 FORMAT (4X,'-45.678',12X,'E10.4',9X,E10.4)
  180 FORMAT (7X,'.0001',12X,'E9.3',9X,E9.3)
      END
```

Fig. 3-21. Program to demonstrate the "E" edit descriptor.

```
VALUE IN MEMORY     FORMAT FIELD     OUTPUT FIELD

     45.678            E10.5          .45678E+02
     45.678            E10.4           .4568E+02
     45.678            E9.5          *********
     45.678            E10.3            .457E+02
    -45.678            E10.6          **********
    -45.678            E12.4             -.4568E+02
    -45.678            E10.4          -.4568E+02
      .0001             E9.3          .100E-03
```

Fig. 3-22. Output from the program in Fig. 3-21.

served for the negative sign. In Apple FORTRAN, the range of reals can go from a negative real with a power of E + 39, to a positive real with a power of E + 38, so the four extra columns to represent scientific notation will always be sufficient. The smallest exponent that can be stored has a power of E − 39.

Apple FORTRAN has a second form of input and output for scientific notation.

*r*E*w*.*d*E*e*
3E7.2E2
2E10.6E2
8E09.4E2

The "E*e*" (Fig. 3-23) edit descriptor outputs data similar to the "E" edit descriptor. Using the same real data and the same field size, the output with the "E" edit descriptor and the "E*e*" edit descriptor is the same when the E2 format is used. If E3 is used, the exponent is displayed in a three-digit field.

Value	Edit Descriptor	Output
45.678	E10.5E2	.45678E+02
45.678	E10.5E3	.04568E+002

```
VALUE IN MEMORY          FORMAT FIELD        OUTPUT FIELD

       45.678             E10.5E2            .45678E+02
       45.678             E10.4E2             .4568E+02
       45.678             E9.5E2            *********
       45.678             E10.3E2              .457E+02
      -45.678             E10.6E2           **********
      -45.678             E12.4E2              -.4568E+02
      -45.678             E10.4E2            -.4568E+02
        .0001              E9.3E2             .100E-03
```

Fig. 3-23. Output from the program in Fig. 3-21 but using the "Ee" edit descriptor.

P Edit Descriptor

In some cases, it is desirable to override the decimal point in the decimal field, and give a new value to data. The "P" edit descriptor is used to change the decimal for floating-point (F) and scientific notation (E) values. The "P" scale factor moves the decimal point in relation to the value of the positive or negative integer preceding the "P" edit descriptor. If the integer is positive, the decimal is moved to the right, equal to the number of places in the integer. If the integer is negative, the decimal is moved to the left, equal to the number of places in the integer.

Value	Edit Descriptor	Output Value
45.678	2P12.4E2	45.6780E+00
45.678	–2P10.4E2	.0046E+04

The program in Fig. 3-24 was written to demonstrate the output of the "P" factor, using a +2P and a –2P edit descriptor. As the decimal point is shifted right or left, the exponent changes to accommodate the change in the characteristic. The output data from the program in Fig. 3-24 is shown in Fig. 3-25.

```
C**** PROGRAM TO DEMONSTRATE OUTPUT USING
C**** THE "P" EDIT DESCRIPTOR FOR SCIENTIFIC
C**** NOTATION
C234567
      PROGRAM W6
      DATA E1/45.678/
      DATA E2/45.678/
      DATA E3/45.678/
      DATA E4/45.678/
      DATA E5/-45.678/
      DATA E6/-45.678/
      DATA E7/-45.678/
      DATA E8/.0001/
      OPEN (6,FILE='PRINTER:')
      WRITE (0,100)
      WRITE (6,100)
      WRITE (0,110) E1
      WRITE (6,110) E1
      WRITE (0,120) E2
      WRITE (6,120) E2
      WRITE (0,130) E3
      WRITE (6,130) E3
      WRITE (0,140) E4
      WRITE (6,140) E4
      WRITE (0,150) E5
      WRITE (6,150) E5
      WRITE (0,160) E6
      WRITE (6,160) E6
      WRITE (0,170) E7
      WRITE (6,170) E7
      WRITE (0,180) E8
      WRITE (6,180) E8
  100 FORMAT (//,'VALUE IN MEMORY',5X,'FORMAT FIELD',5X,
     *'OUTPUT FIELD',/)
  110 FORMAT (5X,'45.678',9X,'2PE12.5E2',9X,2PE12.5E2)
  120 FORMAT (5X,'45.678',9X,'-2PE10.4E2',9X,-2PE10.4E2)
  130 FORMAT (5X,'45.678',9X,'2PE14.5E2',9X,2PE14.5E2)
  140 FORMAT (5X,'45.678',9X,'-2PE10.3E2',9X,-2PE10.3E2)
  150 FORMAT (4X,'-45.678',9X,'2PE10.6E2',9X,2PE10.6E2)
  160 FORMAT (4X,'-45.678',9X,'-2PE12.4E2',9X,-2PE12.4E2)
  170 FORMAT (4X,'-45.678',9X,'2PE10.4E2',9X,2PE10.4E2)
  180 FORMAT (7X,'.0001',9X,'-2PE9.3E2',9X,-2PE9.3E2)
      END
```

Fig. 3-24. Program to demonstrate the "P" edit descriptor.

```
VALUE IN MEMORY     FORMAT FIELD     OUTPUT FIELD

      45.678        2PE12.5E2         45.6780E+00
      45.678        -2PE10.4E2          .0046E+04
      45.678        2PE14.5E2           45.6780E+00
      45.678        -2PE10.3E2          .005E+04
     -45.678        2PE10.6E2        **********
     -45.678        -2PE12.4E2           -.0046E+04
     -45.678        2PE10.4E2        **********
       .0001         -2PE9.3E2          .001E-01
```

Fig. 3-25. Output from the program in Fig. 3-24.

Logical Edit Descriptor

The specification statement LOGICAL is related to the "L" edit descriptor. The logical specification has only two values — TRUE and FALSE. The standard form of the logical specification is the keyword LOGICAL, followed by a variable, a comma, and another variable until the list is complete. LOGICAL does not follow the integer and real alphabetic rule.

LOGICAL ANSWR1, ANSWR2, A(5), D(2,3)

The LOGICAL assignment statement is used to assign a logical value to logical constants.

ANSWR1 = .TRUE.
ANSWR2 = .FALSE.
ANSWR2 = .NOT. ANSWR1

The program in Fig. 3-26 was written to demonstrate the operation of the

```
C**** PROGRAM TO DEMONSTRATE THE USE OF THE
C**** SPECIFICATION LOGICAL AND THE "L"
C**** EDIT DESCRIPTOR
C234567
      PROGRAM LOGIC
      REAL NUM1, NUM2
      LOGICAL ANSWR1, ANSWR2
      OPEN (6,FILE='PRINTER:')
      NUM1 = 40.0
      NUM2 = 13.0
      ANSWR1 = NUM1 .GT. NUM2
      ANSWR2 = ANSWR1 .AND. NUM2 .LT. 10.0
      WRITE (0,10)
      WRITE (6,10)
      WRITE (0,20) ANSWR1, ANSWR2
      WRITE (6,20) ANSWR1, ANSWR2
      WRITE (0,30) ANSWR1, ANSWR2
      WRITE (6,30) ANSWR1, ANSWR2
      WRITE (0,40) ANSWR1, ANSWR2
      WRITE (6,40) ANSWR1, ANSWR2
   10 FORMAT (//,1X,'ANSWR1 IS TRUE, SINCE 40.0 IS GREATER',
     */,' THAN 13.0, AND ANSWR2 IS FALSE, SINCE BOTH',/
     *' CONDITIONS IN AN AND STATEMENT MUST BE TRUE',/,
     *' FOR THE CONDITION TO BE TRUE.')
   20 FORMAT (//,L1,3X,L2,/)
   30 FORMAT (L3,3X,L4,/)
   40 FORMAT (L5,3X,L6,//)
      STOP
      END


 ANSWR1 IS TRUE, SINCE 40.0 IS GREATER
 THAN 13.0, AND ANSWR2 IS FALSE, SINCE BOTH
 CONDITIONS IN AN AND STATEMENT MUST BE TRUE
 FOR THE CONDITION TO BE TRUE.


T   F

  T    F

    T     F
```

Fig. 3-26. Program to demonstrate the "L" edit descriptor.

LOGICAL statement in relation to the "L" edit descriptor. LOGICAL causes ANSWR1 and ANSWR2 to be logical variables. Constant values are assigned to NUM1 and NUM2. The LOGICAL assignment statement is used to compare NUM1 with NUM2. If NUM1 is greater than NUM2, the logical constant .TRUE. is assigned to ANSWR1. If NUM1 is equal to or less than NUM2, the logical constant is assigned to ANSWR1. In this example, NUM1 is greater than NUM2, so the logical constant "T" is printed out. The second LOGICAL statement uses the logical operator ".AND." and the relational operator ".LT." to make comparisons to determine if the logical value is true or false. The logical constant assigned to ANSWR2 is "F" for false.

FORMAT lines 20, 30, and 40 demonstrate the "L" edit descriptor and its multiplier. L1, L2, L3, L4, L5, and L6 are used as edit descriptors and multipliers, but in each case only "T" or "F" is output. The integer multiplier sets the value of the field of output. The output is a single alphabetic character, and blanks fill the rest of the field. The same alphabetic results are printed with L1 as with L6.

Slash Edit Descriptor

The slash (/) edit descriptor is used in DATA statements to indicate the end of the variable list and the end of the constant list. The slash editor is used to close out lines or to skip lines in output. One slash at the beginning of a FORMAT statement causes a line to be skipped. Each additional slash causes a line to be skipped. A slash at the end of a FORMAT statement causes the line to be closed out. This is very useful when a FORMAT statement has continuation lines so literals and data can be placed on separate lines by using only one FORMAT statement. Additional slashes at the end of FORMAT statements, and preceding continuation lines, cause one line to be skipped between lines for each slash.

CHAPTER 4
Loops

A loop is a series of program statements that are repeatedly executed until some condition is met, which causes a branch instruction to jump out of, or default out of, the loop.

Four types of loops will be discussed in this chapter — constructed (or GOTO) loops, DO loops, nested DO loops, and implied DO loops.

CONSTRUCTED LOOPS

The constructed (or GOTO) loop is executed until a condition is met. The constructed loop has four parts:

```
1. Initialization          INT = 0
                           NUM = 10
2. Incrementation      10  INT = INT + 1
3. Body                    X = INT
                           XSQURE = SQRT(X)
                           XQUED = X**2
4. Test                    IF (INT .LT. NUM) GOTO 10
```

The initialization step (Fig. 4-1) sets the index value of the integer variable, INT, to zero. The variable, NUM, contains the value to which INT is compared. In line 10, Fig. 4-1, the variable, INT, is incremented by the statement, INT = INT + 1, each time the loop is executed. The integer value is assigned directly to the real variable by the X = INT statement. This sets the real value of X to the same value as the index variable, INT. In the body of the loop, the square root of X is calculated, and the value of X is squared. The value stored in INT is tested against the value stored in NUM. If the value in INT is less than the value stored in NUM, the test is true and the decision statement causes a branch to line 10. At line 10, one (1) is added to the value stored in INT.

The loop counter increments until the value stored in INT has been incremented 10 times. When the value stored in INT is greater than or equal to the value stored in NUM, the test is false and the program defaults out of the loop and terminates.

PARTS OF A LOOP

Fig. 4-2 is a variation of the constructed loop in which the test statement is at the beginning of the loop:

1. Initialization		INT = 1
		NUM = 10
2. Test	10	IF (INT .GT. NUM) GOTO 20
3. Body		X = INT
		XSQUE = SQRT (X)
4. Incrementation		INT = INT + 1
5. Return		GOTO 10
	20	WRITE

```
C**** PROGRAM TO DEMONSTRATE A CONSTRUCTED LOOP
C**** WHICH INCREMENTS TEN TIMES IN THE LOOP
C**** PROPER, AND COMPUTES THE SQUARE, AND
C**** THE SQUARE ROOT OF THE REALS
C
C234567
      PROGRAM CONSTL
      OPEN (6,FILE='PRINTER:')
      INT = 0
      NUM = 10
      WRITE (0,100)
      WRITE (6,100)
   10 INT = INT + 1
      X = INT
      XSQURE  = SQRT(X)
      XQUED   = X**2
      WRITE (0,200) INT, XSQURE, XQUED
      WRITE (6,200) INT, XSQURE, XQUED
      IF (INT .LT. NUM) GOTO 10
  100 FORMAT (//,5X,'COUNT',5X,'XSQUARE',5X,'XSQUARED',/)
  200 FORMAT (6X,I3,1X,F12.5,7X,F6.2)
      STOP 'FINI'
      END


        COUNT        XSQUARE        XSQUARED

          1          1.00000            1.00
          2          1.41421            4.00
          3          1.73205            9.00
          4          2.00000           16.00
          5          2.23607           25.00
          6          2.44949           36.00
          7          2.64575           49.00
          8          2.82843           64.00
          9          3.00000           81.00
         10          3.16228          100.00
```

Fig. 4-1. Program to demonstrate a constructed loop.

In Fig. 4-2, the integer variable, INT, is initialized to 1, and NUM is initialized to 10. INT is initialized to 1 because the first value is used before INT is incremented. The initialization statements are used in the logical IF as the test, IF (INT .GT. NUM) GOTO 20. Since INT (1) is less than NUM (10), the statement is false and the program defaults to the body of the program to do the computations. When the computations are complete for the first pass of the loop, the incrementing statement adds 1 to the variable INT (1 +

1 = 2). The program defaults to the RETURN statement, GOTO 10. The program unconditionally branches to line 10 to make the test again.

The program repeats the loop until the value stored in INT is greater than the value stored in NUM. When the test is true, the program branches to line 20 to print out the value of INT after the loop is complete. The value output is 11.

```
C**** PROGRAM TO DEMONSTRATE THE USE OF THE
C**** DECISION STATEMENT TO JUMP OUT OF A
C**** CONSTRUCTED LOOP
C
C234567
      PROGRAM COMP
      OPEN (6,FILE='PRINTER:')
      INT = 1
      NUM = 10
      WRITE (0,100)
      WRITE (6,100)
   10 IF (INT .GT. NUM) GOTO 20
      X = INT
      XSQUE = SQRT(X)
      XQUED = X*X
      WRITE (0,200) INT, XSQUE, XQUED
      WRITE (6,200) INT, XSQUE, XQUED
      INT = INT + 1
      GOTO 10
   20 WRITE (6,220) INT
  100 FORMAT (//,5X,'COUNT',5X,'XSQUARE',5X,'XSQUARED',/)
  200 FORMAT (6X,I3,1X,F12.5,7X,F6.2)
  220 FORMAT (//,2X,'WHEN THE LOOP ENDS THE INTEGER VALUE IS:
     *',I3, /)
      STOP 'END'
      END




     COUNT       XSQUARE       XSQUARED

         1       1.00000           1.00
         2       1.41421           4.00
         3       1.73205           9.00
         4       2.00000          16.00
         5       2.23607          25.00
         6       2.44949          36.00
         7       2.64575          49.00
         8       2.82843          64.00
         9       3.00000          81.00
        10       3.16228         100.00

  WHEN THE LOOP ENDS THE INTEGER VALUE IS:  11
```

Fig. 4-2. Program to demonstrate a constructed loop with the test statement at the beginning of the loop.

IMPORTANCE OF CORRECT INITIALIZATION

For output accuracy, the relationship between the initialized value, the placement of the incrementing statement, and the logical operator in the test statement is very important. The program and data in Fig. 4-3 demonstrate this fact. The data in Fig. 4-3B was produced by these program statements.

```
      INT = 0
      NUM = 10
10    X = INT
      XSQURE = SQRT(X)
      XQUED = X**2
      INT = INT + 1
      WRITE (0,200) INT, XSQURE, XQUED
      IF (INT .LE. NUM) GOTO 10
```

The INT value was printed out from 1 to 11. When X = INT was executed, the INT value of zero was assigned to X. When XSQURE and XQUED were computed on the first pass, the value in both variables was zero. When the value in INT was 2, the value in X was 1, XSQURE was 1.00, and XQUED was 1.00. The error continued until the program terminated. In Fig. 4-3C, the program statement initialized INT to 1.

```
      INT = 1
      NUM = 10
10    X = INT
      XSQURE = SQRT(X)
      XQUED = X**2
      INT = INT + 1
      WRITE (0,200) INT, XSQURE, XQUED
      IF (INT .LE. NUM) GOTO 10
```

This version of the program initialized INT to 1. The integer value assigned to the real was 1. On the first pass, the values were printed as 1.00 for the square root and 1.00 for X squared. In this case, the first value in the integer was printed as 2, and the final value was printed as 11. The INT values and the X values were not aligned to produce the correct results.

In Fig. 4-3A the program was manipulated to produce the desired results. This is an example of very bad programming, and shows the programmer did not understand the correct program flow, or how the computer handled the statements. When a program is technically correct and produces the correct results, no gimmicks have to be used. These examples emphasize that a programmer should understand programming and how the computer handles program statements for the program and the output to be correct. Programs that are technically correct and produce the right output can be seen in Figs. 4-1 and 4-2.

To sum up, for correct output (1) the count variable must be initialized to the correct value, (2) the incrementing (counting) statement must be in the correct position in the program, and (3) the correct relational operator must be used in the decision statement. When these three items are correct, the output will be accurate.

```
C**** PROGRAM TO DEMONSTRATE A CONSTRUCTED LOOP
C**** WHICH INCREMENTS TEN TIMES IN THE LOOP
C**** PROPER, AND COMPUTES THE SQUARE, AND
C**** THE SQUARE ROOT OF THE REALS
C
C234567
      PROGRAM CONST1
      OPEN (6,FILE='PRINTER:')
      INT = 0
      XNUM = 10.
      X = 1.
      WRITE (0,100)
      WRITE (6,100)
   10 XSQURE = SQRT(X)
      XQUED  = X**2
      INT = INT + 1
      X = X + 1
      WRITE (0,200) INT, XSQURE, XQUED
      WRITE (6,200) INT, XSQURE, XQUED
      IF (X .LE. XNUM) GOTO 10
  100 FORMAT (//,5X,'COUNT',5X,'XSQUARE',5X,'XSQUARED',/)
  200 FORMAT (6X,I3,1X,F12.5,7X,F6.2)
      STOP 'FINI'
      END
```

(A)

```
   COUNT        XSQUARE        XSQUARED

     1          1.00000          1.00
     2          1.41421          4.00
     3          1.73205          9.00
     4          2.00000         16.00
     5          2.23607         25.00
     6          2.44949         36.00
     7          2.64575         49.00
     8          2.82843         64.00
     9          3.00000         81.00
    10          3.16228        100.00
```

(B) (C)

IF (INT .LE. NUM) GOTO 10

INT = 0			INT = 1		
NUM = 10			NUM = 10		
COUNT	XSQUARE	XSQUARED	COUNT	XSQUARE	XSQUARED
1	0.00000	0.00	2	1.00000	1.00
2	1.00000	1.00	3	1.41421	4.00
3	1.41421	4.00	4	1.73205	9.00
10	3.00000	81.00	11	3.162228	100.00

Fig. 4-3. Constructed loop program illustrating the importance of correct initialization.

DO LOOPS

The DO statement is a command to execute the statements contained in the loop a specific number of times. DO is the keyword that is at the beginning of the loop (Fig. 4-4). The integer 20 relates to the foot of the loop whose statement label is 20, and uses the keyword CONTINUE as the return. The "J" is an integer index variable that is used to initialize, increment, and test the loop functions. The equals sign is the assignment operator that assigns the changing values to the integer variable on the left side of the equals sign. The 1 is the beginning value of the loop index. This may be an integer constant or integer variable with a value of −32768 to 32767. If the value is 32767, there will be no room for the loop to increment, as 32767 is the integer limit of the Apple computer. Fig. 4-5 shows some examples of DO loop statements.

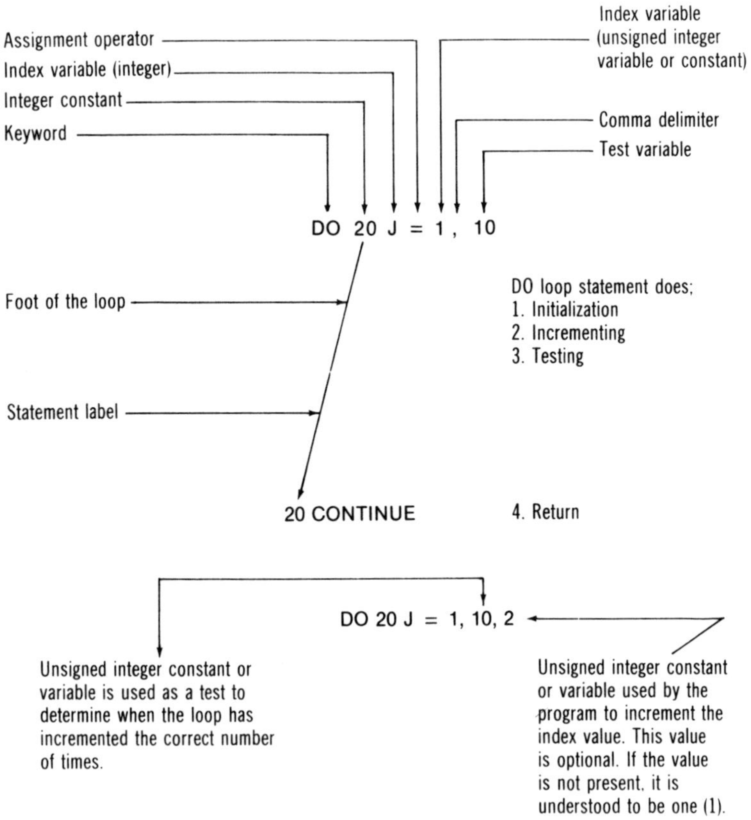

Fig. 4-4. Configuration of a DO loop.

Fig. 4-5. Examples of DO loop statements.

```
     DO 20 INT = 1, 100, 10
     DO 50 J = M, INT, N (M = 3, INT = 99, N = 3)
  10 DO 100 I = 1, 2
9999 DO 200 K = I, J, L (I = 100, J = 1000, L = 100)
```

Cycle of a DO Loop

The cycle of a DO loop is executed according to the following steps:

1. Execution of the DO statement.
2. Incrementation of the index value.
3. Test of the loop variable against the index. If the loop variable is greater than the limit value, the loop terminates execution.

A DO loop consists of all the statements within the range of the DO. The range is determined by the integer following the DO, and the related statement label of an executable statement. In Fig. 4-6, all statements from DO 20 J = 1,5 to and including 20 CONTINUE, are in the range of the DO. The most common practice is to end a DO loop with a CONTINUE statement, but any executable statement with the same statement label as the integer

```
C234567
      PROGRAM DO1
      DIMENSION SCORE (5)
      DATA SCORE/89.,75.,100.,69.,47./
      OPEN (6,FILE='PRINTER:')
      SUM = 0
      DO 20 J = 1,5
      SUM = SUM + SCORE(J)
      WRITE (0,55) SUM
      WRITE (6,55) SUM
 20   CONTINUE
      WRITE (0,50) SUM
      WRITE (6,50) SUM
 50   FORMAT (1X,//,' SUM = ',F10.0//)
      AVG = SUM/5.
      WRITE (0,60) AVG
      WRITE (6,60) AVG
 55   FORMAT (F10.0))
 60   FORMAT (1X,' AVERAGE = ',F10.2,//)
      STOP
      END


       89.
      164.
      264.
      333.
      380.


 SUM =         380.


  AVERAGE =         76.00
```

Fig. 4-6. Program to demonstrate the cycle of a DO loop.

contained in the DO statement will cause the loop to continue the iteration process. The program in Fig. 4-6 could be configured in this manner

```
      DO 20 J = 1,5
      (STATEMENTS WITHIN THE LOOP)
   20 WRITE (6,55) SUM
```

and the loop would execute until it had executed five times. The WRITE (6,55) SUM must be the only line with a statement label of 20. If the WRITE statement to the CRT and the WRITE statement to the printer had both contained the statement label 20, a compile error, "STATEMENT CANNOT HAVE LABEL," would occur.

The DO loop is executed until the index variable is greater than the test variable. When the index variable is greater than the test variable, the conditions of the loop have been satisfied and the loop defaults to the first executable statement below the foot of the loop.

A hexagon is used as the flowchart symbol for the DO loop. Fig. 4-7 shows the flowchart for the program in Fig. 4-6. The flowchart shows the entry to the hexagon, the initialization, incrementation, test, return, and the exit. There are two lines that leave the right side of the hexagon. The upper line is the path that is followed after the index variable is initialized. The lower line is the path that is followed after each test of the limit value. The RETURN line passes through the incrementing statement to the test statement. Both lines that leave the hexagon on the right side join to form one

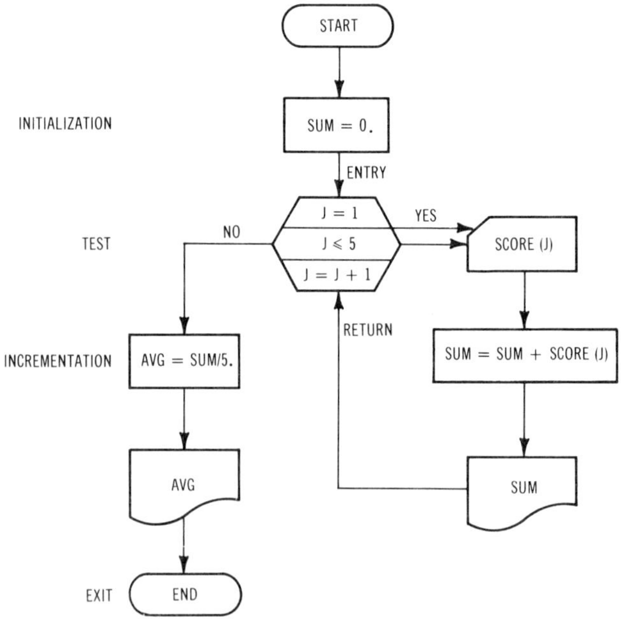

Fig. 4-7. Flowcharting a DO loop.

line that goes through the body of the loop to execute the statements within the body and return to the hexagon. When the test fails (J is greater than 5), the path exits from the left side of the hexagon to complete the program. This exit line is the same as the default when the loop has completed its process.

Rules for Using DO Loops

The rules for using DO loops are as follows:

1. Enter the DO loop through the DO statement.
2. After a DO loop has completed execution, a branch can be directed to the DO statement.
3. Do not enter a DO loop in the body of the loop.
4. After a DO loop has completed execution, do not branch back into the body of the DO loop.
5. When the DO statement is executed, the value is initialized to the value given to the index variable or index constant.
6. A transfer within the loop from one statement to another statement is permitted.
7. A transfer out of the body of the loop is possible without completion of the incrementing process; however, the testing variable may not contain a reliable value.
8. When the loop has completed execution in the normal manner, the testing value may not be reliable after leaving the loop structure.
9. The foot of the loop statement must be an executable statement.
10. When the loop has completed normal execution, it must be followed by an executable statement.
11. The last statement of a DO loop must be an executable statement, but must not be a GOTO, STOP, PAUSE, RETURN, LOGICAL, IF, or DO statement.
12. The DO loop variable must be of the integer type.
13. The referring constant must be of the integer type.
14. The indices must be either integer variables or integer constants.

The CONTINUE statement that is generally the foot of the loop tells the program to continue doing what it is doing. The CONTINUE is an executable statement to mark the end position of the loop (Fig. 4-8).

NESTED DO LOOPS

Nesting loops is a programming technique in which a loop of instructions contains a loop of instructions, etc. Loops may be nested in any of several ways (Fig. 4-9), and are used to create tables of values by using arithmetic expressions. Nested DO loops follow the same rules as single DO loops.

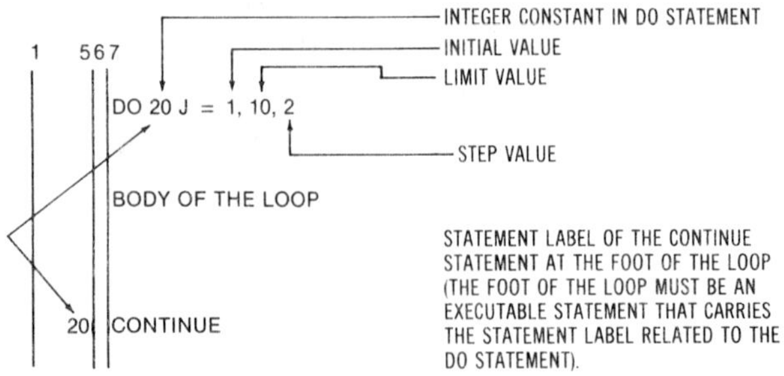

Fig. 4-8. Relationship between the integer constant in the DO and CONTINUE statements.

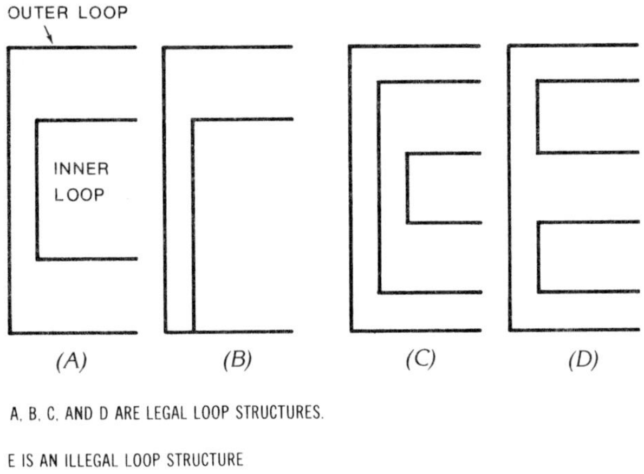

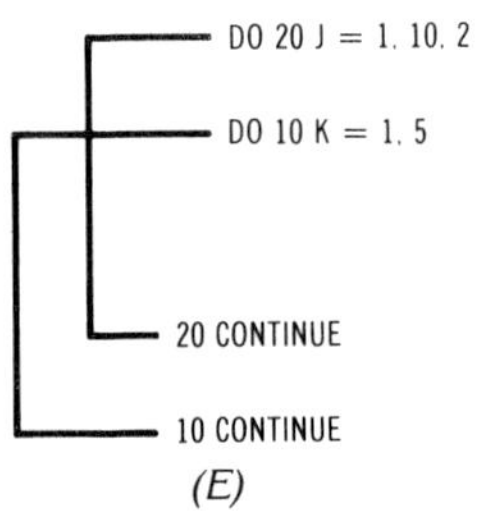

Fig. 4-9. Configuration of nested DO loops.

Doubly Nested DO Loops

In doubly nested DO loops, the outside loop is referred to as the outer loop, and the inside loop is referred to as the inner loop (Fig. 4-9A). When the program defaults into the outer loop, the outer loop executes the first DO statement, so the index is set to the initial value. If the index is 1 (Fig. 4-10), the initial index value is set to 1. The program defaults to the inner DO statement. The inner loop is repeated from the initial value to the limit value. The inner loop then defaults through the body of the loop to the foot of the loop CONTINUE statement to make the test against the limit value. If the loop variable is greater than the limit value, the test fails. The inner loop defaults to the outer loop CONTINUE statement, which causes the outer loop to repeat for the second time. The outer and inner loops continue this incrementing until the limit value of the outer loop is reached.

In the example in Fig. 4-10, the "J" outer loop has an initial value of 1 and a limit value of 3. The "K" inner loop has an initial value of 1 and a limit value of 2.

```
   DO 20 J = 1, 3
   DO 10 K = 1, 2
   .
   .
   .
10 CONTINUE
20 CONTINUE
```

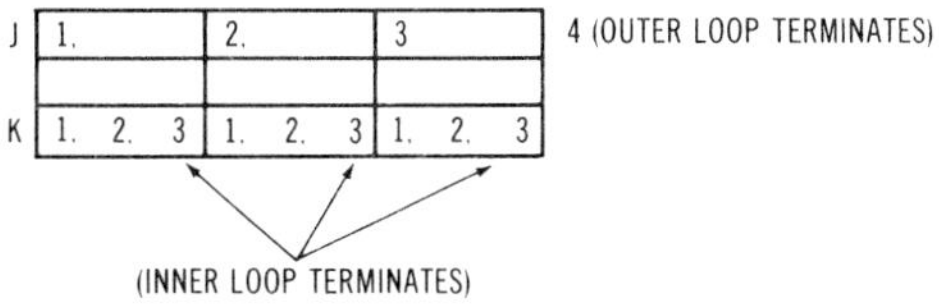

Fig. 4-10. Execution pattern of nested DO loops.

When the program defaults into the "J" loop it sets the initial value to 1. The program defaults to the "K" loop. The "K" loop is executed two times. When the "K" loop variable is greater than the limit value, it defaults to the CONTINUE statement whose label is 20. The "J" loop executes for the second time. The program defaults to the "K" loop. The "K" loop increments twice and defaults to the "J" loop. The "J" loop increments the third time and increments the "J" loop variable to 4. The "K" loop executes for the third time and defaults to the CONTINUE statement whose label is 20. The "J" loop variable has been assigned a value of 4 after the last execution. The "J" variable value 4 is greater than the limit value 3; the test fails, and the loop terminates. A flowchart of this example is shown in Fig. 4-11.

Nested DO loops are formatted according to the needs of the user. Fig. 4-9A is an example of two nested loops that are used to compute the values in a table (Fig. 4-12). Fig. 4-9B is an example of doubly nested DO loops which use the same CONTINUE statement for the foot of the loop. In this example, the outer loop and the inner loop integer constants must be the same value as the statement label of the CONTINUE statement.

```
   DO 50 J = 1,11
   DO 50 K = 3,9
   X(J,10) = X(J,10) + X(J,K)
   IF (X(J,K) .LT. 40.) GOTO 50
   X(J,11) = X(J,11) + X(J,2) * .6
   IF (X(J,K) .LT. 50.) GOTO 50
   X(J,11) = X(J,11) + (X(J,K)-50) * 2.00
50 CONTINUE
```

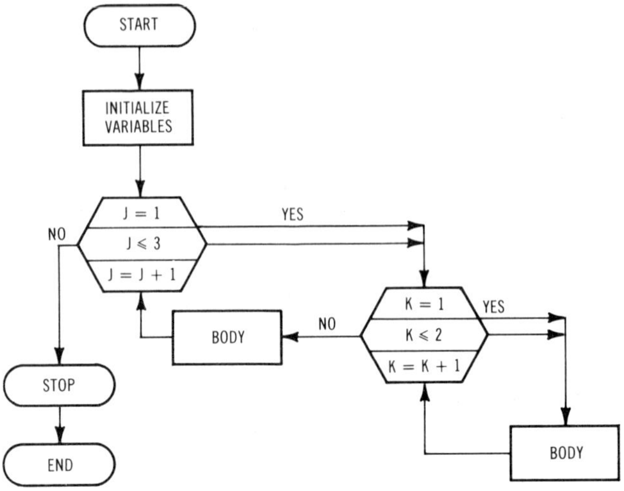


```
      INITIALIZE VARIABLES
      DO 20 J = 1,3
      DO 10 K = 1,2
      BODY
   10 CONTINUE
      BODY
   20 CONTINUE
      STOP
      END
```

Fig. 4-11. Flowchart of a doubly nested DO loop.

The foot of a doubly nested loop does not have to be a CONTINUE statement but must be an executable statement with the same statement label as the integer constant in the DO statement.

```
    DO 80 K = 3,11
    DO 80 J = 1,11
80  X(12,K) = X(12,K) + X(J,K)
    WRITE (0,150)
```

Fig. 4-9C is an example of how triple nested loops would be formatted, and Fig. 4-9D is an example of two nested loops in an outer loop. The inner loops are not nested. Fig. 4-9E is an example of how nested loops should not be formatted.

Rules for Using Nested DO Loops

The rules for using nested loops are as follows:

1. Nested loops are illegal if the index variable in both loops is the same alphabetic character.

   ```
   DO 50 J = 1,11
   DO 40 J = 3,9 (ILLEGAL)
   ```

```
6C**** PROGRAM TO COMPUTE THE BONUS PAY OF
C**** COMPANY MACHINISTS WHO ARE PAID ON THE BASIS
C**** OF PRODUCTION
C234567
      PROGRAM MACH1
      DIMENSION X(12,11)
      DATA X(1,1),X(1,2),X(1,3),X(1,4),X(1,5),X(1,6),
     1X(1,7),X(1,8),X(1,9),X(2,1),X(2,2),X(2,3),X(2,4),
     2X(2,5),X(2,6),X(2,7),X(2,8),X(2,9),X(3,1),X(3,2),
     3X(3,3),X(3,4),X(3,5),X(3,6),X(3,7),X(3,8),X(3,9),X(4,1),
     4X(4,2),X(4,3),X(4,4),X(4,5),X(4,6),X(4,7),X(4,8),
     5X(4,9)/1.,10.50,38.,47.,45.,60.,62.,0.,0.,2.,10.50,
     647.,61.,18.,23.,0.,0.,63.,3.,10.25,60.,62.,49.,.
     738.,0.,0.,70.,4.,11.05,0.,0.,28.,54.,60.,62.,62./
      DATA X(5,1),X(5,2),X(5,3),X(5,4),X(5,5),X(5,6),
     1X(5,7),X(5,8),X(5,9),X(6,1),X(6,2),X(6,3),X(6,4),
     2X(6,5),X(6,6),X(6,7),X(6,8),X(6,9),X(7,1),X(7,2),
     3X(7,3),X(7,4),X(7,5),X(7,6),X(7,7),X(7,8),X(7,9),
     4X(8,1),X(8,2),X(8,3),X(8,4),X(8,5),X(8,6),X(8,7),
     5X(8,8),X(8,9)/5.,8.75,0.,0.,48.,51.,38.,47.,31.,
     66.,9.75,31.,39.,53.,60.,60.,0.,0.,7.,10.00,51.,
     753.,0.,0.,53.,58.,54.,8.,15.75,38.,59.,0.,0.,
     859.,61.,59./
      DATA X(9,1),X(9,2),X(9,3),X(9,4),X(9,5),X(9,6),
     1X(9,7),X(9,8),X(9,9),X(10,1),X(10,2),X(10,3),
     2X(10,4),X(10,5),X(10,6),X(10,7),X(10,8),
     3X(10,9),X(11,1),X(11,2),X(11,3),X(11,4),
     4X(11,5),X(11,6),X(11,7),X(11,8),X(11,9)/
     59.,9.75,0.,0.,40.,53.,29.,49.,50.,10.,
     68.75,60.,60.,0.,0.,59.,58.,58.,11.,11.05,
     758.,43.,21.,0.,0.,46.,49./
      OPEN (6,FILE='PRINTER:')
  150 FORMAT (//,'MACH',55X,'TOTAL')
  160 FORMAT (1H#,6X,3HPAY,4X,3HMON,3X,3HTUE,3X,3HWED,
     *3X,3HTHU,3X,3HFRI,3X ,3HSAT,3X,3HSUN,3X,5HUNITS,
     *2X,5HBONUS,/)
  190 FORMAT (F3.0,3X,F5.2,1X,7(F5.0,1X),F6.0,1X,F7.2)
  200 FORMAT (67(1H-))
  210 FORMAT (5HTOTAL,7X,7(F5.0,1X),F6.0,1X,F7.2)
      DO 10 J = 10,11
      DO 05 K = 1,12
      X(K,J) = 0
   05 CONTINUE
   10 CONTINUE
      DO 15 J = 3,9
      X(12,J) = 0
   15 CONTINUE
      DO 50 J = 1,11
      DO 40 K = 3,9
      X(J,10) = X(J,10) + X(J,K)
      IF (X(J,K) .LT. 40.) GOTO 40
      X(J,11) = X(J,11) + X(J,2) * .6
      IF (X(J,K) .LT. 50.) GOTO 40
      X(J,11) = X(J,11) + (X(J,K)-50.) * 2.00
   40 CONTINUE
   50 CONTINUE
      DO 60 J = 1,11
      IF (X(J,10) .LT. 200.) GOTO 60
      X(J,11) = X(J,11) +(X(J,10)-200.) * .35
   60 CONTINUE
      DO 80 K = 3,11
      DO 70 J = 1,11
      X(12,K) = X(12,K) + X(J,K)
```

Fig. 4-12. Program to demonstrate nested DO loops.

```
70 CONTINUE
80 CONTINUE
   WRITE (0,150)
   WRITE (6,150)
   WRITE (0,160)
   WRITE (6,160)
   DO 90 J = 1,11
   WRITE (0,190) X(J,1),X(J,2),X(J,3),X(J,4),
  *X(J,5),X(J,6),X(J,7),X(J,8),X(J,9),X(J,10),
  *X(J,11)
   WRITE (6,190) X(J,1),X(J,2),X(J,3),X(J,4),X(J,5),
  *X(J,6),X(J,7),X(J,8),X(J,9),X(J,10),X(J,11)
90 CONTINUE
   WRITE (0,200)
   WRITE (6,200)
   WRITE (0,210) X(12,3),X(12,4),X(12,5),X(12,6),
  *X(12,7),X(12,8),X(12,9),X(12,10),X(12,11)
   WRITE (6,210) X(12,3),X(12,4),X(12,5),X(12,6),
  *X(12,7),X(12,8),X(12,9),X(12,10),X(12,11)
   STOP
   END
```

MACH #	PAY	MON	TUE	WED	THU	FRI	SAT	SUN	TOTAL UNITS	BONUS
1.	10.50	38.	47.	45.	60.	62.	0.	0.	252.	87.40
2.	10.50	47.	61.	18.	23.	0.	0.	63.	212.	71.10
3.	10.25	60.	62.	49.	38.	0.	0.	70.	279.	136.25
4.	11.05	0.	0.	28.	54.	60.	62.	62.	266.	125.62
5.	8.75	0.	0.	48.	51.	38.	47.	31.	215.	23.00
6.	9.75	31.	39.	53.	60.	60.	0.	0.	243.	78.60
7.	10.00	51.	53.	0.	0.	53.	58.	54.	269.	92.15
8.	15.75	38.	59.	0.	0.	59.	61.	59.	276.	140.40
9.	9.75	0.	0.	40.	53.	29.	49.	50.	221.	36.75
10.	8.75	60.	60.	0.	0.	59.	58.	58.	295.	149.50
11.	11.05	58.	43.	21.	0.	0.	46.	49.	217.	48.47
TOTAL		383.	424.	302.	339.	420.	381.	496.	2745.	989.24

Fig. 4-12. Program to demonstrate nested DO loops. *(Continued)*

2. The same index variable may be used in DO loops which follow each other but are not nested.

```
    DO 70 J = 1,11
70  CONTINUE
    DO 80 J = 1,11
80  CONTINUE
```

3. An inner DO loop may not redefine the initial or limit value of the outer loop.

```
    DO 60 J = M,N
    DO 50 M = 1,11 (ILLEGAL)
    X(J,10) = X(J,10) + X(J,M)
50  CONTINUE
60  CONTINUE
```

4. Doubly nested DO loops can use the same executable statement at the foot of the loop (continue, computation, write).
5. It is illegal to branch into the middle of an inner or outer loop.

IMPLIED DO LOOPS

Implied DO loops are a modification of the standard DO loop. The rules that pertain to the implied DO loop are similar to the rules that pertain to the standard DO loop, but the implied DO loop has no integer constant that refers to a statement label. The implied DO loop has no CONTINUE, or foot of the loop statement; it is complete in its legal format. The implied DO loop is an efficient method to read and write items that are formatted in a single line.

The implied DO loop (Figs. 3-4 and 4-13) can be used in several combinations to perform the desired action. The READ or WRITE statement can have (1) a single implied DO loop (Fig. 4-13 or Fig. 4-14A), (2) a combination of real and integer variables and an implied DO loop (Fig. 4-14B), (3) two implied DO loops, and (4) a standard DO loop and an implied DO loop (Fig. 4-13) for writing a table.

The implied DO loop can be used only with a READ or WRITE statement. In Apple FORTRAN, there are only two places from which to read — keyboard and disk.

To read from keyboard (Fig. 4-14A), a user prompt is first written to the CRT. The user prompt shows where the data is to be input. The implied DO allows the user to input the data items, one at a time, until three items have been input. The data items are formatted in an F10.2 field, and that is the number of columns available for the input field.

Fig. 4-14B is an example of an array (Z) that has been dimensioned to 10 memory locations. The integer variable "N" has been assigned the value of 10. The READ statement reads an integer value (J) formatted in three columns from the keyboard, and then reads 10 (N = 10) reals from the keyboard, each formatted in six columns (F6.0). The implied DO uses an initial value of 1 and a limit value of 10 stored in the integer variable "N."

Fig. 4-14C is a program in skeletal form that reads a file from disk. The file has to be written to disk (Fig. 4-15E) before it can be read. The file contains 5 elements of data in an array whose variable is "X." The file is opened on device 20 (0 through 12 are reserved for Apple input/output slots). The file is labeled "#5:WRITE," and it is a direct (random) access file. The file was created previously (Fig. 4-15E), thus the STATUS = 'OLD'. The file is formatted, and each record is 30 bytes long. The file is going to be retained for future use, thus the STATUS = 'KEEP' in line 900.

The READ statement is going to read the file on device #20, and will use the FORMAT statement 200. The reading will begin at record #1, and when the file has been read to the end, it will branch to line 900 to close the file.

The file is read by an implied DO loop. The array "X(K)" is to be read from the initial value (1) to the limit value (5). This indicates that each item of data is to be read from the file. If only the first three items of data were to be read, the implied DO would have been "X(K),K = 1, 3." It is permissible to

```
C**** PROGRAM TO COMPUTE THE BONUS PAY OF
C**** COMPANY MACHINISTS WHO ARE PAID ON THE BASIS
C**** OF PRODUCTION
C234567
      PROGRAM MACH1
      DIMENSION X(12,11)
      DATA X(1,1),X(1,2),X(1,3),X(1,4),X(1,5),X(1,6),
     1X(1,7),X(1,8),X(1,9),X(2,1),X(2,2),X(2,3),X(2,4),
     2X(2,5),X(2,6),X(2,7),X(2,8),X(2,9),X(3,1),X(3,2),
     3X(3,3),X(3,4),X(3,5),X(3,6),X(3,7),X(3,8),X(3,9),X(4,1),
     4X(4,2),X(4,3),X(4,4),X(4,5),X(4,6),X(4,7),X(4,8),
     5X(4,9)/1.,10.50,38.,47.,45.,60.,62.,0.,0.,2.,10.50,
     647.,61.,18.,23.,0.,0.,63.,3.,10.25,60.,62.,49.,
     738.,0.,0.,70.,4.,11.05,0.,0.,28.,54.,60.,62.,62./
      DATA X(5,1),X(5,2),X(5,3),X(5,4),X(5,5),X(5,6),
     1X(5,7),X(5,8),X(5,9),X(6,1),X(6,2),X(6,3),X(6,4),
     2X(6,5),X(6,6),X(6,7),X(6,8),X(6,9),X(7,1),X(7,2),
     3X(7,3),X(7,4),X(7,5),X(7,6),X(7,7),X(7,8),X(7,9),
     4X(8,1),X(8,2),X(8,3),X(8,4),X(8,5),X(8,6),X(8,7),
     5X(8,8),X(8,9)/5.,8.75,0.,0.,48.,51.,38.,47.,31.,
     66.,9.75,31.,39.,53.,60.,60.,0.,0.,7.,10.00,51.,
     753.,0.,0.,53.,58.,54.,8.,15.75,38.,59.,0.,0.,
     859.,61.,59./
      DATA X(9,1),X(9,2),X(9,3),X(9,4),X(9,5),X(9,6),
     1X(9,7),X(9,8),X(9,9),X(10,1),X(10,2),X(10,3),
     2X(10,4),X(10,5),X(10,6),X(10,7),X(10,8),
     3X(10,9),X(11,1),X(11,2),X(11,3),X(11,4),
     4X(11,5),X(11,6),X(11,7),X(11,8),X(11,9)/
     59.,9.75,0.,0.,40.,53.,29.,49.,50.,10.,
     68.75,60.,60.,0.,0.,59.,58.,58.,11.,11.05,
     758.,43.,21.,0.,0.,46.,49./
  150 FORMAT (//,'MACH',55X,'TOTAL')
  160 FORMAT (1H#,6X,3HPAY,4X,3HMON,3X,3HTUE,3X,3HWED,
     *3X,3HTHU,3X,3HFRI,3X ,3HSAT,3X,3HSUN,3X,5HUNITS,
     *2X,5HBONUS,/)
  190 FORMAT (F3.0,3X,F5.2,1X,7(F5.0,1X),F6.0,1X,F7.2)
  200 FORMAT (67(1H-))
  210 FORMAT (5HTOTAL,7X,7(F5.0,1X),F6.0,1X,F7.2)
      DO 10 J = 10,11
      DO 05 K = 1,12
      X(K,J) = 0
   05 CONTINUE
   10 CONTINUE
      DO 15 J = 3,9
      X(12,J) = 0
   15 CONTINUE
      DO 50 J = 1,11
      DO 40 K = 3,9
      X(J,10) = X(J,10) + X(J,K)
      IF (X(J,K) .LT. 40.) GOTO 40
      X(J,11) = X(J,11) + X(J,2) * .6
      IF (X(J,K) .LT. 50.) GOTO 40
      X(J,11) = X(J,11) + (X(J,K)-50.) * 2.00
   40 CONTINUE
   50 CONTINUE
      DO 60 J = 1,11
      IF (X(J,10) .LT. 200.) GOTO 60
      X(J,11) = X(J,11) +(X(J,10)-200.) * .35
   60 CONTINUE
      DO 80 K = 3,11
      DO 70 J = 1,11
      X(12,K) = X(12,K) + X(J,K)
   70 CONTINUE
```

Fig. 4-13. Program to demonstrate implied DO loops.

```
80 CONTINUE
   WRITE (0,150)
   WRITE (0,160)
   DO 90 J = 1,11
   WRITE (0,190) (X(J,K),K = 1,11)
90 CONTINUE
   WRITE (0,200)
   WRITE (0,210) (X(12,K),K = 3,11)
   STOP
   END
```

Fig. 4-13. Program to demonstrate implied DO loops. *(Continued)*

read any number of data items in the file, and it is not mandatory that all items be read.

In Apple FORTRAN, a large percentage of the data is read from disk, or placed directly in the program in a DATA statement, so the implied DO is used more for writing than for reading.

In the Apple computer, there are three places to write — CRT, disk, and printer.

(A)

```
     DIMENSION X(3)
     WRITE (0,1)
   1 FORMAT (3(10H!--------*))
     READ (0,5) (X(J), J = 1, 3)
   5 FORMAT (3(F10.2))
```

(B)

```
     DIMENSION Z(10)
     N = 10
     READ (0,10) J, (Z(I), I = 1, N)
  10 FORMAT (I3, 1X, 10(F6.0))
```

(C)
READ FROM DISK

```
     DIMENSION X(5)
     OPEN (20, FILE='#5:WRITE', ACCESS = 'DIRECT',
    *STATUS = 'OLD', FORM = 'FORMATTED',
    *RECL = 30
     READ (20, 200, REC = 1, END = 900) (X(K), K = 1,5)
 200 FORMAT (5(F10.2))
 900 CLOSE (STATUS = 'KEEP')
     STOP
     END
```

Fig. 4-14. Format combinations of the implied DO loop (READ).

HOW LOOPS ARE USED

Fig. 4-14A shows a WRITE statement using an implied DO loop. The WRITE statement is used in the program in Fig. 3-4, and is related to the READ statement in Fig. 4-14A. When the data items are input from the keyboard, they are stored in memory and are written out (Fig. 4-15A) just as they are read in. No manipulations or computations were performed in this example program.

Fig. 4-15C is an example where an integer variable is combined with a real array using an implied DO loop to write out a line of 11 items. This

WRITE statement is related to the READ statement in Fig. 4-14B. The integer variable "N" is assigned a value of 10, and is used in the integer variable form in the implied DO loop.

(A)

```
      DIMENSION X(3)
      WRITE (0, 20)(X(K), K = 1,3)
20    FORMAT (3(F10.2))
```

(B)

```
      DIMENSION Z(3)
      WRITE (0, 100) I, Z, (Z(L), L = 1,3)
100   FORMAT (//, I5, 3X, F10.5, 3X, 3(F10.3))
```

(C)

```
      DIMENSION Z(10)
      WRITE (0, 50) J, (Z(I), I = 1,N)
50    FORMAT (I3, 1X, 10(F6.0))
          (N = 10 PREVIOUSLY DEFINED)
```

(D)

```
      DIMENSION X(12, 11)
      OPEN (6, FILE = 'PRINTER:')
      DO 90 J = 1,11
      WRITE (6, 190)  (X(J,K),K = 1,11
90    CONTINUE
      WRITE (6, 200)
      WRITE (6, 210) (X(12, K), K = 3,11)
190   FORMAT (F3.0, 3X, F5.2, 1X, 7(F5.0,1X),
     * F6.0, 1X, F7.2)
200   FORMAT (67(1H-))
210   FORMAT (5HTOTAL, 7X, 7(F5.0,2X), F6.0, 1X, F7.2)
```

(E)
WRITE TO DISK

```
      DIMENSION X(5)
      DATA X/ 10., 20., 30., 40., 50./

      OPEN (20, FILE = '#5:WRITE', ACCESS = 'DIRECT',
     *STATUS = 'NEW', FORM = 'FORMATTED', RECL = 30)
      WRITE (20, 100, REC = 1, END = 900)
     *(X(J), J = 1,5)
100   FORMAT (5(F10.2))
900   CLOSE (STATUS = 'KEEP')
      STOP
      END
```

Fig. 4-15. Format combinations of the implied DO loop (WRITE).

Fig. 4-15D is taken directly from the program in Fig. 4-12. DIMENSION X(12,11) dimensions a double subscripted array that reserves a 12 × 11 matrix (132 memory locations). The table is to be sent to the printer, so the printer must be opened. The table contains 11 columns and 12 rows. The DO 90 J = 1,11 is used in combination with the implied DO loop, "X(J,K), K = 1,11," to write the 11 × 11 matrix for the table. The implied DO loop writes one row of 11 data items. The standard DO causes the data row of 11 items to be repeated 11 times. After the 11 × 11 table has been written, the WRITE (6,200) causes the table to be underlined with a dashed line in preparation to write the totals of columns 3 to 11. The WRITE (6,210) (X(12,K), K = 3,11) sets up to write one line. Row 12 is the line that contains the totals of columns 3 through 11. The implied DO loop writes these totals by the (X(12,K) specifying that row 12 is to be written with data items in columns 3 through 11.

Fig. 4-15E is a skeletal program to write a file to disk. The array "X" is dimensioned to reserve five memory locations. The data is placed in the program in a DATA statement. Each element of the array, X(1), X(2), etc., is placed in the DATA statement, and each element references one item of data. The file is opened on device #20, and the file is named "WRITE" and is on a disk in disk drive #5. The file is created as a direct (random) access file and its STATUS = 'NEW'. The file is formatted and each record is 30 bytes in length. The WRITE statement is related to the OPEN statement in that the same integer value is used as the device number. The first record to be read is number 1, and when the reading is complete, the END= statement causes the execution of the statement whose label is 900. The file is written by an implied DO loop that writes values in the array named "X," and it writes five values in the array. At line 900 the file is closed, and since the file is to be used for future programs, it is retained with the STATUS = 'KEEP' statement.

CHAPTER 5
Calculation and Control

FORTRAN VARIABLES

A FORTRAN variable is a name whose value can change. When a variable is defined within a program, a memory location is reserved to hold the assigned value. The variable is defined when it receives a value. The value can be assigned to the variable by (1) input from a DATA statement within the program, (2) input from disk, as in Fig. 3-5, or (3) input from the keyboard. When the program is executed, the values assigned to the memory location change, and that memory location can hold only one value at a time. The value in memory remains the same until it is assigned a new value.

FORTRAN variables may contain up to six alphanumeric characters. The variable must begin with an alphabetic character, and not contain any special characters. The arithmetic variable types, integer and real, follow the rule that variables beginning with the letters I–N are integers, and variables beginning with any other letter are reals (Table 1-4). However, the rule can be circumvented by using one of two methods.

IMPLICIT STATEMENTS

```
IMPLICIT INTEGER (A – H)
IMPLICIT REAL (I – N)
```

The IMPLICIT statements must be placed immediately following the program name in the program scheme (Fig. 2-8), or must be the first statement in a program without a program name. When using the IMPLICIT statement, the programmer must realize that integer and real names have been changed as to type, and handle the constant values in the correct relationship to the renamed variables.

Even though the IMPLICIT statement has set the rules for types of variables, these rules can be changed by using the keywords INTEGER and REAL.

```
INTEGER I, J, K
REAL A, B
```

Double shifting variable types should always be avoided, and is considered a bad programming practice.

Other types of variables can be declared immediately after the program name by using IMPLICIT, LOGICAL, or CHARACTER. These variables can be declared in the following ways:

```
IMPLICIT INTEGER (A - H)
IMPLICIT REAL (I - N)
IMPLICIT CHARACTER*20 NAME
```

or

```
INTEGER A, B, C
REAL I, J, K
LOGICAL ANSWR2
CHARACTER*16 N
```

ARITHMETIC EXPRESSIONS

An expression is a means of calculating a new value from one or more known values. Arithmetic expressions follow these rules:

1. A simple arithmetic expression consists of variables and/or constants separated by arithmetic operators (Table 1-7).
2. Two operation symbols must not be written one after another in the expression.
3. An expression may begin with a unary negative sign or a positive sign. The positive sign is optional, and the expression is positive unless otherwise signed.
4. Variables and constants enclosed in parentheses are evaluated first.
5. All variables and constants should be matched as to type, integer or real, except exponentiation. Exponentiation can be handled by either type of variable or constant.

```
COUNT = 0.
KOUNT = 0
AREA = PIE*RADIUS**2.
KAREA = PIE*RADIUS**2
```

ARITHMETIC OPERATORS

Arithmetic expressions are created when constants and/or variables are used with arithmetic operators. Expressions are of the real or integer type.

```
MILES * 4
XMILES * 4.
```

The operators within an arithmetic statement are evaluated according to the precedence of arithmetic operators; (1) exponentiation from left to right, (2) unary negative sign, (3) multiplication and division from left to right, (4) addition and subtraction from left to right, and (5) parentheses overrule precedence (Table 1-7). In evaluating an expression, the computer scans the expression from left to right before any operations are performed. When the initial scan is complete, the processing begins.

HOW THE COMPUTER HANDLES AN EXPRESSION

```
-A * B / D**E**F / G * C - F
```

The expression is scanned by the computer, and since there are no parentheses, the evaluation takes place in the following order:

1. "E" is raised to the power of "F" and the value is stored in temporary location 1 (TL1).
2. "D" is raised to the power of TL1 and the value is stored in TL1.
3. The unary operator negates the value of "A" and places it in temporary location 2 (TL2).
4. "B" is multiplied by TL2 and the value is stored in TL2.
5. The value stored in TL2 is divided by the value stored in TL1 and is stored back in TL1.
6. The value stored in TL1 is divided by the value of "G" and is placed back in TL1.
7. The resulting value is multiplied by "C" and stored in TL1.
8. The value of "F" is subtracted from the result in Step 7, and the final result is assigned to the variable on the left side of the equals sign.

When the computer handles an integer or real expression, it calculates the value of the expression according to type. If the expression is integer type, the results are truncated; that is, the fractional part of the expression is dropped. If the expression is of the real type, the fraction is rounded.

REPLACEMENT OR ASSIGNMENT STATEMENT

The arithmetic replacement statement is identified by the equals (=) sign between a variable on the left side and an expression and/or a variable and/or a constant on the right side. In an assignment statement, the equals sign is not used in the algebraic mode, where the value on the right side of the equals sign is the equivalent value on the left side of the equals sign. In a FORTRAN assignment statement, the value on the right side of the equals sign is assigned to the variable on the left side of the equals sign. The terms assignment and replacement are used interchangeably. The semantics of replacement is that the value held in the variable on the left side of the equals sign is replaced by the value initialized, or computed, on the right side of the equals sign.

HOW THE REPLACEMENT STATEMENT IS USED

The assignment statement can be used in four different ways.

1. To initialize or define variables. This should be done before the variable is used. This places the desired value in the memory location reserved by the variable. This initialization should be performed as a specific known value is placed in a memory location.

```
SUM = 0.
OLDNET = 0.0
KOUNT = 1
PRODT = 1.0
```

2. To calculate a value from an expression composed of variables and/or constants.

```
AVG = SUM/10.
KOUNT = KOUNT + 1
DER = SQRT(B**2 - 4*A*C)
```

3. To store the value of the new calculation into a variable for later use in the program.

```
PROF1 = PROF2
BOKVAL = COST
LTEMP = LIST(J)
LIST(J) = LIST(K)
```

4. To change the type of data from real to integer or integer to real.

```
ISALE = SALES
DATE = MONTH
LIST = YEAR
YEAR = LIST
MONTH = DATE
```

If variable and/or constant values are to be used by the computer to calculate new values, the progression from one calculation to the next must be in a logical order.

```
PIE = 3.1416
RADIUS = 2.3
AREA = PIE * RADIUS**2
```

If the statements were placed in reverse order, the formula for the area of a circle would have no values for the calculation. This is the *incorrect* order of statements:

```
AREA = PIE * RADIUS**2
PIE = 3.1416
RADIUS = 2.3
```

METHODS TO ASSIGN EXPRESSION VALUES

The program (and execution) in Fig. 5-1 is used to demonstrate how Apple FORTRAN handles arithmetic assignment statements in the integer, real, and mixed modes. The variable on the left of the equals sign can be either integer or real. The expression and/or constants on the right side of the equals sign must be integer or real. The assignment statement can assign a real value to an integer variable, or an integer value to a real variable.

```
INTEGER NAME = INTEGER EXPRESSION
INTEGER NAME = REAL EXPRESSION
INTEGER NAME = REAL VALUE
REAL NAME = REAL EXPRESSION
REAL NAME = INTEGER EXPRESSION
REAL NAME = INTEGER VALUE
```

TRUNCATION OF INTEGER VALUES

Fig. 5-1 demonstrates that the real value is output in two decimal places. When the reals are assigned to an integer variable, the value is truncated.

```
X = A + B          K = A + B
X = 2.3 + 7.4      K = 2.3 + 7.4
X = 9.7            K = 9
```

This truncation also carries over when the integer value is assigned to a real variable. Even though the real is output in an F5.2 mode, the two decimal places are zeros.

```
D = M     M= 2     D = 2.00
```

When the real value of "Y" is assigned to the integer variable, the value is truncated.

```
L = Y     Y = 2.00     L = 2
```

COUNTING STATEMENTS

Counting statements are used to count the number of times an action occurs within a FORTRAN program. The assignment statement is used to initialize the count to a specific value. The value generally assigned is zero, but any value can be assigned so the count meets the needs of the program.

```
COUNT = 0.0
KOUNT = 0
```

Each time a specific value is counted, the count is incremented by the correct amount. Items are generally counted by ones, but inventory items in packages could as easily be incremented by the number of items in the package or the case.

```
TEST = TEST + 1.
EGGS = EGGS + 12.
MOTOIL = MOTOIL +24
```

```
&C**** PROGRAM WRITTEN HOW APPLE FORTRAN
C**** HANDLES THE MIXED MODE BETWEEN INTEGERS
C**** AND REALS
C
C234567
      PROGRAM MIXEDM
      DATA I,J,A,B/5,2,2.3,7.4/
      OPEN (6,FILE='PRINTER:')
      X = A + B
      K = A + B
      M = I / J
      Y = I / J
      Z = 5.0 / 2.0
      N = 5.0 / 2.0
      D = M
      L = Y
      WRITE (0,200) X, K, M, Y, Z, N, D, L
      WRITE (6,200) X, K, M, Y, Z, N, D, L
  200 FORMAT (//,'X = ',F5.2,3X,'K = ',I3,3X,'M = ',I3,//,
     *'Y = ',F5.2,3X,'Z = ',F5.2,3X,'N = ',I3,//,
     *3X,'D = ',F5.2,3X,'L = ',I3,//)
      STOP
      END


X =  9.70   K =   9   M =   2

Y =  2.00   Z =  2.50   N =   2

   D =  2.00   L =   2
```

Fig. 5-1. Program to demonstrate how Apple FORTRAN handles arithmetic assignment statements in the integer, real, and mixed modes.

Fig. 5-2 is a program written to demonstrate a counting statement. Five student grades are placed in a DATA statement. The grades are counted, summed, and the average computed for the five grades. The integer variable KOUNT is initialized to zero, so the count is incremented each time a grade is read. The KOUNT is placed inside a DO loop, so it is incremented each time a grade is summed. In this manner, the grades are counted and summed so the relationship between the grade count and the grade is maintained.

SUMMING STATEMENT

The summing statement (Fig. 5-2) is used within the loop to sum the values in the DATA statement, or input from the keyboard if that is the case. The variable SUM is initialized to zero (real), so the value stored in the memory location is a known value. All variables whose values change within the program should be initialized to a specific value before the memory location is used. Each SCORE is added until the loop has incremented five times. After the fifth loop execution, the values stored in

KOUNT and SUM are used in an arithmetic expression to calculate the average of the student's grades. The value calculated is assigned to the variable AVG. The number of scores (KOUNT), the sum of the scores (SUM), and the average (AVG) are then output.

```
C**** PROGRAM TO DEMONSTRATE COUNTING AND
C**** SUMMING STATEMENTS IN RELATION TO
C**** COMPUTING AN AVERAGE
C
C234567
      PROGRAM SUM4
      DIMENSION SCORE (5)
      DATA SCORE/89.,75.,93.,99.,85./
      OPEN (6,FILE='PRINTER:')
      KOUNT = 0
      SUM = 0.0
      DO 50 J = 1,5
      KOUNT = KOUNT + 1
      SUM = SUM + SCORE(J)
   50 CONTINUE
      AVG = SUM / KOUNT
      WRITE (0,200) KOUNT, SUM, AVG
      WRITE (6,200) KOUNT, SUM, AVG
  200 FORMAT (//,'THE AVERAGE OF ',I3,
     *' SCORES WHOSE SUM IS ',F6.2,//,
     *' IS ',F6.2,/)
      STOP
      END




THE AVERAGE OF   5 SCORES WHOSE SUM IS 441.00

 IS  88.20
```

Fig. 5-2. Program to demonstrate counting and summing statements in relation to computing an average.

LOGICAL IF STATEMENT

The program in Fig. 5-3 was written to demonstrate the use of the logical IF statement, and the relationships between relational and logical operators. The format of the logical IF is shown in Fig. 5-4. Many test conditions require that values between specific limits be selected for controlled applications. Specific examples include customer charges for natural gas for heating. A customer who uses 1000 cubic feet of gas per month is charged on a set rate. A customer who uses between 5000 and 8000 cubic feet per month is charged at a different rate than the customer that used 1000 cubic feet per month. A large manufacturer that uses over 100,000 cubic feet per month is charged at a different rate than either of the first two customers. Brokerage houses use a sliding commission rate for stock transactions. The more stock that is purchased on a single order, the cheaper the price of commission per share. This selective process uses the logical IF to select these changing schedules. The relational operators (Table 1-9) and the logical operators (Table 1-10) are used with the logical IF to set the bounds of the area to be selected. The relational operators permit ranges to be selected, and the logical operators permit multiple conditions to be selected in one program statement.

IF THE COST IS GREATER THAN $5.00,
(.AND.) THE COST IS LESS THAN $9.95,
CHARGE THE ITEM.

IF THE COST IS LESS THAN $1000, (.OR.)
THE COST IS GREATER THAN $5000, COUNT
THE ITEM.

IF THE RESULT EQUALS ZERO, (.NOT.)
DISCRIMINANT EQUALS ZERO, SUBTRACT FOUR
FROM THE SUM.

Relational and logical operators use a period before and after the letters or words to let the compiler know these are not variables. The relational and logical operators, without periods, can be used as regular variables.

```
C**** PROGRAM TO DEMONSTRATE THE LOGICAL IF
C**** STATEMENT WITH RELATIONAL AND LOGICAL
C**** OPERATORS
C
C234567
      PROGRAM LOGIC1
      DIMENSION RNUM (10)
      DATA RNUM/3.8,10.75,9.1,4.5,12.21,17.99,
     *7.9,5.2,2.1,0.0/
      OPEN (6,FILE='PRINTER:')
      KOUNT = 1
      SUM = 0.0
      UPPER = 0.
      XLOW = 0.
   10 IF (RNUM(KOUNT) .LT. 2. .OR. RNUM(KOUNT) .LE. 0.0)
     *GOTO 50
      IF (RNUM(KOUNT) .LE. 4.) SUM = SUM + RNUM(KOUNT)
      IF (RNUM(KOUNT) .GT. 4. .AND. RNUM(KOUNT) .LE. 6.1)
     *UPPER = UPPER + RNUM(KOUNT)
      IF (RNUM(KOUNT) .GT. 6.1 .AND. RNUM(KOUNT) .LT. 14.)
     *XLOW = XLOW - RNUM(KOUNT) - 3.2
      IF (RNUM(KOUNT) .GE. 14. .AND. RNUM(KOUNT) .LT. 18.)
     *SUM = SUM /3.0
      KOUNT = KOUNT + 1
      GOTO 10
   50 WRITE (6,200) SUM, UPPER, XLOW, KOUNT
  200 FORMAT (//,'SUM = ',F8.2,3X,'UPPER = ',F8.2,//,
     *' XLOW = ',F8.2,3X,'AND COUNT = ',I3,/)
      STOP
      END


SUM =       3.37    UPPER =        9.70

XLOW =    -52.76    AND COUNT =   10
```

Fig. 5-3. Program to demonstrate the logical IF statement with relational and logical operators.

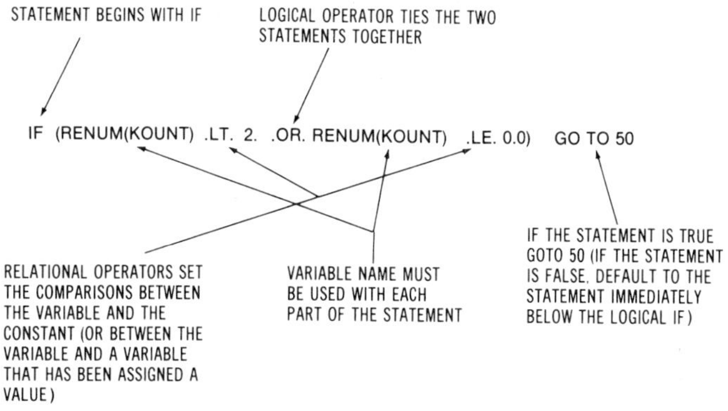

Fig. 5-4. Format of the logical IF statement.

The logical .NOT. has the highest precedence of the three logical operators and causes negation of the assigned value.

IF (.NOT. RENUM(KOUNT) .EQ. 4.) GOTO 20

Without the logical .NOT., if RENUM(KOUNT) was equal to four, the program would branch to statement 20. The .NOT. negates the statement, so any number except four causes a branch to statement 20. The .NOT. operator is used less frequently than the .AND. and .OR., but in some cases can produce more efficient programs (Fig. 5-5). The most efficient program is structured so the greatest number of operations are performed as they default from one statement to the next. In Fig. 5-5A, when J < = 10, the program must branch to three operations on the true (YES) and no operations on the false (NO). With the logic reversed or negated (Fig. 5-5B), when J > 10, the decision is false (NO) and defaults to the next statements to perform the calculations. In many cases, J will be greater than 10 on the last increment, and the program will have to branch only one time.

LOGICAL OPERATORS

The logical operator with the next highest precedence is .AND. . When using relational operators, both statements must be true for the statement to be true.

IF (ISEL .GT. 1 .AND. ISEL .LE. 4) GOTO 10

The .AND. is a logical conjunction with two or more inputs and one output. If all the inputs are true (1), the output will be true (1). If any of the inputs is false (0), the output will be false (0). The logical IF statement in the example requires that the number selected be greater than or equal to one, .AND. that the number be less than or equal to four. When both of these conditions are true, the statement is true. If the number selected is less than one, or if the number selected is greater than four, one of the statements is false, and consequently the entire statement is false.

The logical operator with the lowest precedence is .OR. . When the logical disjunction .OR. joins two comparison statements, only one of the statements must be true for the entire statement to be true.

```
IF (J .LT. 4 .OR. J .GT. 8) GOTO 50
```

The .OR. is a statement with two or more inputs and one output. If either of the inputs is true (1), then the output is true (1).

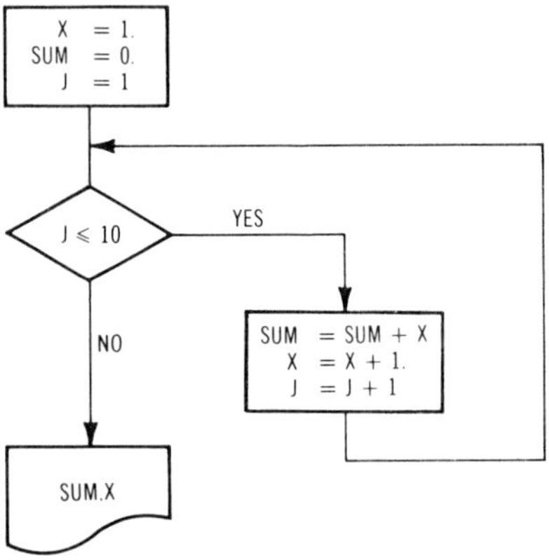

(A) *Normal logic.*

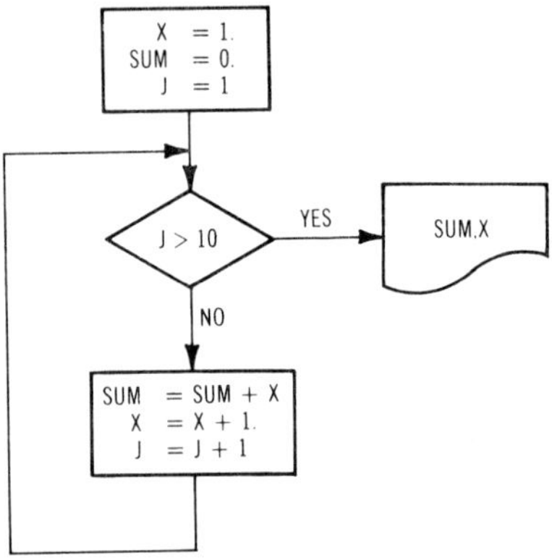

(B) *Negation of logic.*

Fig. 5-5. Flowcharts illustrating the negation of logic.

ARITHMETIC IF STATEMENT

The arithmetic IF statement (Fig. 5-6) is used to test a variable or expression to cause branching to one of three possible program statements. The format of the arithmetic IF (Fig. 5-7) uses the keyword IF followed by the variable or expression in parentheses. Three integer numbers separated by commas follow the closing paranthesis. The program branches to the program statement with the first integer number if the value returned by the variable or expression is less than zero. The program branches to the program statement with the second integer number if the value returned by the variable or expression is equal to zero. The program branches to the program statement with the third integer number if the value returned by the variable or expression is greater than zero.

The arithmetic IF is the ideal statement to be used when a problem has three solutions. The solution to the quadratic formula is a problem that has three normal solutions.

```
X1 = (-B + SQRT((B**2) - 4*A*C))/(2*A)
X2 = (-B - SQRT((B**2) - 4*A*C))/(2*A)
```

```
C**** PROGRAM TO DEMONSTRATE THE
C**** ARITHMETIC IF STATEMENT
C234567
      PROGRAM ARITIF
      DIMENSION X(3)
      OPEN (6,FILE='PRINTER:')
    5 WRITE (0,10)
      WRITE (6,10)
      WRITE (0,20)
      WRITE (6,20)
      READ (0,30) (X(J), J = 1,3)
      A = X(1)
      B = X(2)
      C = X(3)
      IF (A .EQ. 0 . AND. B .EQ. 0 .AND.
     !C .EQ. 0) GOTO 600
      DER1 = (B**2)
      DER2 = (4*A*C)
      DER  = SQRT(ABS(DER1-DER2))
      BASE = -B/(2*A)
      IF (DER1 - DER2 ) 100, 200, 300
  100 XR = BASE
      XI = DER/(2*A)
      WRITE (0,800) XR, XI, XR, XI
      WRITE (6,800) XR, XI, XR, XI
      GOTO 5
  200 WRITE (0,900) BASE
      WRITE (6,900) BASE
      GOTO 5
  300 X1 = (-B + DER)/(2*A)
      X2 = (-B - DER)/(2*A)
  500 WRITE (0,1000) DER, X1, X2
      WRITE (6,1000) DER, X1, X2
      GOTO 5
  600 STOP
   10 FORMAT(/,'ENTER 3 REALS,',
     *' A, B, C',/)
   20 FORMAT (BN,3(5H!---*))
   30 FORMAT (3F5.0)
  800 FORMAT (//,'SOLUTION 1 = ',
     *F9.4,'+',F9.4,'*I',/,'SOLUTION ',
     *'2 = ',F9.4,'-',F9.4,'*I')
  900 FORMAT (//,'THE SINGLE SOLUT',
     *'ION = ',F9.4)
 1000 FORMAT (//,'THE DERIVATIVE'
     *,' = ',F9.4,//,'SOLUTION 1',
     *' = ',F9.4,/,'SOLUTION 2 = ',
     *F9.4)
      END

ENTER 3 REALS, A, B, C

!---*!---*!---*
  1.   2.   1.

THE SINGLE SOLUTION =   -1.0000

ENTER 3 REALS, A, B, C

!---*!---*!---*
  1.   -1.  12.

SOLUTION 1 =     .5000+  10.9430*I
SOLUTION 2 =     .5000-  10.9430*I
```

Fig. 5-6. Program to demonstrate the arithmetic IF statement.

```
ENTER 3 REALS, A, B, C

!----*!----*!----*
  1.   -2.   2.

SOLUTION 1 =     1.0000+   14.1067*I
SOLUTION 2 =     1.0000-   14.1067*I

ENTER 3 REALS, A, B, C

!----*!----*!----*
  1.    5.    6.

THE DERIVATIVE =       1.0000

SOLUTION 1 =    -2.0000
SOLUTION 2 =    -3.0000

ENTER 3 REALS, A, B, C

!----*!----*!----*
  1.   -5.   6

THE DERIVATIVE =       1.0000

SOLUTION 1 =     3.0000
SOLUTION 2 =     2.0000

ENTER 3 REALS, A, B, C

!----*!----*!----*
  0.    0.    0.     (or RETURN)
```

Fig. 5-6. Program to demonstrate the arithmetic IF statement. *(Continued)*

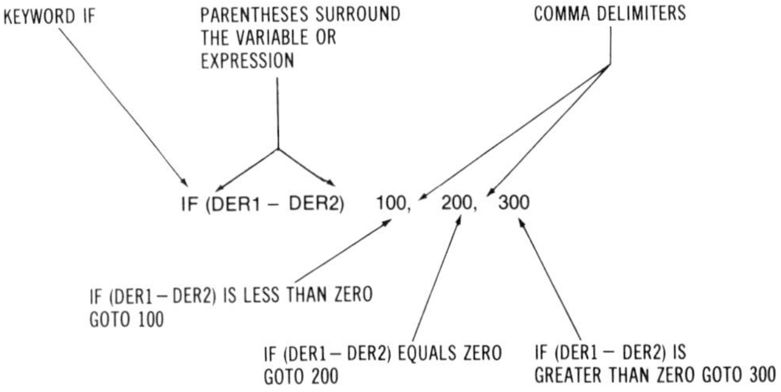

Fig. 5-7. Format of the arithmetic IF statement.

If the value of the discriminant is less than zero, there are two solutions to the quadratic formula; both solutions are irrational. If the discriminant is equal to zero, there are two solutions to the quadratic formula; both are the same solution. If the value of the discriminant is greater than zero, there are two solutions to the quadratic formula; both are real numbers.

In Fig. 5-6, the discriminant had to be separated into two parts, DER1 = B**2 and DER2 = 4*A*C, and the value computed on DER1 – DER2. This was done because the computer cannot take the square root of a negative number. When the discriminant is negative, a special case had to be constructed to produce the correct result.

COMPUTED GOTO STATEMENT

The computed GOTO statement causes control to go to one of several program statements by selection or computation. The program in Fig. 5-8 uses the computed GOTO as a method to select the desired function of angles from zero to 90°. The program sets up a menu with four possible selections.

1. To print out the function of the sine of an angle.
2. To print out the function of the cosine of an angle.
3. To print out the function of the tangent of an angle.
4. To end the program.

When the user makes a selection of 1, 2, 3, or 4, the computed GOTO causes the program to branch to the statement whose label is 100, 200, 300, or 400. The direct correlation is between the selected menu number and the sequence of numbers in the computed GOTO statement. The number selected refers to the position of the number in the computed GOTO statement. If the sequence in the computed GOTO was 400, 300, 200, and 100, then selecting 1 would cause a branch to line 400, selecting 2 would cause a branch to line 300, etc. The relationship between the number selected and the numbers in the computed GOTO is the controlling relationship of where to branch (Fig. 5-9). The computed GOTO is not limited to four branch selections, but can have as many as needed to control the options.

The format of the computed GOTO statement (Fig. 5-10) requires that the keyword GOTO begin in column 7 of the screen. The integer numbers in the statement are enclosed in parentheses and separated by commas. The variable to control the selection follows the closing parenthesis.

INTERACTIVE QUESTION

The program in Fig. 5-8 was also written to demonstrate the interactive question, "DO YOU WISH TO CONTINUE (Y OR N)?," as a method to continue, or end the program. The program also shows the relationship between the CHARACTER and the logical IF statements. If the user wants to continue and make another selection, "Y" is pressed, and then "RETURN." If the user wants to end the program, "N" is pressed, and then "RETURN." To use alphabetic characters in logical FORTRAN statements, the alphabetic character must be assigned to a variable.

```
C**** PROGRAM TO DEMONSTRATE THE COMPUTED
C**** GOTO STATEMENT
C234567
      PROGRAM GOTO
      REAL N
      CHARACTER*1 CHOICE,YES,NO
      DATA YES, NO/'Y','N'/
      RAD = 3.1416/180
      OPEN (6,FILE='PRINTER:')
   10 WRITE (0,1000)
      WRITE (6,1000)
      WRITE (0,1010)
      WRITE (6,1010)
      READ (0,1020) ISEL
      IF (ISEL .GE. 1 .AND. ISEL .LE. 4) GOTO 50
      WRITE (0,1030)
      WRITE (6,1030)
      GOTO 10
   50 GOTO (100,200,300,400) ISEL
  100 WRITE (0,1040)
      WRITE (6,1040)
      WRITE (0,1050)
      WRITE (6,1050)
      DO 20 J = 0,90,10
      X = FLOAT(J)
      Y = SIN(X*RAD)
      WRITE (0,1060) J, Y
      WRITE (6,1060) J, Y
   20 CONTINUE
      GOTO 350
  200 WRITE (0,1040)
      WRITE (6,1040)
      WRITE (0,1070)
      WRITE (6,1070)
      DO 30 J = 0,90,10
      X = FLOAT(J)
      Y = COS(X*RAD)
      WRITE (0,1080) J, Y
      WRITE (6,1080) J, Y
   30 CONTINUE
      GOTO 350
  300 WRITE (0,1040)
      WRITE (6,1040)
      WRITE (0,1090)
      WRITE (6,1090)
      DO 40 J = 0,90,10
      X = FLOAT(J)
      IF (J .EQ. 90) GOTO 18
      Y = TAN(X*RAD)
      WRITE (0,1060) J, Y
      WRITE (6,1060) J, Y
   40 CONTINUE
   18 WRITE (0,2000) J
      WRITE (6,2000) J
  350 WRITE (0,2010)
      WRITE (6,2010)
      READ (0,2020) CHOICE
      IF (CHOICE .EQ. YES) GOTO 10
      IF (CHOICE .EQ. NO) GOTO 400
 1000 FORMAT (/////,16X,'MENU FOR FUNCTION SELECTION',/,
     *16X,27(1H-))
 1010 FORMAT (/,6X,'1.  TO PRINT OUT THE FUNCTION OF THE SINE',
     *' OF AN ANGLE.'/,6X,'2.  TO PRINT OUT THE',
     *' FUNCTION OF THE COSINE OF AN ANGLE.',/,6X,
     *'3.  TO PRINT OUT THE FUNCTION OF THE TANGENT',
```

Fig. 5-8. Program to demonstrate

```
     *' OF AN ANGLE.',/,,6X,'4.  TO END THE PROGRAM.',///,
     *3X,'ENTER SELECTION PLEASE!',3X,'---')
1020 FORMAT (BN,I3)
1030 FORMAT (//,'PLEASE ENTER A NUMBER BETWEEN 1 AND 4 ',
     *'THANKS!')
1040 FORMAT (/,26X,'FUNCTION',/,26X,8(1H-))
1050 FORMAT (22X,'X',14X,'SIN(X)',/,22X,'-',14X,6(1H-))
1060 FORMAT (20X,I3,10X,F10.4)
1070 FORMAT (22X,'X',14X,'COS(X)',/,22X,'-',14X,6(1H-))
1080 FORMAT (20X,I3,10X,F10.4)
1090 FORMAT (22X,'X',14X,'TAN(X)',/,22X,'-',14X,6(1H-))
2000 FORMAT (20X,I3,10X,'******')
2010 FORMAT (/,'DO YOU WISH TO CONTINUE (Y OR N)?',/)
2020 FORMAT (A1)
 400 STOP
     END

                     MENU FOR FUNCTION SELECTION
                     ---------------------------

     1.   TO PRINT OUT THE FUNCTION OF THE SINE OF AN ANGLE.
     2.   TO PRINT OUT THE FUNCTION OF THE COSINE OF AN ANGLE.
     3.   TO PRINT OUT THE FUNCTION OF THE TANGENT OF AN ANGLE.
     4.   TO END THE PROGRAM.

   ENTER SELECTION PLEASE!   ---
 1
                          FUNCTION
                          --------
                      X              SIN(X)
                      -              ------
                      0               .0000
                     10               .1736
                     20               .3420
                     30               .5000
                     40               .6428
                     50               .7660
                     60               .8660
                     70               .9397
                     80               .9848
                     90              1.0000

 DO YOU WISH TO CONTINUE (Y OR N)?

 Y
                     MENU FOR FUNCTION SELECTION
                     ---------------------------

     1.   TO PRINT OUT THE FUNCTION OF THE SINE OF AN ANGLE.
     2.   TO PRINT OUT THE FUNCTION OF THE COSINE OF AN ANGLE.
     3.   TO PRINT OUT THE FUNCTION OF THE TANGENT OF AN ANGLE.
     4.   TO END THE PROGRAM.
   ENTER SELECTION PLEASE!   ---
 2
                          FUNCTION
                          --------
                      X              COS(X)
                      -              ------
                      0              1.0000
                     10               .9848
                     20               .9397
                     30               .8660
                     40               .7660
                     50               .6428
                     60               .5000
```

the computed GOTO statement.

```
                         70                .3420
                         80                .1736
                         90                .0000

  DO YOU WISH TO CONTINUE (Y OR N)?
  Y


                    MENU FOR FUNCTION SELECTION
                    ---------------------------

      1.   TO PRINT OUT THE FUNCTION OF THE SINE OF AN ANGLE.
      2.   TO PRINT OUT THE FUNCTION OF THE COSINE OF AN ANGLE.
      3.   TO PRINT OUT THE FUNCTION OF THE TANGENT OF AN ANGLE.
      4.   TO END THE PROGRAM.


    ENTER SELECTION PLEASE!    ---
 3
                              FUNCTION
                              --------

                          X                TAN(X)
                          -                ------
                          0                .0000
                         10                .1763
                         20                .3640
                         30                .5774
                         40                .8391
                         50               1.1918
                         60               1.7321
                         70               2.7475
                         80               5.6714
                         90           ******

  DO YOU WISH TO CONTINUE (Y OR N)?
  Y


                    MENU FOR FUNCTION SELECTION
                    ---------------------------

      1.   TO PRINT OUT THE FUNCTION OF THE SINE OF AN ANGLE.
      2.   TO PRINT OUT THE FUNCTION OF THE COSINE OF AN ANGLE.
      3.   TO PRINT OUT THE FUNCTION OF THE TANGENT OF AN ANGLE.
      4.   TO END THE PROGRAM.


    ENTER SELECTION PLEASE!    ---
 4
```

Fig. 5-8. Program to demonstrate the computed GOTO statement. *(Continued)*

COMPARISON OF AN ALPHABETIC CHARACTER WITH A VARIABLE

To compare a character variable, CHOICE, and an alphabetic character (Y or N), the alphabetic character may be placed in a variable. The alphabetic character can be placed in a variable in one of two ways — (1) a DATA statement and (2) an assignment statement.

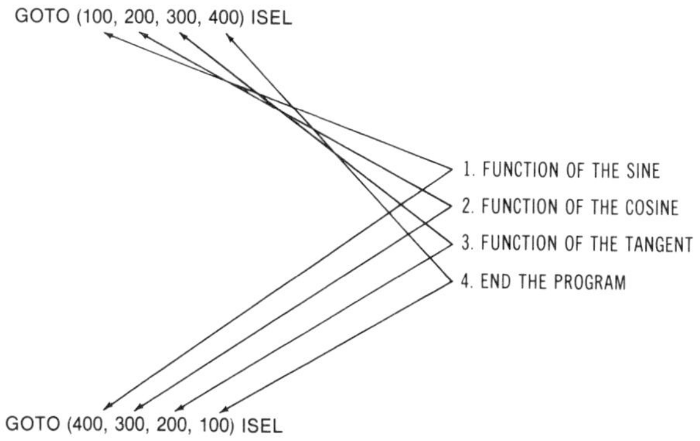

Fig. 5-9. The relationship between the number selected and the numbers in the computed GOTO statement.

1. DATA statement.

```
        REAL N
        CHARACTER*1,CHOICE, YES, NO
        DATA YES, NO / 'Y', 'N'/
        READ(0, 2020) CHOICE
   2020 FORMAT (A1)
        IF (CHOICE .EQ. YES) GOTO 10
        IF (CHOICE .EQ. NO) GOTO 400
```

The character variables must be of the same type — integer or real.

2. Assignment statement.

```
        REAL N
        CHARACTER*1, CHOICE, YES, NO
        YES = 'Y'
        NO = 'N'
        READ (0, 2020) CHOICE
   2020 FORMAT (A1)
        IF (CHOICE .EQ. YES) GOTO 10
        IF (CHOICE .EQ. NO) GOTO 400
```

PAUSE STATEMENT

The PAUSE statement is used to create an interruption in the flow of the program. The program is stopped at the PAUSE statement, and the user causes the program to continue by pressing the spacebar or the RETURN key.

The format of the PAUSE statement is as follows:

```
PAUSE n
PAUSE 1
PAUSE 9999
PAUSE 'AVG'
```

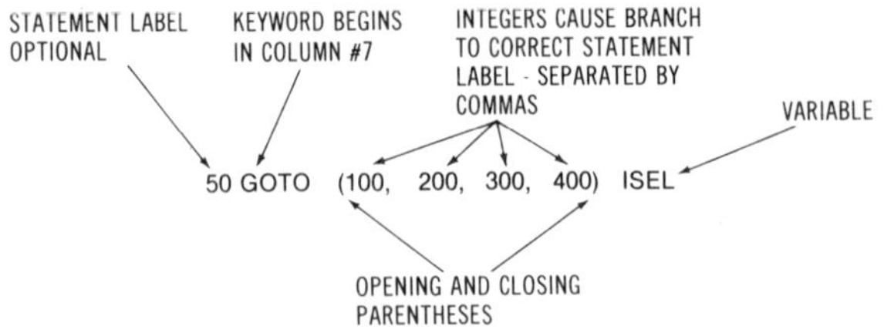

Fig. 5-10. Format of the computed GOTO statement.

The PAUSE statement may contain an integer number of not more than five characters, or a literal of not more than five characters. When the PAUSE statement is executed, the integer number, or literal, is placed on the CRT so the user will know where the program paused.

When a compiled and linked program is executed (Fig. 5-11), the program stops at each PAUSE statement until the user presses the spacebar or RETURN key. In Fig. 5-11, PAUSE 1 is placed inside a DO loop. Each time the loop is repeated, the integer "1" is placed on the CRT to show the location within the program. After the loop has repeated five times, the program defaults to the second PAUSE statement. PAUSE 'AVG' stops the program immediately before the average is computed. PAUSE 2 is placed before the results are printed out.

By judiciously using the PAUSE statements, the program and flow of data through the program can be checked to determine if there are any bugs in the program logic. A program will execute after it has been compiled and linked. The important aspect of any program is that the output be correct.

STOP STATEMENT

The STOP statement causes the computer to stop processing the program. The STOP statement can be formatted in two ways:

1. STOP
2. STOP 'FINI' (Fig. 4-1)

If the program ends with a STOP, the word STOP is printed on the screen at the termination of the program. If the program ends with STOP 'FINI', then STOP*m* and the literal FINI are printed on the screen. The STOP is optional for Apple FORTRAN. All programs should contain a STOP statement immediately preceding the END statement.

END STATEMENT

The END statement is the last statement in every program and subprogram in FORTRAN. If no END statement is at the end of a program or subprogram, the program will not compile. Compile error #91 is "MISSING END STATEMENT."

```
C**** PROGRAM TO DEMONSTRATE PAUSE STATEMENT
C
C234567
      PROGRAM PAUSE
      DIMENSION SCORE (5)
      DATA SCORE/89.,75.,93.,99.,85./
      OPEN (6,FILE='PRINTER:')
      KOUNT = 0
      SUM = 0.0
      DO 50 J = 1,5
      PAUSE 1
      KOUNT = KOUNT + 1
      SUM = SUM + SCORE(J)
   50 CONTINUE
      PAUSE 'AVG'
      AVG = SUM / KOUNT
      PAUSE 2
      WRITE (0,200) KOUNT, SUM, AVG
      WRITE (6,200) KOUNT, SUM, AVG
  200 FORMAT (//,'THE AVERAGE OF ',I3,
     *' SCORES WHOSE SUM IS ',F6.2,//,
     *' IS ',F6.2,/)
      STOP
      END



THE AVERAGE OF   5 SCORES WHOSE SUM IS 441.00

 IS  88.20
```

Fig. 5-11. Program to demonstrate the PAUSE statement.

CLOSE OF A FORTRAN PROGRAM

When a program is closed out after the END statement, the cursor must rest in column 7, just under the "E" in END.

END
■

If the cursor is not under the "E" in END, compile error #4, "FATAL END OF FILE IS ENCOUNTERED," will be printed on the screen.

In EDITOR command, INSERT mode, the cursor is placed below the "E" in END, and CONTROL C is pressed to accept the insertion. Many times, when CONTROL C is pressed, the cursor moves several spaces or lines below the END statement. This erratic movement of the cursor below the END statement causes the fatal end of file condition. After CONTROL C has been pressed, press the RETURN key several times. If the cursor remains directly below the "E" in END, it is in the correct position and no fatal error will be produced. If the cursor moves away from the position directly below the "E" in END, it is in an incorrect position and the fatal error will be produced. There are two methods to correct this problem.

The first solution is to get into the EDIT command and place the cursor directly after the "D" in END.

```
END ■
```

Press "I" for insert, then press RETURN to move the cursor to the next line in column 7 under the "E," and then press CONTROL C. Press RETURN two or three times to determine that the cursor remains in the correct position. If the cursor moves away from the proper position, repeat this procedure until the cursor remains in the correct position.

The second solution is to place the cursor as far away from the END statement as possible by pressing the RETURN key several times. When the cursor no longer moves away from the END statement when RETURN is pressed, it is at its limit away from the END statement. Place the EDIT command in the reverse mode (<EDIT), and press "D" for delete. Using the spacebar, back-arrow key, or the RETURN key, place the cursor under the "E" in the END statement, then press CONTROL C. This may require more than one attempt, so, if necessary, repeat the procedure until the cursor is in the right position.

The cursor placed in an incorrect position will cause many compile errors. The cursor should be checked for proper placement before the program is written to disk.

CHAPTER 6
Single Subscripted Arrays

An array is a collection of many data items of the same kind. An array is an arrangement of data items identified by a variable that has a subscript. The array is constructed in such a manner that the program can examine the specific elements of the list.

A subscript is an identifier, either an integer variable, integer constant, or integer expression, which identifies all or some of the individual elements of a list of data items.

When combined, integer or real array variables and their integer subscripts (variables, constants, or expressions) have formats typified by the following:

```
   X(J)   REAL ARRAY
   N(J)   INTEGER ARRAY
AAA(10)   LOCATION 10 OF AAA ARRAY
   X(2)   LOCATION 2 OF X ARRAY
 A(2*K)   EXPRESSION SUBSCRIPT
```

Arrays are used to eliminate the need for a profusion of simple variables. Using simple variables, an inventory list of 1000 items would be read in this manner:

```
READ (0,100) INV1
READ (0,100) INV2
READ (0,100) INV3
READ (0,100) INV4
—
—
—
—
READ (0,100) INV1000
```

The last item in the list, INV1000, is illegal because it contains seven characters.

Using an array to read the list of inventory items is much simpler.

```
DIMENSION INV (1000)
N = 1000
READ (0,100) (INV(J), J = 1,N)
```

By using one array name and a subscript, the entire list can be read.

The specification statement (DIMENSION, INTEGER, REAL, or COM-

MON) is mandatory when arrays are used. The specification statement reserves memory locations for the data items in the list (Fig. 6-1).

The specification statement, DIMENSION INV(5), reserves five memory locations for the integer array INV. Fig. 6-2 shows five inventory items, 1001 through 1005, stored in five memory locations in the array. The five values in the array can be output in one of three ways:

```
1.     WRITE (0,200) INV(1), INV(2), INV(3), INV(4), INV(5)
2.     DO 20 J = 1,5
       WRITE (0,200) INV(J)
    20 CONTINUE
3.     WRITE (0,200) (INV(J), J = 1,5)
```

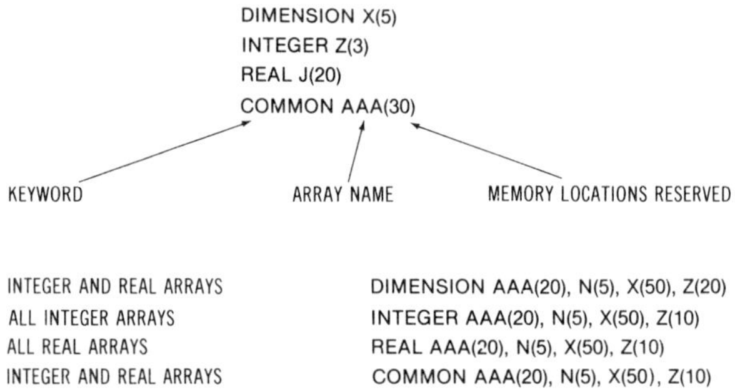

Fig. 6-1. Format of specification statements.

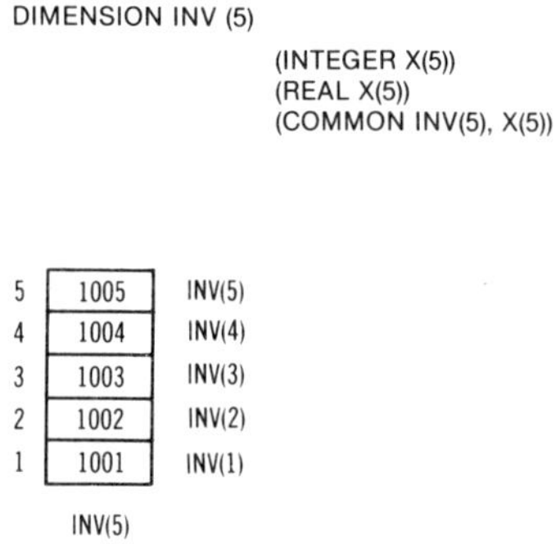

Fig. 6-2. DIMENSION (specification) statement reserves memory locations for an array.

SPECIFICATION STATEMENT RULES

The rules for the use of the specification statement are as follows:

1. The specification statement must be the first statement in the program if there is no program statement, or it must be the second statement in the program if there is a program statement.
2. The program may contain more than one specification statement.

3. An array cannot be dimensioned more than once.
4. A specification statement is not an executable statement (Fig. 1-1), and control cannot be transferred to it.
5. The subscripted arrays are separated by commas, and the subscripts are enclosed in parentheses.
6. Subscripts give the maximum size of the array, and array elements out of the range of the subscript are illegal.

The subscript of an array variable may be an integer variable, an integer constant, or an integer expression (Table 6-1).

Table 6-1. Legal Subscripts

Legal Subscript	Example
Variable	I through J, or an integer created by IMPLICIT or INTEGER.
Constant	3
Variable and a Constant	N + 1 N − 1 N * 2 N / 3
Expression	2*K−1 4*K/L

Many computers, the Apple included, do not zero-out memory locations when they are turned on (booted up). Before data is loaded, it is advisable to zero-out the memory locations where the data is to be placed. For variables that change within the program, such as summing and counting variables, it is mandatory that the locations be set to zero, or set to a desired known value, before the memory locations are used.

Fig. 6-3 is one method to zero-out the reserved array locations before they are used. The array is dimensioned to its limit, DIMENSION X(10). The subscripted array, X(J), is then placed in the standard DO loop to cause the reserved memory locations to be zeroed-out.

ARRAY INPUT

Array data can be read into computer memory from two peripheral locations — keyboard and disk.

Array data can be placed in the program by (1) assignment statements in the program, (2) DATA statements using each element of the array, and (3) DATA statements using only the array variable.

Fig. 6-4 is a program to demonstrate array data input by using assignment statements. Each element of the array is assigned a specific value and placed in a reserved memory location.

```
&C**** PROGRAM TO INITIALIZE THE VALUES STORED
C**** IN AN ARRAY MEMORY LOCATIONS TO ZERO
C
C234567
      PROGRAM ZEROI
      DIMENSION X(10)
      OPEN (6,FILE='PRINTER:')
      DO 20 J = 1,10
      X(J) = 0.
   20 CONTINUE
      WRITE (0,200) (X(K), K = 1,10)
      WRITE (6,200) (X(K), K = 1,10)
  200 FORMAT (//,10(F5.2))
      STOP
      END


  .00  .00  .00  .00  .00  .00  .00  .00  .00  .00
```

Fig. 6-3. Program to demonstrate a method to zero-out reserved array memory locations before they are used.

```
C**** PROGRAM TO DEMONSTRATE DIRECT LOADING
C**** OF ARRAY MEMORY LOCATIONS BY MEANS OF
C**** ASSIGNMENT STATEMENTS
C
C234567
      PROGRAM ARRAY1
      DIMENSION SCORE (5)
      SCORE(1) = 89.
      SCORE(2) = 75.
      SCORE(3) = 93.
      SCORE(4) = 99.
      SCORE(5) = 85.
      OPEN (6,FILE='PRINTER:')
      KOUNT = 0
      SUM = 0.0
      DO 50 J = 1,5
      KOUNT = KOUNT + 1
      SUM = SUM + SCORE(J)
   50 CONTINUE
      AVG = SUM / KOUNT
      WRITE (0,200) KOUNT, SUM, AVG
      WRITE (6,200) KOUNT, SUM, AVG
  200 FORMAT (//,'THE AVERAGE OF ',I3,
     *' SCORES WHOSE SUM IS ',F6.2,//,
     *' IS ',F6.2,/)
      STOP
      END


THE AVERAGE OF   5 SCORES WHOSE SUM IS 441.00

 IS  88.20
```

Fig. 6-4. Program to demonstrate array data input by using assignment statements.

Fig. 6-5 is a program to demonstrate the DATA statement to input values into a specific element of the array. This is the most common way to input large amounts of data in a program.

```
C**** PROGRAM TO DEMONSTRATE ARRAY DATA
C**** PLACED IN EACH ELEMENT OF THE ARRAY
C
C234567
      PROGRAM ARRAY2
      DIMENSION SCORE (5)
      DATA SCORE(1),SCORE(2),SCORE(3),SCORE(4),
     *SCORE(5)/89.,75.,93.,99.,85./
      OPEN (6,FILE='PRINTER:')
      KOUNT = 0
      SUM = 0.0
      DO 50 J = 1,5
      KOUNT = KOUNT + 1
      SUM = SUM + SCORE(J)
   50 CONTINUE
      AVG = SUM / KOUNT
      WRITE (0,200) KOUNT, SUM, AVG
      WRITE (6,200) KOUNT, SUM, AVG
  200 FORMAT (//,'THE AVERAGE OF ',I3,
     *' SCORES WHOSE SUM IS ',F6.2,//,
     *' IS ',F6.2,/)
      STOP
      END




THE AVERAGE OF   5 SCORES WHOSE SUM IS 441.00

 IS  88.20
```

Fig. 6-5. Program to demonstrate data loaded into memory by using a DATA statement.

Fig. 6-6 is a program to demonstrate the DATA statement to input data by using only the array variable. This method saves typing each element of the array, and is acceptable for use with single subscripted arrays.

Input Data from Keyboard

Fig. 6-7 is a program written to input array data from the keyboard. The program reads the data, writes it out to the screen, and prints it as it was input.

Read Array Data from Disk

Fig. 6-8 is a program to read array data from a direct (random) access file. Reading from and writing to disk using a sequential access file can be seen in Figs. 3-5 and 3-6. The file on disk was created by the program in Fig. 6-9, and will be discussed under "ARRAY OUTPUT." The program to read a direct access file from disk (Fig. 6-8) uses the real array "Z" for which five

```
C**** PROGRAM TO DEMONSTRATE DATA INPUT BY
C**** USING ONLY THE ARRAY VARIABLE
C
C234567
      PROGRAM ARRAY3
      DIMENSION SCORE (5)
      DATA SCORE/89.,75.,93.,99.,85./
      OPEN (6,FILE='PRINTER:')
      KOUNT = 0
      SUM = 0.0
      DO 50 J = 1,5
      KOUNT = KOUNT + 1
      SUM = SUM + SCORE(J)
   50 CONTINUE
      AVG = SUM / KOUNT
      WRITE (0,200) KOUNT, SUM, AVG
      WRITE (6,200) KOUNT, SUM, AVG
  200 FORMAT (//,'THE AVERAGE OF ',I3,
     *' SCORES WHOSE SUM IS ',F6.2,//,
     *' IS ',F6.2,/)
      STOP
      END



 THE AVERAGE OF   5 SCORES WHOSE SUM IS 441.00

  IS  88.20
```

Fig. 6-6. Program to demonstrate the DATA statement to input data by using only the array variable.

memory locations are reserved. The program uses device #20 on which to open the file. The file is in disk drive #9 and is named "EXAMP." Disk drive #9 is on a three-disk drive system with the interface card in slot #4. The ACCESS is DIRECT, to reflect the type of file, SEQUENTIAL or DIRECT, used in Apple FORTRAN. The STATUS is OLD, since the file had been previously created. The FORM is FORMATTED, and Apple FORTRAN has two form files — FORMATTED and UNFORMATTED. The length of the record is 51 bytes (RECL = 51). The record length of 51 bytes is related to the READ and FORMAT statements. The READ format specifies 50 bytes (5(F10.2)). The 51 bytes is the length of the (5(F10.2)) FORMAT specification, plus one byte for an end-of-file marker. This relationship exists for records that are read and written with a standard DO loop and an implied DO loop.

```
      OPEN (20,FILE = '#9:EXAMP', ACCESS = 'DIRECT',
     *STATUS = 'OLD', FORM = 'FORMATTED', RECL = 11)
      DO 20 J = 1,5
      READ (20,100, REC = 1, END = 900) X(J)
   20 CONTINUE
  100 FORMAT (F10.2)
  900 DO 30 K = 1,5
      WRITE (0,200) X(J)
  200 FORMAT (F10.2)
   30 CONTINUE
```

```
C**** PROGRAM TO DEMONSTRATE INPUT OF ARRAY
C**** DATA FROM THE KEYBOARD USING AN IMPLIED
C**** DO LOOP
C
C234567
      PROGRAM ARRAYK
      DIMENSION X(3)
      OPEN (6,FILE = 'PRINTER:')
      WRITE (0,1)
      WRITE (6,1)
    1 FORMAT (3(10H!--------*))
      READ (0,5) (X(J),J = 1,3)
    5 FORMAT (3(F10.2))
      WRITE (0,10)
      WRITE (6,10)
   10 FORMAT (//,3(10H!--------*),/)
      WRITE (0,20) (X(K),K = 1,3)
      WRITE (6,20) (X(K),K = 1,3)
   20 FORMAT (3(F10.2))
      STOP
      END


!--------*!--------*!--------*


!--------*!--------*!--------*

    123.33    678.01    222.87
```

Fig. 6-7. Program to demonstrate the input of array data from the keyboard.

```
C**** PROGRAM TO READ A DIRECT ACCESS FILE
C**** FROM DISK
C
C234567
      PROGRAM RDDISK
      DIMENSION Z(5)
      OPEN (20, FILE='#9:EXAMP',ACCESS='DIRECT',
     *STATUS='OLD',FORM='FORMATTED',RECL=51)
      OPEN (6,FILE='PRINTER:')
      READ (20,100,REC=1,END=900) (Z(K),K = 1,5)
  100 FORMAT (10(F10.2))
  900 WRITE (0,200) (Z(K),K = 1,5)
      WRITE (6,200) (Z(K),K = 1,5)
  200 FORMAT (//,5(F10.2))
      CLOSE (20,STATUS='KEEP')
      STOP
      END


      5.00     10.00     15.00     20.00     25.00
```

Fig. 6-8. Program to demonstrate the reading of array data from a direct (random) access file.

```
C**** PROGRAM TO USE AN ARRAY TO CREATE A
C**** FILE ON DISK
C
C234567
      PROGRAM WRDISK
      DIMENSION Z( 5 )
      DATA Z( 1 ),Z( 2 ),Z( 3 ),Z( 4 ),Z( 5 )/5.,10.,15.,20.,
     *25./
      OPEN ( 20,FILE='#9:EXAMP',ACCESS='DIRECT',STATUS='NEW',
     *FORM='FORMATTED',RECL=51 )
      WRITE (20,100,REC=1) (Z( J ), J = 1,5)
  100 FORMAT (5(F10.2))
  900 CLOSE (20,STATUS='KEEP')
      STOP
      END
```

Fig. 6-9. Program to demonstrate the writing of a direct (random) access file to disk.

The standard DO loop reads one value for each line. The record length is 11 bytes per value, 10 columns for the (F10.2) format, and one byte for the end-of-file record. The standard DO loop writes one value per line. The implied DO loop can write all values on one line.

ARRAY OUTPUT

Array data can be output, using the WRITE statement, to three peripheral devices — CRT, disk, and printer. Array data can be written by using the WRITE statement and an output list of (1) the array variable, (2) single or multiple array elements, (3) standard DO loop, and (4) implied DO loop.

WRITE-FORMAT Relationship

FORTRAN output writes one line and closes out that line. The standard DO loop writes one value per line and closes out that line.

```
    DO 20 J = 1,5
    WRITE (0,100) X(J)
 20 CONTINUE
100 FORMAT (F10.2)
```

There are three ways to write all array items on one line of output. The first way is to place each element of the array on one line.

```
    WRITE (0,100) X(1), X(2), X(3), X(4), X(5)
100 FORMAT (5(F10.2))
```

The second method to output all array values on one line (in most cases) is to use an implied DO loop. The result is the same as using all array elements on one line, but is more efficient.

```
    WRITE (0,100) (X(J), J = 1,5)
100 FORMAT (5(F10.2))
```

The third way to output all array values on one line is to use the array variable as the output list (Figs. 6-10, 6-11, and 6-12). When the array variable is used to output the array elements, the FORMAT statement controls how the values are printed.

```
      DIMENSION AA(10), BB(10)
      WRITE (0,200) AA, BB
  200 FORMAT (10(F5.0))
```

```
C**** PROGRAM TO CREATE DUPLICATE ARRAYS AA
C**** AND BB.  AA IS THE ORIGINAL ARRAY THAT
C**** CONTAINS THE VALUES.
C
C234567
      PROGRAM ARRAYX
      DIMENSION AA( 10 ), BB( 10 )
      DATA AA( 1 ),AA( 2 ),AA( 3 ),AA( 4 ),AA( 5 ),AA( 6 ),
     *AA( 7 ),AA( 8 ),AA( 9 ),AA( 10 )/5.,18.,-30.,-2.,4.,
     *7.,9.,-1.,10.,12./
      OPEN ( 6,FILE='PRINTER:' )
      DO 20 J = 1,10
      BB( J ) = AA( J )
   20 CONTINUE
      WRITE ( 0,200 ) AA, BB
      WRITE ( 6,200 ) AA, BB
  200 FORMAT (//,10( F5.0 ))
      STOP
      END




   5.   18.  -30.   -2.    4.    7.    9.   -1.   10.   12.
   5.   18.  -30.   -2.    4.    7.    9.   -1.   10.   12.
```

Fig. 6-10. Program to demonstrate the direct transfer of values from one array to another.

Each element of the arrays "AA" and "BB" is output using the FORMAT statement labeled 200. All 10 elements of the array "AA" are output, each in a floating-point field of F5.0. When the "AA" list has been output, array "BB" then outputs its 10 elements using the same (10(F5.0)) FORMAT statement.

When the FORMAT statement is changed (Fig. 6-12), the "X" array variable outputs each of 10 elements, but this time the FORMAT statement, 200 FORMAT (5(F5.0),/), causes five elements to be printed on one line. A line is skipped, and the last five elements are printed on the next line. The "Y" array then prints each of its 10 elements using the same FORMAT statement.

```
      DIMENSION X(10), Y(10)
      WRITE (0,200) X, Y
  200 FORMAT (5(F5.0),/)
```

The WRITE statement controls what is output, and the FORMAT statement is the secondary control. The WRITE statement can output any, or all, of the array elements, but they are printed according to the FORMAT statement.

```
      DIMENSION F(20)
      WRITE (0,200) F
200   FORMAT (F10.0)
```

When the array elements of "F" are written, all 20 elements of the array will be written, but they will be written one element value per line.

```
      DIMENSION F(20)
      WRITE (0,200) F
200   FORMAT (10(F5.0))
```

In this example, all 20 elements of the "F" array will be written, but they will be written 10 elements per line.

```
      DIMENSION F(20)
      WRITE (0,200) (F(J), J = 1,20, 5)
200   FORMAT (20(F5.0))
```

In this example, elements F(1), F(6), F(11), and F(17) will be written on one line. The FORMAT statement specifies 20 fields to be written. Only four elements of the array will be written. The implied DO loop controls the number of elements written, and the excess fields in the FORMAT statement are ignored.

```
C****  PROGRAM TO EXCHANGE TO ARRAY POSITIONS
C****  COMPLETELY FROM POSITION 1 TO POSITION 10
C
C
C234567
       PROGRAM COMPEX
       DIMENSION AA( 10 ), BB( 10 )
       DATA AA( 1 ),AA( 2 ),AA( 3 ),AA( 4 ),AA( 5 ),AA( 6 ),
      *AA( 7 ),AA( 8 ),AA( 9 ),AA( 10 )/5.,18.,-30.,-2.,4.,
      *7.,9.,-1.,9.,12./
       OPEN ( 6,FILE='PRINTER:' )
       DO 20 J = 1,10
       K = 11 - J
       BB( K ) = AA( J )
   20  CONTINUE
       WRITE ( 0,200 ) AA, BB
       WRITE ( 6,200 ) AA, BB
  200  FORMAT (//,10( F5.0 ))
       STOP
       END





   5.   18.  -30.   -2.    4.    7.    9.   -1.    9.   12.
  12.    9.   -1.    9.    7.    4.   -2.  -30.   18.    5.
```

Fig. 6-11. Program to demonstrate the transfer of values from one array to another in reverse order.

```
C**** PROGRAM TO PLACE THE LOWER HALF OF X ARRAY,
C**** INTO THE TOP HALF OF Y ARRAY, AND TO PLACE
C**** THE UPPER HALF OF X ARRAY INTO THE LOWER HALF
C**** OF Y ARRAY
C
C234567
      PROGRAM EXCHGE
      DIMENSION X( 10 ), Y( 10 )
      DATA X( 1 ),X( 2 ),X( 3 ),X( 4 ),X( 5 ),X( 6 ),X( 7 ),X( 8 ),
     *X( 9 ),X( 10 )/5.,18.,-30.,-2.,4.,7.,9.,-1.,9.,
     *12./
      OPEN ( 6,FILE='PRINTER:' )
      DO 20 J = 1,5
      K = J + 5
      Y( K ) = X( J )
   20 CONTINUE
      DO 30 J = 6,10
      K = J - 5
      Y( K ) = X( J )
   30 CONTINUE
      WRITE ( 0,200 ) X, Y
      WRITE ( 6,200 ) X, Y
  200 FORMAT ( 5( F5.0 ),/ )
      STOP
      END


   5.  18. -30.  -2.   4.

   7.   9.  -1.   9.  12.

   7.   9.  -1.   9.  12.

   5.  18. -30.  -2.   4.
```

Fig. 6-12. Program to demonstrate the transfer of values from the lower half of one array to the upper half of a second array, and from the upper half of the first array to the lower half of the second array.

Write to CRT (0)

Array data is written to the CRT using single array elements, standard DO loops, or the array variable by using WRITE (0,100) or WRITE (*,100), followed by the output list.

Write to Printer (6)

Array data is output to the printer, first by opening the printer, and then using the printer device number in the WRITE statement.

```
      OPEN (6,FILE='PRINTER:')
      —
      —
      —
      WRITE (6,200) (X(J), J = 1,5)
  200 FORMAT (5(F10.2))
```

Write to Disk

Fig. 6-9 is a program to write array data to disk using a direct access file.

```
      DIMENSION Z(5)
      OPEN (20,FILE='#9:EXAMP',
     *ACCESS='DIRECT',STATUS='NEW',
     *FORM='FORMATTED',RECL=51)
      WRITE (20,100,REC=1)(Z(J),J=1,5)
  100 FORMAT (5(F10.2))
  900 CLOSE (20,STATUS = 'KEEP')
```

The file is opened on device #20. Numbers 1 through 12 are reserved for Apple hardware devices. The file was created on a three-disk drive system, and the file "EXAMP" is created on a disk in disk drive #9. The ACCESS is DIRECT, *and direct access files must be given a specific number of bytes into which the records are placed.* There are five array values, each placed in 10 columns, (5(F10.2)), and this requires 50 bytes of space. The file requires 1 byte of space for the end-of-file marker, thus 51 bytes of space are required for each array record.

The WRITE (20,100,REC = 1) relates the OPEN statement to device #20 on which the file is written. The second integer number, 100, ties the FORMAT statement, 5(F10.2), to the record length. In FORTRAN, the record begins with #1, not #0, as in BASIC or Pascal. The implied DO loop causes the five array values of "Z" to be written on one line. Line 900, CLOSE (20,STATUS = 'KEEP'), closes the file opened on device #20, and preserves the file for future use. If the file was to be removed from the disk, the STATUS = 'DELETE', would be used.

ARRAY MANIPULATION

One definition of manipulation is "skillful handling or treatment." Data in array form is one of the powerful tools used by the computer to produce information. The manipulative expressions contained in the body of the loop produce desired results with a minimum of program statements and a minimum of memory. If simple variables were used in computation instead of arrays, programs would be much larger, more difficult to handle and type, and more time-consuming to load.

There are almost a limitless number of ways in which loops and arrays can be manipulated to produce information. One of the most common ways to use arrays is to sum a list of values (Figs. 6-4, 6-5, and 6-6) and to compute the average of the list.

Fig. 6-5 is a program to sum the scores in a list, count the number of scores in the list, and compute the average (AVG). The array SCORE is DIMENSIONED to five (5), and five scores are placed in the array. The KOUNT = 0 and KOUNT = KOUNT + 1 statements are unnecessary in this program because the DIMENSION statement and the loop both have the same final value. The AVG = SUM/KOUNT statement could have been AVG = SUM/5 and would have produced the same results. If a limit had been set to count only a certain number of grades, the KOUNT would have been useful to compute the average.

```
      SUM = SUM + SCORE(J)
      IF (KOUNT .EQ. 4) GOTO 60
      KOUNT = KOUNT + 1
   50 CONTINUE
   60 AVG = SUM/KOUNT
```

The decision statement caused the program to jump out of the loop when the KOUNT is equal to four (4), and compute the average on the basis of four scores instead of five.

Fig. 6-10 is a program that transfers the values of array "AA" directly into array "BB."

```
      DIMENSION AA(10), BB(10)
      DO 20 J = 1,10
      BB(J) = AA(J)
   20 CONTINUE
```

The assignment statement places one value stored in "AA" into "BB" on each loop execution. After the loop repeats 10 times, "BB" has received the 10 values stored in "AA." Different elements of "AA" could be placed in "BB" by changing the subscripts.

```
      DO 20 J = 1,9
      BB(J) = AA(J+1)
   20 CONTINUE
      BB(10) = AA(1)
```

In this example, elements 2 through 10 of "AA" are assigned to elements 1 through 9 of "BB." When the loop execution is completed, element AA(1) is assigned to BB(10).

Fig. 6-11 is a program to reverse the positions of the values stored in "AA" and place them in "BB." AA(1) is assigned to BB(10), AA(2) is assigned to BB(9), etc. The statement "BB(K) = AA(J)" is then used to place the values stored in "AA" in reverse order into "BB."

Fig. 6-12 is a program that causes the five values in array elements X(1) through X(5) to be placed in array elements Y(6) through Y(10), and array elements X(6) through X(10) to be placed in array elements Y(1) through Y(5). The program uses a standard DO loop to select off array elements 1 through 5. The variable "K" is assigned the values 6 through 10 depending on the value of "J."

A second standard DO loop that increments from 6 through 10 sets up the array locations to be transferred into Y(1) through Y(5). In this case, 5 is subtracted from the value of "J" and assigned to the variable "K." On each "J" loop repetition from 6 through 10, the value of "K" is incremented from 1 to 5. When the transfers are complete, the "X" and "Y" arrays are written out using only the array variable to print out the complete list of array values. The FORMAT statement sets the pattern for the output, so five values are printed on one line, and one line is skipped before the next line of five values is printed out.

```
      DO 30 J = 6,10
      K = J - 5
      Y(K) = X(J)
   30 CONTINUE
      WRITE (0,200) X, Y
  200 FORMAT (5(F5.0),/)
```

Fig. 6-13 is a program written to count the number of grades in a specific grade range, and the total number of grades. The items to be counted are: (1) those grades greater than 90; (2) those grades greater than or equal to 80, and those grades less than or equal to 90; (3) those grades less than 80; and (4) the total number of grades.

Decision statements, using relational and logical operators, are used to

```
C**** PROGRAM TO SELECT AND COUNT GRADE RANGES
C**** GREATER THAN 90, FROM 80 TO 90,BELOW
C**** 90, AND COUNT THE TOTAL NUMBER OF GRADES
C
C234567
      PROGRAM NGRDE
      DIMENSION N(15)
      DATA N/78,89,96,100,77,45,99,85,97,98,
     *87,89,65,100,97/
      OPEN (6,FILE='PRINTER:')
      K1 = 0
      K2 = 0
      K3 = 0
      K4 = 0
      NUM = 15
      DO 20 J = 1,NUM
      IF (N(J) .GT. 90) K1 = K1 + 1
      IF (N(J) .GE. 80 .AND. N(J) .LE. 90) K2 = K2 + 1
      IF (N(J) .LT. 80) K3 = K3 + 1
      K4 = K4 + 1
   20 CONTINUE
      WRITE (0,200) K1, K2, K3, K4
      WRITE (6,200) K1, K2, K3, K4
  200 FORMAT (//,'NUMBER OF GRADES GREATER THAN 90: ',
     *I4,/,'NUMBER OF GRADES 80 TO 90 ARE:     ',I4,/,
     *'NUMBER OF GRADES BELOW 80 ARE:      ',I4,/,
     *'AND TOTAL NUMBER OF GRADES ARE:    'I4)
      STOP
      END


NUMBER OF GRADES GREATER THAN 90:      7
NUMBER OF GRADES 80 TO 90 ARE:         4
NUMBER OF GRADES BELOW 80 ARE:         4
AND TOTAL NUMBER OF GRADES ARE:       15
```

Fig. 6-13. Program to count the number of grades in a specific grade range, and the total number of grades.

select the values stored in the array. Each logical IF statement terminates with a counting statement, so the proper count is recorded with each grade selection. The total number of grades are counted, so K4 = K4 + 1 (total count) is incremented as each grade is passed through the program.

Fig. 6-14 is a program written to count the number of times a selected grade value occurs within a list of grades. The grade selected to be counted is 100 (NSPECL = 100). A logical IF statement is used to compare the array values and the specific grade value.

```
IF (N(J) .EQ. NSPECL) K1 = K1 + 1
```

As the standard DO loop increments from 1 to 15, each array value is compared to a specific value, NSPECL = 100. If the array value is equal to 100, the array value is counted. When the DO loop has repeated 15 times, it defaults to the WRITE statement to output the number of times the specific value occurred in the list of array values.

```
C**** PROGRAM TO COUNT THE NUMBER OF TIMES A
C**** SPECIFIC VALUE OCCURS IN A LIST OF
C**** NUMBERS
C
C234567
      PROGRAM COUNT
      DIMENSION N(15)
      DATA N/78,89,96,100,77,45,99,85,97,98,
     *87,89,65,100,97/
      OPEN (6,FILE='PRINTER:')
      K1 = 0
      NSPECL = 100
      NUM = 15
      DO 20 J = 1,NUM
      IF (N(J) .EQ. NSPECL) K1 =  K1 + 1
   20 CONTINUE
      WRITE (0,200) K1
      WRITE (6,200) K1
  200 FORMAT (//,'THE NUMBER OF TIMES THAT THE ',/,
     *'GRADE 100 OCCURRED IN THE GRADE LIST WAS:',I4,//)
      STOP
      END




THE NUMBER OF TIMES THAT THE
GRADE 100 OCCURRED IN THE GRADE LIST WAS:   2
```

Fig. 6-14. Program to count the number of times a selected grade value occurs within a list of grades.

The program in Fig. 6-15 is used to locate the lowest grade in a list of array values, and to determine the position of the lowest grade in the list. Using the location of the lowest grade in the list, a logical IF statement causes the lowest grade in the list to be dropped when the grades are summed. The position of the lowest grade in the list, and the lowest grade are selected in the first DO loop.

```
      LOWEST = N(1)
      LOC = 1
      NUM = 15
      DO 20 J = 2,NUM
      IF (N(J) .GE. LOWEST) GOTO 20
      LOWEST = N(J)
      LOC = J
   20 CONTINUE
```

```
C**** PROGRAM TO DROP THE LOWEST GRADE FROM
C**** THE LIST, SUM THE GRADES IN THE LIST,
C**** AND COMPUTE THE AVERAGE GRADE
C
C234567
      PROGRAM ELIM
      DIMENSION N(15)
      DATA N/78,89,96,100,77,45,99,85,97,98,
     *87,89,65,100,97/
      OPEN (6,FILE='PRINTER:')
      NSUM = 0
      LOWEST = N(1)
      LOC = 1
      NUM = 15
      DO 20 J = 2,NUM
      IF (N(J) .GE. LOWEST) GOTO 20
      LOWEST = N(J)
      LOC = J
   20 CONTINUE
      DO 30 K = 1,NUM
      IF (K .EQ. LOC) GOTO 30
      NSUM = NSUM + N(K)
   30 CONTINUE
      NAVG = NSUM/(NUM-1)
      WRITE (0,200) N
      WRITE (6,200) N
      WRITE (0,210) LOWEST, LOC, NSUM, NAVG
      WRITE (6,210) LOWEST, LOC, NSUM, NAVG
  200 FORMAT (/,5(I4))
  210 FORMAT (///,'THE LOWEST GRADE IS: ',I4,/,
     *'THE LOCATION OF THE LOWEST GRADE IS: ',I4,/,
     *'THE SUM OF ALL THE GRADES IS: ',I4,/,
     *'AND THE AVERAGE IS: ',I4)
      STOP
      END


  78  89  96 100  77
  45  99  85  97  98
  87  89  65 100  97


THE LOWEST GRADE IS:   45
THE LOCATION OF THE LOWEST GRADE IS:    6
THE SUM OF ALL THE GRADES IS: 1257
AND THE AVERAGE IS:   89
```

Fig. 6-15. Program to drop the lowest grade from a list of grades, sum the grades in the list, and compute the average grade.

When the position of the lowest grade, and the lowest grade have been determined, the program defaults to the second DO loop. The second DO loop uses a logical IF statement to eliminate the position of the lowest grade from the summing statement. When the position of the lowest grade is compared to the loop value, and the two values are equal, the decision statement jumps to the foot of the loop. On all other loop repetitions the grades are summed in the summing statement.

When the lowest grade is dropped, it must be reflected when the grades are averaged. The number of grades was initialized to 15 (NUM = 15). If all 15 grades were to be summed and averaged, the averaging statement would be

```
NAVG = SUM/NUM.
```

The lowest grade was dropped from the list, and this must be reflected in the averaging statement by subtracting one grade from the number of grades in the list.

```
NAVG = SUM/(NUM-1)
```

SORTING

Figs. 6-16, 6-17, 6-18, and 6-19 deal with sorting items in a list, so the list is put in a specific order. A definition of sorting is to arrange items, values, or information according to a specific usable pattern. Items recognized as being sorted according to a specific pattern include integers from least to greatest; for example, from 1 to 10. The words in a dictionary are sorted according to the letters in the alphabet. Bulk mail is sorted according to the ZIP code, from least number to the greatest number.

Sorting depends on sequencing the items according to a key. Congressional representatives' names are generally sorted by three keys. The alphabetic key, where the surname is sorted alphabetically, is probably the most frequently used key. The second key would be by Senate or House. The list of Senators in Congress would use the alphabetic key and the Senate key. The House members would use the alphabetic key and the House key. A third list might contain three keys alphabetized by name, state, and branch of Congress.

In the following example, a list of five integers is sorted from least integer to greatest integer. The list is input from the greatest integer to the least integer, so the maximum number of passes and exchanges will occur. The array variable "N" is dimensioned to five.

```
N(1) = 100
N(2) = 96
N(3) = 89
N(4) = 78
N(5) = 77
```

A pass in a sort is equated to one execution of the outer loop. The outer loop accounts for the number of passes. The inner loop makes the comparisons between pairs of numbers in the list.

If a list of numbers has "N" number of elements, the maximum number of passes needed to sort the list is "N – 1." This example contains five numbers, so there will be four (5 – 1) passes.

The number of required passes and exchanges depends on the order of the initial list. If the initial list is in correct order, there will be no exchanges. The number of passes will be executed to fulfill the requirements of the program.

```
      DIMENSION N(5)
      DATA N /100,96,89,78,77/
      DO 20 J = 1,4
      DO 10 K = 1,4
      IF (N(K) .LE. N(K+1)) GOTO 10
      NTEMP = N(K)
      N(K) = N(K+1)
      N(K+1) = NTEMP
   10 CONTINUE
   20 CONTINUE
```

SORT PASSES

Fig. 6-16 is the printout of a special program written to output the sequence of passes and exchanges from the sort.

Pass 1

a. The numbers in the first two positions of the list are compared, and the larger number is placed in the second position in the list.
b. This comparison continues for each pair of numbers in the list.
c. The largest number will be in the last position in the list.

Pass 2

a. The numbers in the list are compared in pairs, and the largest number is placed in the second position in the list.
b. This comparison continues until the next to largest number in the list has been moved to the next to last position in the list.

Pass 3

a. The numbers in the first two positions in the list are compared and the larger number is placed in the second position in the list.
b. This comparison continues until the third largest number in the list has been moved to the third position from the end of the list.

Pass 4

a. The numbers in the first two positions in the list are compared and the largest number is placed in the second position in the list.
b. On the last pass, one comparison is done and the list is sorted.

```
&
]RUN
100   96   89   78   77

N(1 )=  100  EXCHANGED  WITH  N( 2 )=  96
N(2 )=  100  EXCHANGED  WITH  N( 3 )=  89
N(3 )=  100  EXCHANGED  WITH  N( 4 )=  78
N( 4 )=  100  EXCHANGED  WITH  N( 5 )=  77


96   89   78   77   100

N( 1 )=  96  EXCHANGED  WITH  N( 2 )=  89
N( 2 )=  96  EXCHANGED  WITH  N( 3 )=  78
N( 3 )=  96  EXCHANGED  WITH  N( 4 )=  77
N( 4 )  AND  N( 5 )NOT  EXCHANGED


89   78   77   96   100

N( 1 )=  89  EXCHANGED  WITH  N( 2 )=  78
N( 2 )=  89  EXCHANGED  WITH  N( 3 )=  77
N( 3 )  AND  N( 4 )NOT  EXCHANGED
N( 4 )  AND  N( 5 )NOT  EXCHANGED


78   77   89   96   100

N( 1 )=  78  EXCHANGED  WITH  N( 2 )=  77
N( 2 )  AND  N( 3 )NOT  EXCHANGED
N( 3 )  AND  N( 4 )NOT  EXCHANGED
N( 4 )  AND  N( 5 )NOT  EXCHANGED


77   78   89   96   100
```

Fig. 6-16. Printout of a program written to output the sequence of passes and exchanges from a sort.

Fig. 6-17 is a chart of the passes, the exchanges, and the list of numbers after each pass.

The progam in Fig. 6-18 demonstrates the *bubble* sort, a more efficient way to sort. This sort discovers the smallest value in the list and places it in the first position. This is accomplished by incrementing the initial value of the inner loop on each pass of the outer loop. The program in Fig. 6-18 sorts a list of 15 numbers, and prints out the initial list and the sorted list in five columns and three rows.

A special program was written to cause five numbers to be sorted. The program that sorts five numbers and 15 numbers accomplishes the same purpose.

PASS	LIMIT	J	K	N(1)	N(2)	N(3)	N(4)	EXCH	K + 1	N(2)	N(3)	N(4)	N(5)	LIST				
0	5	1	1						2					100	96	89	78	77
1	5	1	1	100				1	2	96								
					100			2			89							
						100		3				78						
							100	4					77					
2	5	2	2						3					96	89	78	77	100
2	5	2	2	96				1	3	89								
					96			2			78							
						96		3				77						
							N(4) and						N(5) not exchanged					
3	5	3	3						4					89	78	77	96	100
	5	3	3	89				1	4	78								
					89			2			77							
						N(3) and						N(4) not exchanged						
							N(4) and						N(5) not exchanged					
4	5	4	4						5					78	77	89	96	100
4	5	4	4	78				1	5	77								
					N(2) and						N(3) not exchanged							
						N(3) and						N(4) not exchanged						
							N(4) and						N(5) not exchanged					
														77	78	89	96	100

Fig. 6-17. Chart of the passes, exchanges, and list of numbers after each pass for the printout in Fig. 6-16.

```
&C**** PROGRAM TO DEMONSTRATE THE BUBBLE SORT,
C**** AND SORT A LIST OF NUMBERS FROM LEAST
C**** TO GREATEST
C
C234567
      PROGRAM SORTLG
      DIMENSION N(15)
      DATA N/78,89,96,100,77,45,99,85,97,98,
     *87,89,65,100,97/
      OPEN (6,FILE='PRINTER:')
      WRITE (0,100)
      WRITE (6,100)
  100 FORMAT (///,'THIS IS THE LIST AS INPUT',//)
      WRITE (0,210) N
      WRITE (6,210) N
      L = 15
      M = L-1
      DO 30 J = 1,M
      JPLUS1 = J + 1
      DO 20 K = JPLUS1,L
      IF (N(J) .LE. N(K)) GOTO 20
      NTEMP = N(J)
      N(J) = N(K)
      N(K) = NTEMP
   20 CONTINUE
   30 CONTINUE
      WRITE (0,200)
      WRITE (6,200)
  200 FORMAT (///,'THIS IS THE SORTED LIST',//)
      WRITE (0,210) N
      WRITE (6,210) N
  210 FORMAT (5I6)
      STOP
      END



THIS IS THE LIST AS INPUT


    78    89    96   100    77
    45    99    85    97    98
    87    89    65   100    97



THIS IS THE SORTED LIST


    45    65    77    78    85
    87    89    89    96    97
    97    98    99   100   100
```

Fig. 6-18. Program to demonstrate the bubble sort with numbers sorted from least to greatest.

```
DIMENSION N(5)
DATA N /100,96,89,78,77/
L = 5
M = L-1
DO J = 1,M
```

```
      JPLUS1 = J + 1
      DO 20 K = JPLUS1,L
      IF (N(J) .LE. N(K)) GOTO 20
      NTEMP = N(J)
      N(J) = N(K)
      N(K) = NTEMP
   20 CONTINUE
   30 CONTINUE
```

In this example, the "J" loop goes from 1 to 4, and the "K" loop goes from 2 to 5 on the initial series of executions. The "K" loop then goes from 3 to 5, 4 to 5, and 5 to 5 on the final executions. Fig. 6-19 is a printout of this program written to show the sequence of passes and exchanges from the sort.

This loop configuration, the logical IF, and the exchange routine search the list of numbers until the smallest number is found, and place it in the first array element. The second number is discovered, and placed in the second array element, etc., until the list is in order. This sorting technique reduces the number of comparisons by 33%. If the original list is in the correct order, no exchanges will be made, but "N – 1" passes will be made to satisfy program requirements. Fig. 6-20 is a chart of the passes, exchanges, and the list of numbers after each pass.

The program in Fig. 6-21 sorts a list of numbers from the greatest number to the least number. There is only one program statement that is different in Fig. 6-18 and Fig. 6-21, and that is the logical IF statement. In Fig. 6-21, the statement

```
]PR#1
]RUN
100   96   89   78   77

N(1 )=  100 EXCHANGED WITH N( 2 )=  96
N(1 )=  96 EXCHANGED WITH N( 3 )=  89
N(1 )=  89 EXCHANGED WITH N( 4 )=  78
N( 1 )=  78 EXCHANGED WITH N( 5 )=  77


77   100   96   89   78

N( 2 )=  100 EXCHANGED WITH N( 3 )=  96
N( 2 )=  96 EXCHANGED WITH N( 4 )=  89
N( 2 )=  89 EXCHANGED WITH N( 5 )=  78


77   78   100   96   89

N( 3 )=  100 EXCHANGED WITH N( 4 )=  96
N( 3 )=  96 EXCHANGED WITH N( 5 )=  89


77   78   89   100   96

N( 4 )=  100 EXCHANGED WITH N( 5 )=  96


77   78   89   96   100
```

Fig. 6-19. Printout of a bubble sort exchange.

PASS	L	M(L-1)	J	N(1)	N(2)	N(3)	N(4)	EXCH	JPLUS1	K	N(2)	N(3)	N(4)	N(5)	LIST				
0	5	4	1												100	96	89	78	77
1	5	4	1	100				1	2	2	96								
				96				2				89							
				89				3					78						
				78				4						77					
2	5	4	2						3	3					77	100	96	89	78
2	5	4	2		100			1	3	3		96							
					96			2					89						
					89			3						78					
3	5	4	3						4	4					77	78	100	96	89
3	5	4	3			100		1	4	4			96						
						96		2						89					
4	5	4	4						5	5					77	78	89	100	96
4	5	4	4				100	1	5	5				96					
															77	78	89	96	100

Fig. 6-20. Chart of the passes, exchanges, and list of numbers after each pass for the printout in Fig. 6-19.

IF (N(J) .GE. N(K)) GOTO 20

causes the program to sort from greatest to least. In Fig. 6-18, the statement

IF (N(J) .LE. N(K)) GOTO 20

causes the program to sort from least to greatest.

```
C**** PROGRAM TO DEMONSTRATE THE BUBBLE SORT,
C**** AND SORT A LIST OF NUMBERS FROM GREATEST
C**** TO LEAST
C
C234567
      PROGRAM SORTGL
      DIMENSION N(15)
      DATA N/78,89,96,100,77,45,99,85,97,98,
     *87,89,65,100,97/
      OPEN (6,FILE='PRINTER:')
      WRITE (0,100)
      WRITE (6,100)
  100 FORMAT (///,'THIS IS THE LIST AS INPUT',//)
      WRITE (0,210) N
      WRITE (6,210) N
      L = 15
      M = L-1
      DO 30 J = 1,M
      JPLUS1 = J + 1
      DO 20 K = JPLUS1,L
      IF (N(J) .GE. N(K)) GOTO 20
      NTEMP = N(J)
      N(J) = N(K)
      N(K) = NTEMP
   20 CONTINUE
   30 CONTINUE
      WRITE (0,200)
      WRITE (6,200)
  200 FORMAT (///,'THIS IS THE SORTED LIST',//)
      WRITE (0,210) N
      WRITE (6,210) N
  210 FORMAT (5I6)
      STOP
      END



 THIS IS THE LIST AS INPUT


     78    89    96   100    77
     45    99    85    97    98
     87    89    65   100    97


 THIS IS THE SORTED LIST


    100   100    99    98    97
     97    96    89    89    87
     85    78    77    65    45
```

Fig. 6-21. Program to demonstrate the bubble sort with numbers sorted from greatest to least.

CHAPTER 7
Double Subscripted Arrays

INTRODUCTION

A double subscripted array is an array whose variable has two subscripts. These subscripts can be thought of as a table whose format contains rows that extend from left to right in a horizontal fashion, and whose columns extend from top to bottom in a vertical fashion (Fig. 7-1).

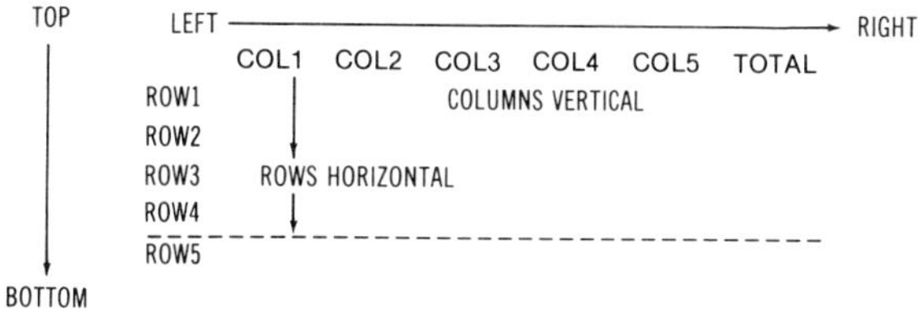

Fig. 7-1. Table format of a double subscripted array.

SPECIFICATION STATEMENT

A specification statement is used to reserve memory space for the array.

```
DIMENSION X(10,10), N(5,31)
INTEGER X(10,10), AAA(31,5)
REAL N(3,2), K(14,32)
COMMON /ATS/ X(10,10), X(5,31)
```

Most tables contain two parts — (1) that portion of the table into which the data is placed and (2) that portion of the table that is computed from the given data.

The specification statement reserves memory locations for the complete table, the given data, and the columns and rows of computed information. When the problem and solution are set up, the specification statement must reflect the total memory needs. Fig. 7-2 uses a DIMENSION N(5,6) statement to reserve memory. The given data is placed in a 4 × 5 matrix. The computed information, TOTAL, uses rows 1 through 5 in column 6 to write the totals computed from adding columns 1 through 5. The totals of each column are computed and placed in row 5 of columns 1 through 6.

```
C**** PROGRAM TO DEMONSTRATE ROW AND COLUMN
C**** SET-UP OF DOUBLE SUBSCRIPTED ARRAYS
C234567
      PROGRAM ROWCOL
      DIMENSION N(5,6)
      DATA N(1,1),N(1,2),N(1,3),N(1,4),N(1,5)/11,12,13,14,15/
      DATA N(2,1),N(2,2),N(2,3),N(2,4),N(2,5)/21,22,23,24,25/
      DATA N(3,1),N(3,2),N(3,3),N(3,4),N(3,5)/31,32,33,34,35/
      DATA N(4,1),N(4,2),N(4,3),N(4,4),N(4,5)/41,42,43,44,45/
      OPEN (6,FILE='PRINTER:')
      DO 5 NROW = 1,5
      N(NROW,6) = 0
    5 CONTINUE
      DO 10 NCOL = 1,5
      N(5,NCOL) = 0
   10 CONTINUE
      DO 20 NROW = 1,4
      DO 20 NCOL = 1,5
      N(NROW,6) = N(NROW,6) + N(NROW,NCOL)
   20 CONTINUE
      DO 30 NCOL = 1,6
      DO 30 NROW = 1,4
      N(5,NCOL) = N(5,NCOL) + N(NROW,NCOL)
   30 CONTINUE
      WRITE (0,100)
      WRITE (6,100)
  100 FORMAT (8X,'COL1   COL2   COL3   COL4   COL5   TOTAL',/)
      DO 40 NROW = 1,4
      WRITE (0,110) NROW, (N(NROW,NCOL),NCOL = 1,6)
      WRITE (6,110) NROW, (N(NROW,NCOL),NCOL = 1,6)
   40 CONTINUE
  110 FORMAT ('ROW ',I2,6(I6))
      WRITE (0,120)
      WRITE (6,120)
  120 FORMAT (41(1H-))
      WRITE (0,130) (N(5,NCOL),NCOL = 1,6)
      WRITE (6,130) (N(5,NCOL),NCOL = 1,6)
  130 FORMAT ('TOTAL ',6(I6))
      STOP
      END
```

Fig. 7-2. Program to demonstrate row and column setup of double subscripted arrays.

DATA INPUT IN A DOUBLE SUBSCRIPTED MATRIX

The given data in Fig. 7-2, a 4 × 5 matrix, reflects the row number and column number of the related element in the matrix.

N(1,1) = 11
N(1,5) = 15
N(2,3) = 23
N(3,5) = 35
N(4,1) = 41

The execution of the program in Fig. 7-2 produced the matrix in Fig. 7-3.

Loops are used to input and output data and information in the matrix. A matrix can be filled in one of two directions — horizontally or vertically (top down). When a matrix is filled horizontally, the rows are filled first (Fig. 7-4).

```
          COL1    COL2    COL3    COL4    COL5    TOTAL

ROW  1     11      12      13      14      15       65
ROW  2     21      22      23      24      25      115
ROW  3     31      32      33      34      35      165
ROW  4     41      42      43      44      45      215
-------------------------------------------------------
TOTAL     104     108     112     116     120      560
```

Fig. 7-3. Output of program in Fig. 7-2.

```
    DO 20 NROW = 1,4
    DO 10 NCOL = 1,5
    WRITE (0,100) N(NROW,NCOL)
 10 CONTINUE
 20 CONTINUE
100 FORMAT (5(F5.0))
    STOP
    END
```

THIS PROGRAM PRINTS OUT ONE VALUE PER LINE FOR 20 LINES

HORIZONTAL ROW, COLUMN RELATIONSHIP

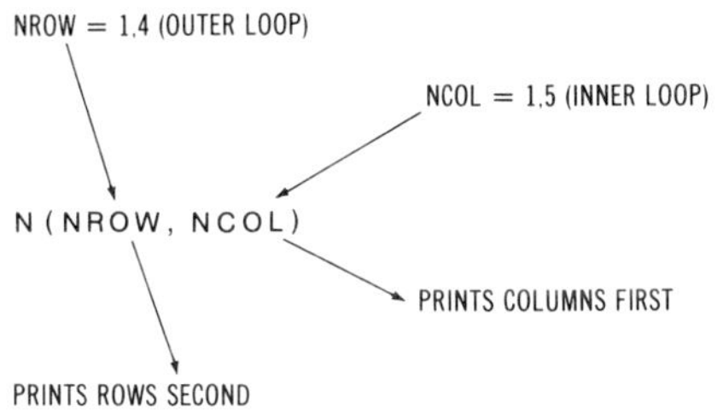

Fig. 7-4. Horizontal relationship of loops, rows, and columns.

READ DATA FROM KEYBOARD

To read a 4 × 5 matrix horizontally from the keyboard, one of the two following examples could be used:

```
    DO 20 NROW = 1,4
    READ(0,200) N(NROW,1),N(NROW,2),
   *N(NROW,3),N(NROW,4),N(NROW,5)
 20 CONTINUE
200 FORMAT (5(F5.0))
```

or

```
    DO 20 NROW = 1,4
    READ(0,200)(N(NROW,NCOL),NCOL=1,5)
 20 CONTINUE
200 FORMAT (5(F5.0))
```

In each example the data is input in rows from column 1 to column 5, using either the single array element or the implied DO loop. When the first row is filled, the outer loop increments to receive the data input for the next row.

```
      DO 20 NCOL = 1,5
      DO 10 NROW = 1,4
      READ(0,200)(N(NROW,NCOL))
   10 CONTINUE
   20 CONTINUE
  200 FORMAT (F5.0)
```

When the data is input in a vertical mode, the inner loop controls the row when the NROW subscript is in the first subscript position. In this case, the outer loop sets up columns 1 through 5, and the inner loop sets up rows 1 through 4. When the first row of data is complete, the outer loop increments to receive the data for column 2, rows 1 through 4.

TOTAL ROWS

When the rows are to be totaled, the horizontal mode is used. In Fig. 7-2, the rows are totaled, and the total is placed in column 6.

```
      DO 20 NROW = 1,4
      DO 10 NCOL = 1,5
      N(NROW,6)=N(NROW,6)+N(NROW,NCOL)
   10 CONTINUE
   20 CONTINUE
```

When columns are operated on in the vertical mode, the loops and subscripts are reversed (Fig. 7-5). The outer loop moves slower than the inner

```
      DO 20 NCOL = 1,6
      DO 10 NROW = 1,5
      N(5,NCOL) = N(5,NCOL) + N(NROW,NCOL)
   10 CONTINUE
   20 CONTINUE
```

EACH COLUMN IS SUMMED AND EACH TOTAL IS PLACED IN ROW 1 THROUGH ROW 6.

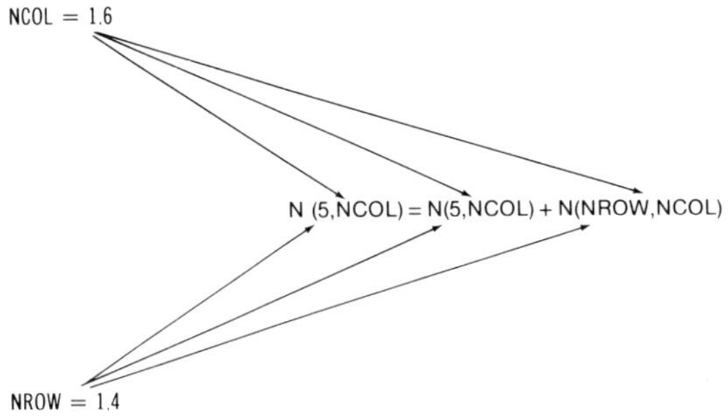

Fig. 7-5. Vertical relationship of loops, rows, and columns.

loop, and controls the columns. The inner loop and the inner loop subscript in the first position executes faster and controls the rows.

```
      DO 20 NCOL = 1,6
      DO 10 NROW = 1,4
      N(5,NCOL)=N(5,NCOL)+N(NROW,NCOL)
   10 CONTINUE
   20 CONTINUE
```

The four rows in column 1 are summed and placed in N(5,1) on the first execution of the outer loop. The outer loop executes the second time and, with four repetitions of the inner loop, sums the rows in column 2, and places the results in N(5,2). This summing continues until all six columns have been summed, and the results placed in row 5.

ZERO-OUT MEMORY LOCATIONS

Those memory locations, rows and columns, that are to have their values taken out, modified, and put back in the same position must be zeroed-out before the computations are made. This is true with simple variables, single subscripted arrays, and multiple subscripted arrays.

Computations processed within the program are to be placed in column 6, rows 1 through 5, and row 5, columns 1 through 5.

These program statements zero column 6, rows 1 through 5.

```
      DO 20 NROW = 1,5
      N(NROW,6) = 0
   20 CONTINUE
```

These program statements zero row 5, columns 1 through 5.

```
      DO 10 NCOL = 1,5
      N(5,NCOL) = 0
   10 CONTINUE
```

The variable of a double subscripted array can be used in the DATA statement to designate the values in each element of the array. When the array variable is used, the data values must be placed in the correct relationship according to rows and columns (Fig. 7-6).

The array variable can be used as the output list in a WRITE statement (Fig. 7-7). When only the array variable is used in the DATA and WRITE statements, the DIMENSION and FORMAT statements control the output.

In Fig. 7-6, the data is input columnwise, and the WRITE (6,110) N uses a FORMAT (5(I6)) to output the five array values on one line. The default value prints four lines containing five values on each line.

Fig. 7-7 uses the same array variable, and the array values in the same order as in Fig. 7-5. The DIMENSION N(5,4) sets aside a 5 × 4 matrix in memory, and the WRITE (6,110) N uses a FORMAT (4(I6)) to output a 5 × 4 matrix.

```
C**** PROGRAM TO DEMONSTRATE THE DEFAULT
C**** CONDITION OF READING AND WRITING A
C**** DOUBLE SUBSCRIPTED ARRAY USING ONLY
C**** THE ARRAY VARIABLE IN THE DATA
C**** STATEMENT AND THE ARRAY VARIABLE AS
C**** THE OUTPUT LIST IN THE WRITE STATEMENT
C234567
      PROGRAM DEFALT
      DIMENSION N( 4,5 )
      DATA N/11,12,13,14,15,21,22,23,24,25,31,32,33,34,
     *35,41,42,43,44,45/
      OPEN (6,FILE='PRINTER:' )
      WRITE (0,110 ) N
      WRITE (6,110 ) N
  110 FORMAT (5( I6 ),/ )
      STOP
      END



     11     12     13     14     15

     21     22     23     24     25

     31     32     33     34     35

     41     42     43     44     45
```

Fig. 7-6. Program to demonstrate the use of a double subscripted array variable to read and write a 4 × 5 matrix.

WEAKNESS OF DATA AND WRITE STATEMENTS

There is a great drawback when using only the array variable in DATA and WRITE statements. The memory must be reserved for the exact array space in the DIMENSION statement. DIMENSION N(4,5), Fig. 7-5, reserves 20 memory locations. When DIMENSION N(5,6) is used to reserve more memory locations for computations, the program will not compile, and consequently cannot be executed. Fig. 7-5, using DIMENSION N(5,6), causes COMPILE-TIME ERROR #79 — NUMBER OF VARIABLES DOES NOT MATCH THE NUMBER OF VALUES IN THE DATA LIST.

INPUT

Double subscripted array data can be input directly from the program, from the keyboard, or from disk.

Double subscripted array data can be input directly into the program using

(1) assignment statements

```
DIMENSION N(1,4)
N(1,1) = 11
```

```
N(1,2) = 12
N(1,3) = 13
N(1,4) = 14
```

(2) DATA statements using each array element, or

```
DIMENSION N(1,3)
DATA N(1,1),N(1,2),N(1,3)/11,12,13/
```

(3) DATA statements using only the array variable

```
DIMENSION N(1,3)
DATA N/11,12,13/
```

```
C**** PROGRAM TO DEMONSTRATE THE DEFAULT
C**** CONDITION OF READING AND WRITING A
C**** DOUBLE SUBSCRIPTED ARRAY USING ONLY
C**** THE ARRAY VARIABLE IN THE DATA
C**** STATEMENT AND THE ARRAY VARIABLE AS
C**** THE OUTPUT LIST IN THE WRITE STATEMENT
C234567
      PROGRAM DEFAL1
      DIMENSION N(5,4)
      DATA N/11,12,13,14,15,21,22,23,24,25,31,32,33,34,
     *35,41,42,43,44,45/
      OPEN (6,FILE='PRINTER:')
      WRITE (0,110) N
      WRITE (6,110) N
  110 FORMAT (4(I6),/)
      STOP
      END




    11    12    13    14

    15    21    22    23

    24    25    31    32

    33    34    35    41

    42    43    44    45
```

Fig. 7-7. Program to demonstrate the use of a double subscripted array variable to read and write a 5 × 4 matrix.

Input from Keyboard

Input from the keyboard is similar to the input in Figs. 3-3, 3-4, and 6-7. In Fig. 7-8, the input from the keyboard into a double subscripted array takes a standard DO loop as the outer loop, and an implied DO loop as the inner loop.

```
DO 20 NROW = 1,4
WRITE (0,100)
```

```
      READ (0,105)(N(NROW,NCOL),NCOL=1,5)
   20 CONTINUE
  100 FORMAT (/,5(2H**,1X),/)
  105 FORMAT (5(I2,1X))
```

A user prompt, 100 FORMAT, is placed on the screen to show where the integers should be placed so they will be in the proper locations. FORMAT lines 100 and 105 align the user prompt and the READ statement.

Zero-Out Memory Locations

In Fig. 7-8 all 30 reserved locations of the 5 × 6 matrix are zeroed-out. This is accomplished by double nested DO loops.

```
      DO 5 NROW = 1,5
      DO 5 NCOL = 1,6
```

```
C**** PROGRAM TO READ FROM THE KEYBOARD
C**** USING A DOUBLE SUBSCRIPTED ARRAY
C234567
      PROGRAM KEYBRD
      COMMON /ATS/ N(5,6)
      DO 5 NROW = 1,5
      DO 5 NCOL = 1,6
      N(NROW,NCOL) = 0
    5 CONTINUE
  100 FORMAT (/,5(2H!*,1X),/)
      DO 20 NROW = 1,4
      WRITE (0,100)
      READ (0,105) (N(NROW,NCOL),NCOL = 1,5)
   20 CONTINUE
  105 FORMAT (5(I2,1X))
      CALL COLADD
      CALL ROWADD
      WRITE (0,110)
  110 FORMAT (8X,'COL1  COL2  COL3  COL4  COL5  TOTAL',/)
      DO 30 NROW = 1,4
      WRITE (0,120) NROW, (N(NROW,NCOL),
     *NCOL = 1,6)
   30 CONTINUE
  120 FORMAT ('ROW ',I2,6I6)
      WRITE (0,130)
  130 FORMAT (41(1H-))
      WRITE (0,140) (N(5,NCOL),NCOL = 1,6)
  140 FORMAT ('TOTAL ',6I6)
      STOP
      END
      SUBROUTINE COLADD
      COMMON /ATS/ N(5,6)
      DO 20 NROW = 1,4
      DO 20 NCOL = 1,5
      N(NROW,6) = N(NROW,6) + N(NROW,NCOL)
   20 CONTINUE
      RETURN
      END
      SUBROUTINE ROWADD
      COMMON /ATS/ N(5,6)
      DO 20 NCOL = 1,6
      DO 20 NROW = 1,4
      N(5,NCOL) = N(5,NCOL) + N(NROW,NCOL)
   20 CONTINUE
      RETURN
      END
```

Fig. 7-8. Program to read from the keyboard using a double subscripted array.

```
      N(NROW, NCOL) = 0
    5 CONTINUE
```

It is not necessary to zero-out memory locations into which data is placed. It is absolutely necessary to zero-out memory locations which are to be used for summing purposes. When the program is run without zeroing-out those memory locations into which computations are placed, a different value is returned on each execution of the program.

Zeroing all memory locations of the 5 × 6 matrix in Fig. 7-8 is a different approach from that in Fig. 7-2. In Fig. 7-2, only the memory locations in column 6 and row 5 were zeroed. In Fig. 7-2, column 6 and row 5 were locations into which computed values were placed.

Fig. 7-9 is a program to read (input) a direct access file of a double subscripted array from disk. The program to write (output) the file to disk (Fig. 7-10) will be discussed under output.

```
C**** PROGRAM TO READ A DOUBLE SUBSCRIPTED
C**** ARRAY THAT HAS BEEN PLACED IN A FILE
C**** ON DISK - #9:ARRAY.TEXT
C234567
      PROGRAM READFL
      DIMENSION N(5,6)
      OPEN (6,FILE='PRINTER:')
      OPEN(20,FILE='#9:ARRAY.TEXT',
     !STATUS='OLD',ACCESS='DIRECT',
     !FORM='FORMATTED',
     !RECL=37)
      DO 40 NROW = 1,5
      READ(20,110,REC=NROW)
     !(N(NROW,NCOL),NCOL = 1,6)
   40 CONTINUE
  110 FORMAT (6(I6))
      CLOSE(20,STATUS='KEEP')
      WRITE (0,100)
      WRITE (6,100)
  100 FORMAT (8X,'COL1   COL2   COL3   COL4   COL5   TOTAL',/)
      DO 50 NROW = 1,4
      WRITE (0,140) NROW, (N(NROW,NCOL),NCOL = 1,6)
      WRITE (6,140) NROW, (N(NROW,NCOL),NCOL = 1,6)
   50 CONTINUE
  140 FORMAT ('ROW ',I2,6(I6))
      WRITE (0,120)
      WRITE (6,120)
  120 FORMAT (41(1H-))
      WRITE (0,130) (N(5,NCOL),NCOL = 1,6)
      WRITE (6,130) (N(5,NCOL),NCOL = 1,6)
  130 FORMAT ('TOTAL ',6(I6))
      STOP
      END
```

Fig. 7-9. Program to read a double subscripted array from a direct access file on disk.

Read from Disk

The read (input) from disk program (Fig. 7-9) has one important feature that has not been previously discussed.

```
DO 40 NROW = 1,5
READ(20,110,REC=NROW)
```

```
    *(N(NROW,NCOL),NCOL=1,6)
 40 CONTINUE
110 FORMAT (6(I6))
```

In the OPEN statement the record length is 37 bytes. This is computed by multiplying 6 × I6 = 36 (100 FORMAT), and adding one end-of-record byte for a total of 37 bytes. This 37 bytes accommodates one row of the table, and is read on the first execution of the DO 40 NROW = 1,5. This takes care of REC = 1. However, the REC = option must be incremented five times. REC = NROW is related to the standard DO 40 NROW = 1,5, so the record number will be incremented five times to read the five records in the table.

The table placed on the disk is without row markers, column markers, a line between the table and the totals, or totals as in Fig. 7-11. Fig. 7-11 is created by the program in Fig. 7-9 after it is read from disk.

```
C**** PROGRAM TO WRITE A DOUBLE SUBSCRIPTED
C**** ARRAY TO DISK
C234567
      PROGRAM WRTFLE
      DIMENSION N(5,6)
      DATA N(1,1),N(1,2),N(1,3),N(1,4),N(1,5)/11,12,13,14,15/
      DATA N(2,1),N(2,2),N(2,3),N(2,4),N(2,5)/21,22,23,24,25/
      DATA N(3,1),N(3,2),N(3,3),N(3,4),N(3,5)/31,32,33,34,35/
      DATA N(4,1),N(4,2),N(4,3),N(4,4),N(4,5)/41,42,43,44,45/
      DO 5 NROW = 1,5
      N(NROW,6) = 0
    5 CONTINUE
      DO 10 NCOL = 1,5
      N(5,NCOL) = 0
   10 CONTINUE
      DO 20 NROW = 1,4
      DO 20 NCOL = 1,5
      N(NROW,6) = N(NROW,6) + N(NROW,NCOL)
   20 CONTINUE
      DO 30 NCOL = 1,6
      DO 30 NROW = 1,4
      N(5,NCOL) = N(5,NCOL) + N(NROW,NCOL)
   30 CONTINUE
      OPEN(20,FILE='#9:ARRAY.TEXT',
     !STATUS='NEW',ACCESS='DIRECT',
     !FORM='FORMATTED',
     !RECL=37)
      DO 40 NROW = 1,5
      WRITE(20,110,REC=NROW)
     !(N(NROW,NCOL),NCOL=1,6)
   40 CONTINUE
  110 FORMAT (6(I6))
      CLOSE(20,STATUS='KEEP')
      STOP
      END
```

Fig. 7-10. Program to write a double subscripted array to a direct access file on disk.

OUTPUT

The WRITE statement causes information to be output to the CRT, printer, and disk.

```
            COL1   COL2   COL3   COL4   COL5   TOTAL

ROW  1       11     12     13     14     15      65
ROW  2       21     22     23     24     25     115
ROW  3       31     32     33     34     35     165
ROW  4       41     42     43     44     45     215
----------------------------------------------------
TOTAL       104    108    112    116    120     560
```

Fig. 7-11. Output of program in Fig. 7-9.

Output to CRT

```
      DO 40 NROW = 1,4
      WRITE(0,110)NROW,(N(NROW,NCOL),
     *NCOL=1,6)
   40 CONTINUE
  110 FORMAT ('ROW',I2,6(I6))
```

The preceding program statements (Fig. 7-2) cause the 4 × 6 matrix to be written to the CRT. The integer zero (0) in WRITE (0,110) causes the output to go to the CRT. The integer 110 is the FORMAT statement to designate how one row of the table is to be written. The standard DO loop causes four lines of the table to be written to the CRT.

Output to Printer

```
      OPEN (6,FILE='PRINTER:')
      DO 40 NROW = 1,4
      WRITE(6,110)NROW,(N(NROW,NCOL),
     *NCOL = 1,6)
   40 CONTINUE
  110 FORMAT ('ROW',I2,6(I6))
```

The preceding program statements (Fig. 7-2) cause the output to go to the printer. The printer file must be opened, and the integer 6 in the WRITE statement references the printer. A 4 × 6 matrix is written to the printer.

Output to Disk

Fig. 7-10 is a program to write (output) a double subscripted array to disk. The data is input as individual elements in a DATA statement. Column 6 and row 5 are zeroed-out. The computations are made to fill column 6 and row 5.

The direct access file with a record length of 37 bytes is opened.

```
      OPEN(20,FILE='#9:ARRAY.TEXT',
     *STATUS='NEW',ACCESS='DIRECT',
     *FORM='FORMATTED',RECL=37)
```

The file has five records. The file begins with record #1, and increments to record #5. To increment the record number, the REC = must be placed in a loop to change the record number as each record is written to disk.

```
      DO 40 NROW = 1,5
      WRITE(20,110,REC=NROW)
     *(N(NROW,NCOL),NCOL=1,6)
   40 CONTINUE
  100 FORMAT (6(I6))
```

When the five records have been output to disk, the file is closed, and the file is maintained on disk for future use.

```
      CLOSE(20,STATUS='KEEP')
```

SAMPLE PROGRAM USING DOUBLE SUBSCRIPTED ARRAYS

Fig. 7-12 is a program to compute the daily and weekly bonuses of 11 machinists. The machinists are paid a flat rate for less than 40 items produced each day, and do not qualify for a weekly bonus unless more than 200 items are produced per week. If the machinist produces more than 40 items per day, and less than 51 items, he gets a bonus of 60% of base pay. When the machinist produces more than 50 items per day, he gets a $2.00 bonus for each item over 50. If the machinist produces over 200 items per week, he gets a $0.35 bonus for each item over 200. Fig. 7-13 shows the results generated by the program.

The DIMENSION X(12,11) reserves memory for the matrix. Each element of the double subscripted array is placed in the DATA statement. Apple FORTRAN allows only nine continuation lines, so there are three DATA statements to accommodate the array elements and the data. The printer is activated by the OPEN(6,FILE = 'PRINTER:').

The FORMAT statements are all grouped together at the beginning of the program. FORMAT statements can be placed anywhere in the program after the PROGRAM statement.

Zero-Out Memory Locations

Columns 10 and 11, rows 1 through 12 are to be used for summing purposes, so they must be zeroed. Row 12, columns 3 through 9 (10 and 11 were previously zeroed) are also zeroed before the summed values can be placed in them.

```
      DO 10 J = 10,11
      DO 05 K = 1,12
      X(K,J) = 0
   05 CONTINUE
   10 CONTINUE
      DO 15 J = 3,9
      X(12,J) = 0
   15 CONTINUE
```

Counting the Units Produced

The program then adds the total number of items produced each day by each machinist and places this total in column 10, rows 1 through 11.

```
C**** PROGRAM TO COMPUTE THE BONUS PAY OF
C**** COMPANY MACHINISTS WHO ARE PAID ON THE BASIS
C**** OF PRODUCTION
C234567
      PROGRAM MACH2
      DIMENSION X(12,11)
      DATA X(1,1),X(1,2),X(1,3),X(1,4),X(1,5),X(1,6),
     1X(1,7),X(1,8),X(1,9),X(2,1),X(2,2),X(2,3),X(2,4),
     2X(2,5),X(2,6),X(2,7),X(2,8),X(2,9),X(3,1),X(3,2),
     3X(3,3),X(3,4),X(3,5),X(3,6),X(3,7),X(3,8),X(3,9),X(4,1),
     4X(4,2),X(4,3),X(4,4),X(4,5),X(4,6),X(4,7),X(4,8),
     5X(4,9)/1.,10.50,38.,47.,45.,60.,62.,0.,0.,2.,10.50,
     647.,61.,18.,23.,0.,0.,63.,3.,10.25,60.,62.,49.,
     738.,0.,0.,70.,4.,11.05,0.,0.,28.,54.,60.,62.,62./
      DATA X(5,1),X(5,2),X(5,3),X(5,4),X(5,5),X(5,6),
     1X(5,7),X(5,8),X(5,9),X(6,1),X(6,2),X(6,3),X(6,4),
     2X(6,5),X(6,6),X(6,7),X(6,8),X(6,9),X(7,1),X(7,2),
     3X(7,3),X(7,4),X(7,5),X(7,6),X(7,7),X(7,8),X(7,9),
     4X(8,1),X(8,2),X(8,3),X(8,4),X(8,5),X(8,6),X(8,7),
     5X(8,8),X(8,9)/5.,8.75,0.,0.,48.,51.,38.,47.,31.,
     66.,9.75,31.,39.,53.,60.,60.,0.,0.,7.,10.00,51.,
     753.,0.,0.,53.,58.,54.,8.,15.75,38.,59.,0.,0.,
     859.,61.,59./
      DATA X(9,1),X(9,2),X(9,3),X(9,4),X(9,5),X(9,6),
     1X(9,7),X(9,8),X(9,9),X(10,1),X(10,2),X(10,3),
     2X(10,4),X(10,5),X(10,6),X(10,7),X(10,8),
     3X(10,9),X(11,1),X(11,2),X(11,3),X(11,4),
     4X(11,5),X(11,6),X(11,7),X(11,8),X(11,9)/
     59.,9.75,0.,0.,40.,53.,29.,49.,50.,10.,
     68.75,60.,60.,0.,0.,59.,58.,58.,11.,11.05,
     758.,43.,21.,0.,0.,46.,49./
      OPEN (6,FILE='PRINTER:')
  150 FORMAT (//,'MACH',55X,'TOTAL')
  160 FORMAT (1H#,6X,3HPAY,4X,3HMON,3X,3HTUE,3X,3HWED,
     *3X,3HTHU,3X,3HFRI,3X,3HSAT,3X,3HSUN,3X,5HUNITS,
     *2X,5HBONUS,/)
  190 FORMAT (F3.0,3X,F5.2,1X,7(F5.0,1X),F6.0,1X,F7.2)
  200 FORMAT (67(1H-))
  210 FORMAT (5HTOTAL,7X,7(F5.0,1X),F6.0,1X,F7.2)
      DO 10 J = 10,11
      DO 05 K = 1,12
      X(K,J) = 0
   05 CONTINUE
   10 CONTINUE
      DO 15 J = 3,9
      X(12,J) = 0
   15 CONTINUE
      DO 50 J = 1,11
      DO 40 K = 3,9
      X(J,10) = X(J,10) + X(J,K)
      IF (X(J,K) .LT. 40.) GOTO 40
      X(J,11) = X(J,11) + X(J,2) * .6
      IF (X(J,K) .LT. 50.) GOTO 40
      X(J,11) = X(J,11) + (X(J,K)-50.) * 2.00
   40 CONTINUE
   50 CONTINUE
      DO 60 J = 1,11
      IF (X(J,10) .LT. 200.) GOTO 60
      X(J,11) = X(J,11) +(X(J,10)-200.) * .35
   60 CONTINUE
      DO 80 K = 3,11
      DO 70 J = 1,11
      X(12,K) = X(12,K) + X(J,K)
   70 CONTINUE
```

Fig. 7-12. Program to compute the daily and weekly bonus pay of 11 machinists.

```
80 CONTINUE
   WRITE (0,150)
   WRITE (6,150)
   WRITE (0,160)
   WRITE (6,160)
   DO 90 J = 1,11
   WRITE (0,190) (X(J,K),K = 1,11)
   WRITE (6,190) (X(J,K),K = 1,11)
90 CONTINUE
   WRITE (0,200)
   WRITE (6,200)
   WRITE (0,210) (X(12,K),K = 3,11)
   WRITE (6,210) (X(12,K),K = 3,11)
   STOP
   END
```

Fig. 7-12. Program to compute the daily and weekly bonus pay of 11 machinists. *(Continued)*

MACH #	PAY	MON	TUE	WED	THU	FRI	SAT	SUN	TOTAL UNITS	BONUS
1.	10.50	38.	47.	45.	60.	62.	0.	0.	252.	87.40
2.	10.50	47.	61.	18.	23.	0.	0.	63.	212.	71.10
3.	10.25	60.	62.	49.	38.	0.	0.	70.	279.	136.25
4.	11.05	0.	0.	28.	54.	60.	62.	62.	266.	125.62
5.	8.75	0.	0.	48.	51.	38.	47.	31.	215.	23.00
6.	9.75	31.	39.	53.	60.	60.	0.	0.	243.	78.60
7.	10.00	51.	53.	0.	0.	53.	58.	54.	269.	92.15
8.	15.75	38.	59.	0.	0.	59.	61.	59.	276.	140.40
9.	9.75	0.	0.	40.	53.	29.	49.	50.	221.	36.75
10.	8.75	60.	60.	0.	0.	59.	58.	58.	295.	149.50
11.	11.05	58.	43.	21.	0.	0.	46.	49.	217.	48.47
TOTAL		383.	424.	302.	339.	420.	381.	496.	2745.	989.24

Fig. 7-13. Output of program in Fig. 7-12.

Column 1 (J,1) holds the machinist's number. Column 2 (J,2) holds the rate of pay of the machinists. Columns three (J,3) through nine (J,9) hold the items produced each day. This is placed in the array elements by the DATA statement. The loops and arrays are configured to add in a horizontal fashion and place the results in the UNITS column (J,10).

```
DO 50 J = 1,11
DO 40 K = 3,9
X(J,10) = X(J,10) + X(J,K)
```

Computing Pay and Bonus

Also within the nested loops are the computational statements to compute the bonus if over 40 or less than 51 units are produced per day, and the computational statement to compute the daily bonus when over 50 units are produced.

```
    IF (X(J,K) .LT. 40.) GOTO 40
    X(J,11) = X(J,11)+X(J,2)*.6
    IF (X(J,K) .LT. 50.) GOTO 40
    X(J,11) = X(J,11)+(X(J,K)– 50.)*2.00
 40 CONTINUE
 50 CONTINUE
```

If over 40 units per day are produced, the bonus is a flat rate of hourly pay (J,2) times .6. If over 50 units per day are produced, a bonus of $2.00 per unit is paid. The CONTINUE statements close the loops, and the total daily bonus is placed in column 11 (J,11).

To column 11 (J,11), a weekly bonus is added if each machinist has produced over 200 units for the week. This weekly bonus is added to the amount of the daily bonus.

```
      DO 60 J = 1,11
      IF (X(J,10) .LT. 200.) GOTO 60
      X(J,11) = X(J,11)+(X(J,10)- 200.)*.35
   60 CONTINUE
```

Total Columns

When the daily and weekly bonus computations are completed, and the totals are placed in column 11 (J,11), columns 3 through 11 are totaled, and the results are placed in row 12, columns 3 through 11.

The columns are added vertically from column 3 through column 11, so the variable subscripts and loops are placed in a different relationship than when the columns are added horizontally. In this case, the columns are added vertically, row by row, so the inner J loop is represented as the first subscript in the array. The column number is represented by the outer K loop, and is the second subscript in the array. The totals are placed in columns 3 through 11.

```
      DO 80 K = 3,11
      DO 70 J = 1,11
      X(12,K) = X(12,K)+X(J,K)
   70 CONTINUE
   80 CONTINUE
```

Output Results to CRT and Printer

When all computations are complete and placed in the correct row and column position, the results are printed out to the CRT and the printer.

```
      WRITE (0,150)
      WRITE (6,150)
      WRITE (0,160)
      WRITE (6,160)
  150 FORMAT (//,'MACH',55X,'TOTAL')
  160 FORMAT (1H#,6X,3HPAY,4X,3HMON, 3X,
     *3HTUE,3X,3HWED,3X,3HTHU,3X, 3HFRI,
     *3X,3HSAT,3X,3HSUN,3X,5HUNITS,
     *2X,5HBONUS,/)
```

Write Headings — The four WRITE statements and their related FORMAT statements print out the table headings. For this exercise, the printer DIP switches were adjusted to output 10 characters per inch, so Fig. 7-13 would fit on the 9 × 11.5-inch fanfold tractor-type paper. Other programs are output on 8.3 characters per inch.

Write Matrix Data — A standard DO loop and an implied DO loop write out the 11 × 11 matrix of information.

```
      DO 90 J = 1,11
      WRITE (0,190)(X(J,K),K=1,11)
      WRITE (6,190)(X(J,K),K=1,11)
   90 CONTINUE
  190 FORMAT (F3.0,3X,F5.2,1X, 7(F5.0,1X),
     *F6.0,1X,F7.2)
```

Underline Matrix — When the 11 × 11 matrix has been output, a line is drawn prior to the row 12 totals.

```
      WRITE (0,200)
      WRITE (6,200)
  200 FORMAT (67(1H—))
```

The 1H is one Hollerith character (—) that is printed 67 times to underline the 11 × 11 matrix.

Write Column Totals — The final row of totals is then printed to complete the program in Fig. 7-12, and prepare to print the report in Fig. 7-13.

```
      WRITE (0,210)(X(12,K),K=3,11)
      WRITE (6,210)(X(12,K),K=3,11)
  210 FORMAT (5HTOTAL,7X,7(5.0,1X),
     *F6.0,1X,F7.2)
```

CHAPTER 8
Triple Subscripted Arrays

INTRODUCTION

A triple subscripted array is an array variable that has three subscripts. The triple subscripted array in Fig. 8-1 has an array variable TERTRY. The first subscript value (2) sets up the number of tables that can be stored in an array. The table is configured to the second subscript (3) and the third subscript (4).

Single elements of a triple subscripted array are referenced by using the array variable name and three specific subscripts (Fig. 8-3).

```
TERTRY (1,1,1) = 34.98
TERTRY (2,1,1) = 40.32
TERTRY (1,3,4) =  7.30
TERTRY (2,3,4) = 32.50
```

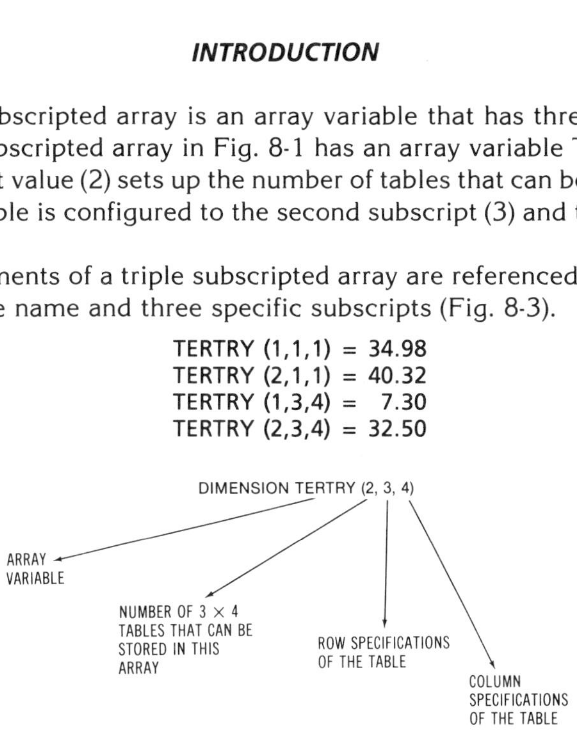

Fig. 8-1. Format of a triple subscripted array.

The example in Fig. 8-2 was written to demonstrate a triple subscripted array whose data is input from the keyboard and output to the printer and disk, where a sequential file is created. The data is not output to the CRT. Fig. 8-4 is a program to read the sequential file on disk created by the program in Fig. 8-2, and output the file to the CRT and printer. The file is output to the printer in two forms — (1) as it is read from disk and (2) as it is read from memory and output to the printer using != as a prompt to differentiate the two outputs.

The tables are input and output using two nested standard DO loops and a single implied DO loop. The outer standard DO loop creates the execution level of the number of tables. The inner standard DO loop creates the number of rows in the table. The implied DO loop creates the number of columns in the table.

The file is named "#9:TRIPDT.DATA" and is placed on file number 20. The first 12 devices are reserved for Apple hardware. The file was created on a three-disk drive system. The third disk interface is in slot number 4, so the first disk drive is number 9. This is the reason the file is referenced by #9:TRIPDT.DATA.

```
&C**** PROGRAM TO DEMONSTRATE TRIPLE SUBSCRIPTED
C**** ARRAY. READ FROM KEYBOARD; WRITE TO DISK.
C234567
      PROGRAM TRIPLE
      DIMENSION TERTRY(2,3,4)
  100 FORMAT(4('*---------!'))
  110 FORMAT(5F10.2)
      OPEN (6,FILE='PRINTER:')
      DO 50 J=1,2
      WRITE(0,100)
      WRITE(6,100)
      DO 50 K=1,3
      READ (0,110) (TERTRY(J,K,L),L=1,4)
      WRITE(6,110) (TERTRY(J,K,L),L=1,4)
   50 CONTINUE
      OPEN(20,FILE='#9:TRIPDT.DATA',
     *STATUS='NEW')
      DO 60 J=1,2
      DO 60 K=1,3
      WRITE(20,110) (TERTRY(J,K,L),
     *L=1,4)
      WRITE(6,110) (TERTRY(J,K,L),L=1,4)
   60 CONTINUE
      CLOSE (20,STATUS='KEEP')
      CLOSE (6)
      STOP
      END
```

Fig. 8-2. Program to demonstrate a triple subscripted array whose data is read from keyboard and written to disk and printer.

```
*---------!*---------!*---------!*---------!
     34.48     392.30     104.50     23.40
     35.90     305.23     150.30     12.30
     38.04     250.32     194.30      7.30
*---------!*---------!*---------!*---------!
     40.32     194.30     240.32      6.30
     30.22     134.62     280.32      4.70
     26.32      89.32     350.32     32.50
--------------------------------------------
     34.48     392.30     104.50     23.40
     35.90     305.23     150.30     12.30
     38.04     250.32     194.30      7.30
     40.32     194.30     240.32      6.30
     30.22     134.62     280.32      4.70
     26.32      89.32     350.32     32.50
```

THIS DATA IS READ FROM THE KEYBOARD AND WRITTEN TO PRINTER.

THIS DATA IS WRITTEN TO DISK AND PRINTER.

Fig. 8-3. Data input and output from the program in Fig. 8-2.

The first section of Fig. 8-3 is the input as it is read from the keyboard and output to the printer. The second section of Fig. 8-3 is the output as it is written to disk and echoed to the printer.

The first section of Fig. 8-5 is the file read from disk and echoed to the

```
C**** PROGRAM TO DEMONSTRATE TRIPLE SUBSCRIPTED
C**** ARRAY. READ FROM DISK; WRITE TO SCREEN.
C234567
      PROGRAM TRIPWR
      DIMENSION TERTRY( 2,3,4 )
      OPEN( 20,FILE='#9:TRIPDT.DATA' )
      OPEN( 6,FILE='PRINTER:' )
  100 FORMAT ( 4( F10.2 ) )
  110 FORMAT ( 4( '! = ',F10.2 ) )
      DO 10 J=1,2
      DO 10 K=1,3
      READ( 20,100 ) ( TERTRY( J,K,L ),L=1,4 )
      WRITE( 6,100 ) ( TERTRY( J,K,L ),L=1,4 )
   10 CONTINUE
      CLOSE( 20 )
      DO 20 J=1,2
      DO 20 K=1,3
      WRITE( 0,110 ) ( TERTRY( J,K,L ),L=1,4 )
      WRITE( 6,110 ) ( TERTRY( J,K,L ),L=1,4 )
   20 CONTINUE
      CLOSE ( 6 )
      STOP
      END
```

Fig. 8-4. Program to demonstrate a triple subscripted array whose data is read from disk and written to CRT and printer.

```
      34.48     392.30     104.50      23.40
      35.90     305.23     150.30      12.30
      38.04     250.32     194.30       7.30
      40.32     194.30     240.32       6.30
      30.22     134.62     280.32       4.70
      26.32      89.32     350.32      32.50
! =      34.48! =     392.30! =     104.50! =      23.40
! =      35.90! =     305.23! =     150.30! =      12.30
! =      38.04! =     250.32! =     194.30! =       7.30
! =      40.32! =     194.30! =     240.32! =       6.30
! =      30.22! =     134.62! =     280.32! =       4.70
! =      26.32! =      89.32! =     350.32! =      32.50
```

DATA READ FROM DISK AND ECHOED TO THE PRINTER

DATA STORED IN MEMORY THAT IS WRITTEN TO THE CRT AND THE PRINTER IN A DIFFERENT FORMAT THAN THE DATA READ FROM DISK

Fig. 8-5. Data input and output from the program in Fig. 8-4.

printer. The second section in Fig. 8-5 is the file as it is output to the CRT and the printer.

HOW MULTIPLE SUBSCRIPTED ARRAYS ARE USED

Multiple subscripted arrays are used in industry to track production. Companies that produce several models of a product, with several styles per model and several options per style, use multiple arrays to count the different categories of production. When the model, style, and option of an item is shipped to the wholesaler and/or retailer-dealer, an IBM punch card (or other method to count the item) with the same information is shipped with the item. When the item is sold, the IBM card is returned to the manufacturer. This feedback information is used for several reports. An inventory report is issued to determine whether production should be increased or decreased. High-level sales and low-level sales reports are issued to determine which items are selling and which items are not selling. A geographic report is issued to determine which items are selling in which sales region. A profit projection report is issued as to the profitability on each item in each sales region. These and other reports are part of a management information system (MIS) that is so vital to the profitability of the company.

Some computers accept up to 60 subscripts with an array variable. This type of power can produce reports of voluminous detail.

SAMPLE PROGRAM USING A TRIPLE SUBSCRIPTED ARRAY

Fig. 8-6 is an example of a program using a triple subscripted array to count the items manufactured on one work turn. The DIMENSION ICOUNT(5,4,8) reserves memory for five model numbers (Fig. 8-8), four styles per model, and eight option packages. In this program example, the manufactured outputs are manually input into the READ statements, READ (0,110) MODEL, 65 READ (0,110) STYLE, and READ (0,110) OPTION. This is an unsophisticated method to input information, but this program is just an example to teach triple subscripted arrays.

Each model, style, and option is to hold a computed value, so the memory locations must be initialized. The standard way to initialize the table would be in triple nested loops.

```
      DO 10 J = 1,5
      DO 10 K = 1,4
      DO 10 L = 1,8
      ICOUNT (J,K,L) = 0
   10 CONTINUE
```

In Fig. 8-6, the multiple subscripted array is initialized to zero by using a DATA statement.

```
      DATA ICOUNT/160*0/
```

The ICOUNT array contains a total of 160 memory locations (5*4*8). The DATA ICOUNT/160*0/ is one method to initialize the total memory storage area to zero.

A check is input to determine if the program is to end if zero is input. If a value of one to five is input, the program will continue.

```
      IF (MODEL .GT. 0) GOTO 20
```

The program is terminated when zero (0) is input when ENTER MODEL # (0 FOR END OF SHIFT) is printed on the CRT and the printer. FORTRAN loops can begin with an initial loop value of 1.

```
C**** PROGRAM USING TRIPLE SUBSCRIPTED ARRAYS
C**** TO COUNT CARS BEING PRODUCED.
C234567
      PROGRAM COUNT
      DIMENSION ICOUNT(5,4,8),
     *ISTYLE(5),IOPTSN(5,4)
      REAL MODEL
      CHARACTER*12 EOS
      DATA EOS /'END OF SHIFT'/
      DATA ISTYLE /3,4,2,4,1/
      DATA IOPTSN /8,4,8,7,3,6,5,5,5,
     *0,8,7,0,4,0,0,3,0,7,0/
      DATA ICOUNT /160*0/
      OPEN (6,FILE='PRINTER:')
   15 WRITE (0,100) EOS
      WRITE (6,100) EOS
      READ (0,110)MODEL
      WRITE(6,115)MODEL
      IMODEL=IFIX(MODEL)
      IF (IMODEL.GT.5.OR.IMODEL.LT.0)
     *GOTO 40
      IF (IMODEL.GT.0)GOTO 20
      WRITE (0,120)EOS
      WRITE (6,120)EOS
      DO 25 J=1,5
      WRITE(0,122)J
      WRITE(6,122)J
      K=ISTYLE(J)
      DO 25 KK=1,K
      WRITE(0,124)KK
      WRITE(6,124)KK
      L=IOPTSN(J,KK)
      WRITE(0,126) (LL,LL=1,L)
      WRITE(6,126) (LL,LL=1,L)
      WRITE(0,128)(ICOUNT(J,KK,LL),
     *LL=1,L)
      WRITE(6,128)(ICOUNT(J,KK,LL),
     *LL=1,L)
   25 CONTINUE
      STOP
   40 WRITE (0,140)
      WRITE (6,140)
      GOTO 15
   20 K=ISTYLE(IMODEL)
   50 IF (K.EQ.1)GOTO 60
      WRITE(0,150)K
      WRITE(6,150)K
   65 READ (0,110)STYLE
      WRITE(6,115)STYLE
      ISSTYL=IFIX(STYLE)
      IF (ISSTYL.LE.K.AND.ISSTYL.GT.0)
     *GOTO 70
      WRITE (0,160)
      WRITE (6,160)
      GOTO 65
   60 ISSTYL=K
   70 L=IOPTSN(IMODEL,ISSTYL)
   75 WRITE(0,170)L
      WRITE(6,170)L
      READ (0,110)OPTION
      WRITE(6,115)OPTION
      IOPTN=IFIX(OPTION)
      IF (IOPTN.LE.L.AND.IOPTN.GT.0)
     *GOTO90
      WRITE(0,180)
```

Fig. 8-6. Program using a triple subscripted array to count items being produced.

```
      WRITE(6,180)
      GOTO 75
   90 ICOUNT(IMODEL,ISSTYL,IOPTN)=
     *ICOUNT(IMODEL,ISSTYL,IOPTN)+1
      GOTO 15
C**** FORMAT LISTINGS FOLLOW!
  100 FORMAT (//,'ENTER MODEL #',/,
     *'(0   FOR ',A12,' )',/)
  110 FORMAT (F5.4)
  115 FORMAT (F5.3)
  120 FORMAT(///,'STATISTICS AT ',
     *A12,////)
  122 FORMAT (//,'MODEL # ',I2)
  124 FORMAT (/,6X,'STYLE # ',I2)
  128 FORMAT (9(1X,I4,2X))
  126 FORMAT(/,12X,'OPTION PACKAGE ',
     *'TOTALS',/,9(' # ',I2,2X),/)
  140 FORMAT(//,'ILLEGAL VALUE OF ',
     *'MODEL WAS SELECTED',///)
  150 FORMAT(/,'ENTER STYLE #(1...',
     *,I2,' )' )
  160 FORMAT(//,'ILLEGAL VALUE FOR',
     *' STYLE WAS SELECTED',/)
  170 FORMAT(///,'ENTER OPTION PACK',
     *'AGE # (1...',I2,' )', )
  180 FORMAT(///,'ILLEGAL PACKAGE ',
     *'# WAS SELECTED',//)
      END
```

Fig. 8-6. Program using a triple subscripted array to count items being produced. *(Continued)*

The program has three checks to alert the user when an illegal value has been input. The legal range of inputs is limited by the dimension statement, DIMENSION ICOUNT(5,4,8),ISTYLE(5),IOPTSN(5,4). The legal range is from 1 to the limit of the array subscript in the related subscript item. The three checks are,

1. IF (IMODEL .GT. 5 .OR. IMODEL .LT. 0) GOTO 40
2. IF (ISSTYL .LE. K .AND. ISSTYL .GT. 0) GOTO 70
3. IF (IOPTN .LE. L .AND. IOPTN .GT. 0) GOTO 90

If the model input is illegal, ILLEGAL VALUE OF MODEL WAS SELECTED is output, and the program jumps to line number 15 to set up the model input routine again.

If an illegal style value is input, ILLEGAL VALUE FOR STYLE WAS SELECTED is output, and the program jumps to line number 65 to set up the style input again.

If an illegal option value is input, ILLEGAL PACKAGE # WAS SELECTED is output, and the program jumps to line number 75 to set up the option input again.

When the count is completed and/or the shift is ended, ENTER MODEL # (0 FOR END OF SHIFT) is output. When zero (0) is input in answer to the END OF SHIFT prompt, the program terminates. This termination causes the count report to be generated. The count report (Fig. 8-7) is a count of the styles and option packages for each model produced during the period.

```
"
ENTER MODEL #
(0  FOR END OF SHIFT)

1.000

ENTER STYLE #(1... 3)
1.000


ENTER OPTION PACKAGE # (1... 8)
1.000


ENTER MODEL #
(0  FOR END OF SHIFT)

1.000

ENTER STYLE #(1... 3)
4.000

ILLEGAL VALUE FOR STYLE WAS SELECTED

1.000


ENTER OPTION PACKAGE # (1... 8)
1.000


ENTER MODEL #
(0  FOR END OF SHIFT)

5.000


ENTER OPTION PACKAGE # (1... 3)
3.000


ENTER MODEL #
(0  FOR END OF SHIFT)

5.000


ENTER OPTION PACKAGE # (1... 3)
2.000


ENTER MODEL #
(0  FOR END OF SHIFT)

5.000


ENTER OPTION PACKAGE # (1... 3)
1.000
```

Fig. 8-7. Input and output from the program in Fig. 8-6.

```
ENTER MODEL #
(0  FOR END OF SHIFT)

6.000


ILLEGAL VALUE OF MODEL WAS SELECTED




ENTER MODEL #
(0  FOR END OF SHIFT)

2.000

ENTER STYLE #(1... 4)
3.000


ENTER OPTION PACKAGE # (1... 7)
7.000


ENTER MODEL #
(0  FOR END OF SHIFT)

3.000

ENTER STYLE #(1... 2)
2.000


ENTER OPTION PACKAGE # (1... 5)
3.000


ENTER MODEL #
(0  FOR END OF SHIFT)

4.000

ENTER STYLE #(1... 4)
4.000


ENTER OPTION PACKAGE # (1... 7)
7.000


ENTER MODEL #
(0  FOR END OF SHIFT)

 .000


STATISTICS AT END OF SHIFT
```

Fig. 8-7. Input and output

```
MODEL #  1

        STYLE #  1

                OPTION PACKAGE TOTALS
 #  1    #  2    #  3    #  4    #  5    #  6    #  7    #  8    #
    2       0       0       0       0       0       0       0

        STYLE #  2

                OPTION PACKAGE TOTALS
 #  1    #  2    #  3    #  4    #  5    #  6    #
    0       0       0       0       0       0

        STYLE #  3

                OPTION PACKAGE TOTALS
 #  1    #  2    #  3    #  4    #  5    #  6    #  7    #  8    #
    0       0       0       0       0       0       0       0

MODEL #  2

        STYLE #  1

                OPTION PACKAGE TOTALS
 #  1    #  2    #  3    #  4    #
    0       0       0       0

        STYLE #  2

                OPTION PACKAGE TOTALS
 #  1    #  2    #  3    #  4    #  5    #
    0       0       0       0       0

        STYLE #  3

                OPTION PACKAGE TOTALS
 #  1    #  2    #  3    #  4    #  5    #  6    #  7    #
    0       0       0       0       0       0       1

        STYLE #  4

                OPTION PACKAGE TOTALS
 #  1    #  2    #  3    #
    0       0       0

MODEL #  3

        STYLE #  1

                OPTION PACKAGE TOTALS
 #  1    #  2    #  3    #  4    #  5    #  6    #  7    #  8    #
    0       0       0       0       0       0       0       0

        STYLE #  2

                OPTION PACKAGE TOTALS
 #  1    #  2    #  3    #  4    #  5    #
    0       0       1       0       0
```

from the program in Fig. 8-6. *(Continued)*

```
MODEL #  4

         STYLE #  1

                  OPTION PACKAGE TOTALS
 #  1   #  2   #  3   #  4   #  5   #  6   #  7   #
    0      0      0      0      0      0      0

         STYLE #  2

                  OPTION PACKAGE TOTALS
 #  1   #  2   #  3   #  4   #  5   #
    0      0      0      0      0

         STYLE #  3

                  OPTION PACKAGE TOTALS
 #  1   #  2   #  3   #  4   #
    0      0      0      0

         STYLE #  4

                  OPTION PACKAGE TOTALS
 #  1   #  2   #  3   #  4   #  5   #  6   #  7   #
    0      0      0      0      0      0      1

MODEL #  5

         STYLE #  1

                  OPTION PACKAGE TOTALS
 #  1   #  2   #  3   #
    1      1      1
```

Fig. 8-7. Input and output from the program in Fig. 8-6. *(Continued)*

MODEL #	# OF STYLES
1	3
2	4
3	2
4	4
5	1

MODEL #	STYLE #	# OF OPTION PACKAGES
1	1	8
1	2	6
1	3	8
1	4	0
2	1	4
2	2	5
2	3	7
2	4	3
3	1	8
3	2	5
3	3	0
3	4	0
4	1	7
4	2	5
4	3	4
4	4	7
5	1	3
5	2	0
5	3	0
5	4	0

MODEL #1 has 3 styles
STYLE #1 has 8 option packages

Fig. 8-8. Dimensions for model, style, and option packages for the program in Fig. 8-6.

CHAPTER 9
Subroutines

A subroutine is a self-contained program that is referenced by the main program to perform more than one computation, or operation, to augment the main program.

A subprogram can be referenced by a CALL statement from any location within the main program. When the subroutine has performed its actions, control is returned to the main program by a RETURN statement that is placed somewhere within the subroutine. In Apple FORTRAN, control is returned to the main program in the program statement immediately below the CALL statement.

SUBROUTINES DIVIDE THE PROGRAM INTO SMALLER PARTS

Subroutines are used to divide the program into smaller parts that are more easily coded and debugged. Each subroutine can be coded as a separate part of the main program to perform a well-defined task. When the subroutine is called from the main program, a WRITE statement can be placed within the subprogram to help determine where incorrect results are produced (Fig. 9-1). This debugging technique traces the execution of the program.

FORTRAN subroutines have been written to perform many specific tasks. These proven subroutines incorporated in a program are an aid to solving problems by using the computer. These pretested and preprogrammed subroutines make programming easier and quicker.

Memory space is saved by writing a subroutine and calling it from the main program, instead of writing the same procedure in the main program each time it is needed.

In many large programs it is necessary for more than one programmer to develop a program. By breaking the program into subroutines, different individuals can work to complete different sections of the program.

Subroutines simplify the total program because as a part of the program they are easier to understand, easier to correct, and easier to modify.

CALL STATEMENT

Control from the main program is passed to the subroutine in a CALL statement, and control is returned to the main program from the subroutine in a RETURN statement (Fig. 9-2).

The main program and subroutines are separate programs that must have a standardized format (Fig. 9-3). The main program follows the outline in

```
C**** THIS PROGRAM DEMONSTRATES THE USE OF
C**** A SUBROUTINE TO CHECK THE VALUE OF A
C**** REAL NUMBER INPUT FROM THE KEYBOARD
C**** AND PASSES A SINGLE PARAMETER FROM A
C**** CALL TO THE ARGUMENT OF A SUBROUTINE
C234567
      PROGRAM SUBRT1
      OPEN (6, FILE = 'PRINTER:')
      SUM = 0
      KOUNT = 0
 10   WRITE (0,900) 'ENTER A REAL: '
      WRITE (6,900) 'ENTER A REAL: '
900   FORMAT (A$)
      READ (0,910) X
      CALL CHECK (X)
      WRITE (6,910) X
910   FORMAT (BN, F7.2)
      IF (X .LE. 0.00) GOTO 20
      KOUNT = KOUNT + 1
      SUM = SUM + X
      GOTO 10
 20   AVG = SUM/KOUNT
      WRITE (0,920) KOUNT, SUM, AVG
      WRITE (6,920) KOUNT, SUM, AVG
920   FORMAT (///,'NUMBERS ENTERED = ',
     *I3,' SUM = ',F10.2,' AND AVG = ',
     2F7.2)
      STOP
      END
      SUBROUTINE CHECK (X)
      IF (X .LE. 9999.99) RETURN
      WRITE (0,930)
      WRITE (6,930)
930   FORMAT (///,'REAL IS TOO LARGE',//)
      WRITE (0,940)
      WRITE (6,940)
940   FORMAT ('ENTER A NUMBER BELOW 10000',//)
      STOP
      END


 ENTER A REAL:


 REAL IS TOO LARGE


 ENTER A NUMBER BELOW 10000



 ENTER A REAL:  100.00
 ENTER A REAL:  200.00
 ENTER A REAL:  300.00
 ENTER A REAL:     .00



 NUMBERS ENTERED =   3 SUM =      600.00 AND AVG =  200.00
```

Fig. 9-1. Program to demonstrate the use of a subroutine.

Fig. 9-3, and ends with a STOP and an END. The subroutine must begin with the SUBROUTINE statement and have a RETURN statement within the subroutine to return control to the main program. Since the subroutine is a separate program, an END statement must be the last statement in the subroutine.

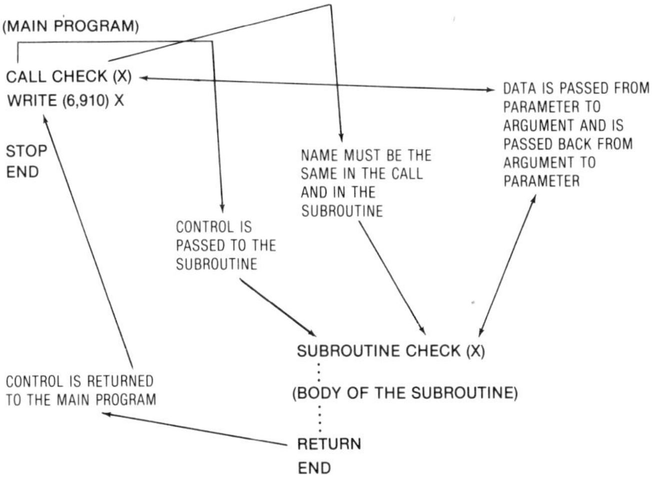

Fig. 9-2. Passing control from the main program to the subroutine, and returning control from the subroutine to the main program.

```
PROGRAM WRITE2       (THE PROGRAM NAME IS OPTIONAL)
SPECIFICATION
DATA
INITIALIZATION
CALL CHECK (X)
WRITE (6,910) X
  :
(BODY OF THE MAIN PROGRAM)
  :
  :
STOP
END

                             SUBROUTINE CHECK (X)
                               :
                             (BODY OF THE SUBROUTINE)
                               :
                             RETURN
                             END
```

Fig. 9-3. Format of the main program and the subroutine.

PASS DATA FROM MAIN PROGRAM TO SUBROUTINE

For the subroutine to perform its task, data is passed from the main program to the subroutine, and computations or results must be passed from the subroutine to the main program. Data is passed by one of two methods — (1) from parameters in the CALL statement to dummy arguments in the SUBROUTINE statement or (2) in the COMMON statement.

Parameters in a CALL statement are enclosed between parentheses, and if there is more than one parameter, they are separated by commas. Parameters are passed to arguments in the SUBROUTINE statement. Arguments are enclosed between parentheses and, if there is more than one argument, they are separated by commas.

Data is passed from the parameters in a CALL statement to the arguments in a SUBROUTINE statement. When the subroutine has performed its actions, the results must be passed from the argument in the SUBROUTINE statement to the parameter in the CALL statement. The parameters and arguments are a two-way street. Data and information must be passed from the main program to the subroutine. The subroutine performs its actions and an avenue must be open for these results to be passed from the subroutine to the main program. If there is more than one parameter/argument set, the last parameter/argument set is used to pass the information to the main program. More than one parameter/argument set may be used to pass information from the subroutine to the main program.

CORRESPONDENCE BETWEEN MAIN PROGRAM AND SUBROUTINE

When parameters are passed in a call to a subroutine, the correspondence must agree according to the following rules:

1. The arguments and parameters must contain the same number of items. If there are three parameters, there must be three arguments.
2. The arguments and parameters must be in the correct order (Fig. 9-4). If they are not in the correct order, the data and results will be passed to the wrong correspondent.
3. The parameter and its related arguments must be of the same type — integer, real, logical, or character.
4. The names of the parameters and arguments may be the same, but they may be different as long as they comply with rules 1, 2, and 3 (Fig. 9-5).

PASSING DATA IN A PARAMETER

A parameter is sometimes called a formal argument or formal parameter. An argument is sometimes called an actual argument, actual parameter, or a dummy argument (Fig. 9-6). The terminology used henceforth will be: a

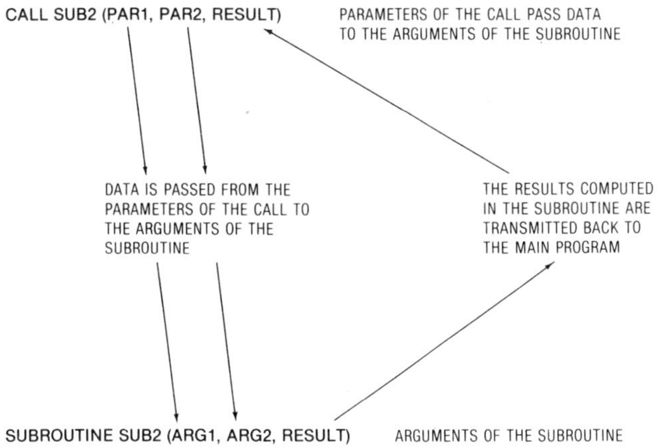

Fig. 9-4. Parameters of the CALL statement; arguments of the SUBROUTINE statement.

parameter is passed in a CALL statement to an argument in a SUBROUTINE statement, and vice versa.

Parameters and arguments can be of two general types — (1) scalar and (2) array. The scalar values are passed between the correspondents on a one-to-one basis, and can be seen in Fig. 9-7.

When single subscripted arrays are passed in a parameter (Fig. 9-7), the array variable is passed, and the subscript is passed as an integer constant. The argument receives the single subscripted array into the same type of variable, but the subscript is received into an integer variable. The single subscripted array may be passed by using only the variable, and no subscript. When the variable is passed with no subscript, the default value of the subscript is the dimensioned (SPECIFICATION statement) subscript value.

When a double subscripted array is passed in a parameter (Fig. 9-7), the

```
CALL SUB1         (ARG1, ARG2, RESULT)

SUBROUTINE SUB1   (ARG1, ARG2, RESULT)


CALL SUB1         (ARG1, ARG2, RESULT)

SUBROUTINE SUB1   (X,  Y,  Z )
```

Fig. 9-5. Parameters and arguments may or may not have the same names.

CALL	SUBROUTINE
PARAMETER	ARGUMENT
FORMAL PARAMETER	ACTUAL ARGUMENT
ACTUAL or FORMAL ARGUMENT	DUMMY ARGUMENT

Fig. 9-6. Multiple names for parameters and arguments.

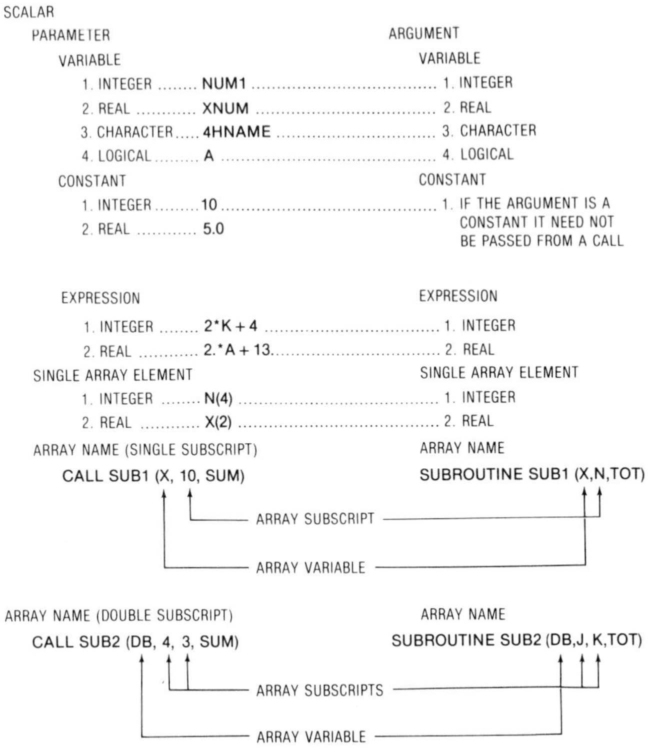

Fig. 9-7. Correspondence between parameters and arguments.

array variable is passed, and the two integer subscripts are passed as integer constants. The argument receives the double subscripted array into the same type variable, and the two integer subscripts as integer variables. The double subscripted array can be passed by using only the variable. When the double subscripted array is passed using only the variable, the default values of the subscripts are the same as those in the DIMENSION (SPECIFICATION) statement.

PASSING DATA IN COMMON

The second method of passing data from the main program to a subroutine is through the COMMON statement.

COMMON is a specification statement that can reserve memory as do DIMENSION X(10), INTEGER X(10), and REAL X(10), but COMMON X(10) makes the same memory locations available for use by all parts of the program. Since the main program and subroutines are separate entities, each part of the program that uses the common data must include the COMMON statement after the initial PROGRAM statement or SUBROUTINE statement.

Scalar values and arrays can be used in common to reserve memory. The scalars and arrays used in the main programs and subprograms can be the same identifiers or names, or they can be different. The variables are related by order of listing in the COMMON statement.

```
MAIN PROGRAM — COMMON LIMIT, SIDE(3), ANGLE(3)
  SUBROUTINE — COMMON LIMIT, SIDE(3), ANGLE(3)

MAIN PROGRAM — COMMON LIMIT, SIDE(3), ANGLE(3)
  SUBROUTINE — COMMON J, TRI (3), RANGE(3)
```

If the scalars and arrays are different types, the arguments in common storage must be properly arranged according to order and type, so no conflicts will occur in reserved memory. The COMMON statement may contain dummy variables in order to provide the correct arrangement throughout the program.

Parameters passed in a CALL statement and COMMON statement can be used in the same program. In Fig. 9-8, COMMON/ATS/LIMIT is used to reserve memory for the final loop value of the array (X), and COMMON is used in each subroutine for the same purpose. The array itself is passed as a parameter to an argument in the subroutine.

```
CALL MINMAX (X)
SUBROUTINE MINMAX (X)
```

An array value can be passed in a CALL statement in one of two ways:

1. DIMENSION X(10)
   CALL MINMAX (X)
   SUBROUTINE MINMAX (X)
   DIMENSION X(10)
2. CALL MINMAX (X,10)
   SUBROUTINE MINMAX (X,N)

If no subscript is passed in the parameter, the array must be placed in a specification statement in each part of the program. When the array variable and subscript constant are passed in the parameter, the argument must have a related array variable and a variable subscript to receive the subscripted array.

It is illegal for the array to be dimensioned in two specification statements.

```
COMMON X(10)
DIMENSION X(10) (illegal)
```

The preferred method for reserving memory when there is a main program and one or more subroutines is to use the specification statement COMMON.

```
COMMON X(10)
```

Memory can be reserved for variables and arrays by using the common block statement. The common block statement must be the same in each part of the program.

```
6C**** PROGRAM TO DEMONSTRATE THE PASSING OF
C**** A PARAMETER IN THE COMMON STATEMENT
C234567
      PROGRAM SUBRT2
      DIMENSION X(10)
      COMMON /ATS/ LIMIT
      DATA X/-5.,-1.,-50.,2.,6.,8.,30.,
     132.,69.,1./
      OPEN (6,FILE='PRINTER:')
      LIMIT = 10
      WRITE (0,90) (X(I),I = 1,LIMIT)
      WRITE (6,90) (X(I),I = 1,LIMIT)
   90 FORMAT (5(F5.0),/)
      XMAX = X(1)
      XMIN = X(1)
      DO 20 J = 2, LIMIT
      IF (X(J) .GE. XMAX) XMAX = X(J)
      IF (X(J) .LE. XMIN) XMIN = X(J)
 20   CONTINUE
      WRITE (0, 100) XMAX, XMIN
      WRITE (6, 100) XMAX, XMIN
100   FORMAT (//,'THE LARGEST IS',F5.0,
     *' AND SMALLEST IS ',F5.0,//)
      CALL MINMAX (X)
      CALL SORT (X)
      CALL REMOVE (X)
      STOP
      END
      SUBROUTINE MINMAX (X)
      DIMENSION X(10)
      COMMON /ATS/ LIMIT
      XMAX = X(1)
      XMIN = X(1)
      DO 20 J = 2,LIMIT
      IF (X(J) .GE. XMAX) XMAX = X(J)
      IF (X(J) .LE. XMIN) XMIN = X(J)
 20   CONTINUE
      WRITE (0,110) XMAX,XMIN
      WRITE (6,110) XMAX,XMIN
 110  FORMAT (//,'THE LARGEST IS ',
     *F5.0,' AND THE SMALLEST IS ',F5.0,//)
      RETURN
      END
      SUBROUTINE SORT (X)
      DIMENSION X(10)
      COMMON /ATS/ LIMIT
      DO 30 J = 1,LIMIT-1
      JPLUS1 = J + 1
      DO 20 K = JPLUS1,LIMIT
      IF (X(J) .LE. X(K)) GOTO 20
      TEMP = X(J)
      X(J) = X(K)
      X(K) = TEMP
 20   CONTINUE
 30   CONTINUE
      DO 40 J = 1,LIMIT,5
      M = J + 4
      IF (M .GE. LIMIT) M = LIMIT
      WRITE (0, 120) (X(K),K = J,M)
      WRITE (6, 120) (X(K),K = J,M)
 40   CONTINUE
 120  FORMAT (/,5(F5.0),/)
      RETURN
      END
```

Fig. 9-8. Program to demonstrate the passing

```
      SUBROUTINE REMOVE (X)
      DIMENSION X(10)
      COMMON /ATS/ LIMIT
      DO 50 J = 1,LIMIT
      IF (X(J) .LE. 22.3) GOTO 50
      ITEMP = J
      WRITE (0,9010) ITEMP
      WRITE (6,9010) ITEMP
 9010 FORMAT (//,'ITEMP = ',I4,//)
      GOTO 60
 50   CONTINUE
      WRITE (0,130)
      WRITE (6,130)
130   FORMAT (//,'ALL LESS THAN 22.3',//)
      RETURN
 60   DO 70 K = ITEMP,LIMIT
      X(K-ITEMP+1) = X(K)
      WRITE (0,9020) X(K-ITEMP+1)
      WRITE (6,9020) X(K-ITEMP+1)
9020  FORMAT (1X,/,'X(K-ITEMP+1) = ',F5.0,/)
 70   CONTINUE
      DO 80 J = LIMIT - ITEMP + 2, LIMIT
      X(J) = 0
 80   CONTINUE
      DO 90 J = 1,LIMIT,5
      M = J + 4
      IF (M .GE. LIMIT) M = LIMIT
      WRITE (0,140) (X(K),K = J,M)
      WRITE (6,140) (X(K),K = J,M)
 90   CONTINUE
 140  FORMAT (/,5(F5.0))
      RETURN
      END
```

```
   -5.  -1. -50.   2.   6.

    8.  30.  32.  69.   1.


THE LARGEST IS  69. AND SMALLEST IS  -50.


THE LARGEST IS   69. AND THE SMALLEST IS  -50.


  -50.  -5.  -1.   1.   2.

    6.   8.  30.  32.  69.


ITEMP =      8
```

of a parameter in the COMMON statement.

```
        X(K-ITEMP+1) =    30.

        X(K-ITEMP+1) =    32.

        X(K-ITEMP+1) =    69.

          30.    32.    69.     0.     0.
           0.     0.     0.     0.     0.
```

Fig. 9-8. Program to demonstrate the passing of a parameter in the COMMON statement. *(Continued)*

MAIN PROGRAM — COMMON A,B,X(20)
1st SUBROUTINE — COMMON A,B,X(20)
2nd SUBROUTINE — COMMON A,B,X(20)

If the variables and arrays are not all used in each subroutine, the common can be separated into labeled common block divisions, so each subroutine can be assigned only those variables and arrays which it uses.

MAIN PROGRAM — COMMON/ATS1/A,X(10)/ATS2/B,Y(20/ATS3/C,Z(20)
1st SUBROUTINE — COMMON/ATS1/A,X(10)
2nd SUBROUTINE — COMMON/ATS2/B,Y(20)
3rd SUBROUTINE — COMMON/ATS3/C,Z(20)

Breaking the COMMON statement into labeled common blocks allows the main program to communicate with all subprograms. The subprograms do not need to communicate with each other, so they are assigned the necessary variables and arrays.

The names assigned to the labeled common block subroutine statements may be different from the labeled common block in the main program, but the names must agree in order and type with the labeled common block in the main program.

MAIN PROGRAM — COMMON/ATS1/A,X(10)/ATS2/B,Y(20)/ATS3/C,Z(20)
1st SUBROUTINE — COMMON/ATS1/D,P(10)
2nd SUBROUTINE — COMMON/ATS2/E,Q(20)
3rd SUBROUTINE — COMMON/ATS3/F,R(20)

EQUIVALENCE STATEMENT

The EQUIVALENCE statement is used to specify that two or more variables or arrays share the same memory storage. The variables or arrays are of the same type — integer or real. Memory is similar to a tall ladder. The individual locations are similar to the spaces between the rungs of the ladder. When variables and subscripted arrays are stored in memory, they are stored between specific rungs in the ladder at a specific address until the values are all stored. This is a rather simple explanation of the concept of how variables and arrays are stored.

HOW MATRIX VALUES ARE STORED IN MEMORY

When double subscripted array values are stored between the rungs of the ladder, they cannot be stored in recognizable table form. To determine how Apple FORTRAN stores double subscripted arrays, an EQUIVALENCE statement is used to compare the relationship of a double subscripted array with 10 memory locations, and a single subscripted array with 10 memory locations (Fig. 9-9). The output from the program in Fig. 9-9 is the information in Table 9-1.

Table 9-1. Double Subscripted Array Equivalenced to a Single Subscripted Array

Loop Values	IB(10)	IA(2,5)
11	IB(1)	IA(1,1)
12	IB(2)	IA(1,2)
21	IB(3)	IA(2,1)
22	IB(4)	IA(2,2)
31	IB(5)	IA(3,1)
32	IB(6)	IA(3,2)
41	IB(7)	IA(4,1)
42	IB(8)	IA(4,2)
51	IB(9)	IA(5,1)
52	IB(10)	IA(5,2)

```
C**** PROGRAM TO DEMONSTRATE THE USE OF
C**** EQUIVALENCE STATEMENT
C234567
      PROGRAM EQUIV
      DIMENSION IA( 2,5 ),IB( 10 )
      EQUIVALENCE ( IA,IB )
      OPEN ( 6,FILE='PRINTER:' )
      DO 20 J = 1,2
      DO 20 K = 1,5
      IA( J,K ) = J + K*10
   20 CONTINUE
      DO 30 I = 1,10
      WRITE ( 0,100 ) IB( I )
      WRITE ( 6,100 ) IB( I )
   30 CONTINUE
  100 FORMAT ( 10X,I5 )
      STOP
      END
```

Fig. 9-9. Program to demonstrate the use of the EQUIVALENCE statement.

A 2 × 5 matrix, IA(2,5), is input by means of nested DO loops. The output created by the single subscripted array, IB(10), shows how Apple FORTRAN stores the double subscripted array.

```
   DO 20 J = 1,2
   DO 20 K = 1,5
   IA(J,K) = J + K*10
20 CONTINUE
```

The keyword EQUIVALENCE is used to specify that two or more variables or arrays share the same memory space. In Fig. 9-9, EQUIVALENCE assigns the same 10 memory locations to the double subscripted array, IA(2,5), as it does to the single subscripted array, IB(10). The double subscripted array, IA(2,5), is a table with two rows and five columns. When IA(2,5) is stored in memory, it is stored sequentially according to the arrangement of the subscripts. To determine the arrangement by which Apple FORTRAN stores a double subscripted array in memory, the double subscripted array is placed inside doubly nested loops, and the statement, IA(J,K) = J + K * 10, is used to compute the values stored in memory. When the 10 values of the double subscripted array are computed and stored in memory, IB(10), a single subscripted array, is used to output the same 10 equivalent memory locations (Table 9-1). The output shows that Apple FORTRAN uses column-major, row-minor form. That is, the columns are stored first, and then the rows are stored. To determine the relationship between memory, single subscripted arrays, and double subscripted arrays (OFFSET), a formula is derived from the output:

```
I = (J-1)*NUMBER OF ROWS + K
I = (J-1)*5 + K
```

In this example, the 2-row by 5-column matrix shows the values in column-major, row-minor form (Table 9-1). The output is column 1, row 1; column 1, row 2; column 2, row 1; column 2, row 2; etc., until all the values are output.

In beginning FORTRAN programming, the EQUIVALENCE statement is not used very often. It is useful to convert double subscripted arrays to single subscripted arrays. The desired operations can be carried out on the single subscripted array, and printed out in the double subscripted array.

Fig. 9-8 is a program that demonstrates the use of the specification statement, DIMENSION X(10), to reserve 10 memory locations for the real array X. The array variable is passed in the parameter of three calls to the arguments of three subroutines. The limit value of the loops is passed in common from the main program to the subroutines.

The program is the solution to a problem to select the least and the greatest values from the array list. This is done in the main program and the subroutine MINMAX to demonstrate two places where MINMAX can be used. The subroutine SORT then sorts the array list from least to greatest using a selection with interchange bubble sort.

The third subroutine in the program, REMOVE, takes the sorted list and removes all values in the list below 22.3. It then shifts all values greater than or equal to 22.3 to the first three positions in the array list, and fills the remaining positions in the list with zeros. This is a programming exercise to test the capability of the programmer.

EXAMPLE PROGRAM TO DETERMINE THE SIDES AND ANGLES OF A TRIANGLE

Program GMETRY (Fig. 9-10) is a program written to compute the sides and angles of a triangle when specific data is entered into the program. The flowchart of GMETRY is shown in Fig. 9-11. The program is written using subroutines for efficiency and ease in debugging. Each subroutine contains a WRITE statement, and associated FORMAT statement, that outputs the name of the subroutine that is processing the data. When an error occurs that causes the program to stop executing because of a WRITE CODE ERROR, the last subroutine name is the place where the error occurred. This debugging method tells the programmer where the error has occurred and, consequently, is a clue to solving the program logic, or data error.

Solving the Problem

A logic error would occur if the data given was three sides of a triangle, and the LAW OF SINES subroutine was called to solve this problem. The LAW OF COSINES subroutine must be used to solve the problem when three sides are given.

A data input error (WRITE CODE ERROR) occurs when the sine or cosine computed is greater than the value of plus or minus one (+1 or −1). The value of the sine is zero (0) at 0° and 180°, plus one (+1) at 90°, and minus one (−1) at 270°. The value of the cosine is zero (0) at 90° and 270°, plus one (+1) at 0°, and minus one (−1) at 180°. Any data input that causes the range of the sine or cosine to fall outside the magnitude of zero (0), plus one (+1), to minus one (−1), causes a WRITE CODE ERROR.

How Data Is Input

To compute the sides and angles of a triangle, the real data is input from the keyboard in the following format:

1. Columns 1–10, side A.
2. Columns 11–20, side B.
3. Columns 21–30, side C.
4. Columns 31–40, angle opposite side A.
5. Columns 41–50, angle opposite side B.
6. Columns 51-60, angle opposite side C.

For the program to process input data properly, only three real values are accepted for processing — three real sides, two real sides and one real

```
&C234567
      PROGRAM GMETRY
      INTRINSIC ACOS,SQRT,COS,MOD,SIN,ASIN
      COMMON /ATS/SIDE(3),ANGLE(3)
      OPEN (6,FILE = 'PRINTER:')
 10   CALL READCR
      CALL COUNTA(ISIDE,IANGLE)
      IF (ISIDE+IANGLE.EQ.0)GOTO 999
      IF (ISIDE+IANGLE.GT.3)GOTO 780
      IF (ISIDE+IANGLE.LT.3
     *.OR.IANGLE.EQ.3)GOTO 800
      IF (ISIDE.EQ.3)GOTO 700
      CALL DEGRAD
      CALL EVLUAT(ITYPE,ISIDE,IANGLE)
      CALL ORDER
      GOTO (600,200,300),ITYPE
 200  CALL SINANG(SIDE(1),ANGLE(1),SIDE(2),ANGLE(2))
 300  CALL ANG180
      CALL ALLANG
      GOTO 710
 600  CALL COSSID(SIDE(3),SIDE(1),SIDE(2),ANGLE(3))
 700  CALL ALLSID
 710  CALL SRTREC
      CALL RADDEG
      GOTO 820
 780  WRITE(*,790)
      WRITE(6,790)
 790  FORMAT(/,20HTOO MUCH INFORMATION)
      GOTO 820
 800  WRITE(*,810)
      WRITE(6,810)
 810  FORMAT(/,24HINSUFFICIENT INFORMATION)
 820  CALL PRTREC
      GOTO 10
 999  STOP
      END
      SUBROUTINE READCR
      COMMON /ATS/ SIDE(3),ANGLE(3)
      READ (0,6) A
    6 FORMAT (F5.0)
      WRITE(*,5)
      WRITE(6,5)
 5    FORMAT(///,6(10H!---------*))
      READ (*,10)(SIDE(J),J=1,3),
     *(ANGLE(I),I=1,3)
      WRITE(6,10)(SIDE(J),J=1,3),
     *(ANGLE(I),I=1,3)
 10   FORMAT(6(F10.2))
            RETURN
            END
      SUBROUTINE COUNTA(ISIDE,IANGLE)
      COMMON /ATS/ SIDE(3),ANGLE(3)
      ISIDE=0
      IANGLE=0
      DO 10 J=1,3
      IF(SIDE(J).GT.0)ISIDE=ISIDE+1
      IF(ANGLE(J).GT.0)IANGLE=IANGLE+1
 10   CONTINUE
      WRITE(*,20)ISIDE,IANGLE
      WRITE(6,20)ISIDE,IANGLE
 20   FORMAT(///,12H# OF SIDES= ,I3,3X,13H# OF ANGLES= ,I5,//)
            RETURN
            END
```

Fig. 9-10. Geometry

```
      SUBROUTINE PRTREC
      COMMON /ATS/ SIDE(3),ANGLE(3)
      WRITE(*,10)(SIDE(J),J=1,3),
     *(ANGLE(I),I=1,3)
      WRITE(6,10)(SIDE(J),J=1,3),
     *(ANGLE(I),I=1,3)
10    FORMAT(/,6(F10.2))
            RETURN
            END
      SUBROUTINE ALLSID
      COMMON /ATS/ S(3),A(3)
      WRITE(*,1)
      WRITE(6,1)
1     FORMAT(26H-- IN ALLSID SUBROUTINE --)
      CALL COSANG(S(1),S(2),S(3),A(1))
      CALL COSANG(S(2),S(3),S(1),A(2))
      CALL COSANG(S(3),S(1),S(2),A(3))
            RETURN
            END
      SUBROUTINE COSANG(SA,SB,SC,AA)
      WRITE(*,1)
      WRITE(6,1)
1     FORMAT(26H-- IN COSANG SUBROUTINE --)
      IF (AA.GT.0)RETURN
      AA=ACOS(((SB**2)+(SC**2)-(SA**2)
     !)/(2*SB*SC))
10          RETURN
            END
      SUBROUTINE COSSID(S1,S2,S3,A1)
      WRITE(*,1)
      WRITE(6,1)
1     FORMAT(26H-- IN COSSID SUBROUTINE --)
      S1=SQRT((S2**2)+(S3**2)-2*S2*S3*COS(A1))
            RETURN
            END
      SUBROUTINE DEGRAD
      COMMON /ATS/ SIDE(3),ANGLE(3)
      WRITE(*,1)
      WRITE(6,1)
1     FORMAT(26H-- IN DEGRAD SUBROUTINE --)
      DO 10 J=1,3
      ANGLE(J)=ANGLE(J)/57.2958
10    CONTINUE
            RETURN
            END
      SUBROUTINE RADDEG
      COMMON /ATS/ SIDE(3),ANGLE(3)
      WRITE(*,1)
      WRITE(6,1)
1     FORMAT(26H-- IN RADDEG SUBROUTINE --)
      DO 10 J=1,3
      ANGLE(J)=ANGLE(J)*57.2958
10    CONTINUE
            RETURN
            END
      SUBROUTINE SINSID(S1,A1,S2,A2)
      WRITE(*,1)
      WRITE(6,1)
1     FORMAT(26H-- IN SINSID SUBROUTINE --)
      IF (S2.GT.0)RETURN
      S2=S1*SIN(A2)/SIN(A1)
            RETURN
            END
```

program.

```
      SUBROUTINE ALLANG
      COMMON /ATS/ S(3),A(3)
      WRITE(*,1)
      WRITE(6,1)
1     FORMAT(26H-- IN ALLANG SUBROUTINE --)
      DO 10 J=1,2
      CALL SINSID(S(J),A(J),S(J+1),A(J+1))
10    CONTINUE
            RETURN
            END
      SUBROUTINE SRTREC
      COMMON /ATS/ SIDE(3),ANGL(3)
      WRITE(*,1)
      WRITE(6,1)
1     FORMAT(26H-- IN SRTREC SUBROUTINE --)
      DO 20 L=1,2
      ILS=L
      DO 10 J=L+1,3
      IF (SIDE(J).GT.SIDE(ILS))ILS=J
10    CONTINUE
      IF (ILS.EQ.L)GOTO 20
      CALL TRNSFR(ILS,L)
20    CONTINUE
            RETURN
            END
      SUBROUTINE TRNSFR(I,J)
      COMMON /ATS/ SIDE(3),ANGLE(3)
      WRITE(*,1)
      WRITE(6,1)
1     FORMAT(26H-- IN TRNSFR SUBROUTINE --)
      TS = SIDE(I)
      SIDE(I)=SIDE(J)
      SIDE(J)=TS
      TS=ANGLE(I)
      ANGLE(I)=ANGLE(J)
      ANGLE(J)=TS
            RETURN
            END
      SUBROUTINE EVLUAT(ITYPE,ISIDE,IANGLE)
      COMMON /ATS/ SIDE(3),ANGLE(3)
      WRITE(*,1)
      WRITE(6,1)
1     FORMAT(26H-- IN EVLUAT SUBROUTINE --)
      IF (IANGLE.EQ.2)THEN
         ITYPE=3
         GOTO 50
         ENDIF
      DO 20 J=1,3
      IF (SIDE(J).EQ.O.AND.ANGLE(J).EQ.O)GOTO10
      GOTO20
10    ITYPE=2
      GOTO 50
20    CONTINUE
      ITYPE=1
50          RETURN
            END
      SUBROUTINE ANG180
      COMMON /ATS/ SIDE(3),ANGLE(3)
      WRITE(*,1)
      WRITE(6,1)
1     FORMAT(26H-- IN ANG180 SUBROUTINE --)
      CALL ZROANG(I)
```

Fig. 9-10. Geometry

```
      ANGLE(I)=3.1416-ANGLE(MOD(I,3)+1)-
     !ANGLE(MOD(I+1,3)+1)
             RETURN
             END
      SUBROUTINE ORDER
      COMMON /ATS/ S(3),A(3)
      DIMENSION IV(3)
      WRITE(*,1)
      WRITE(6,1)
1     FORMAT(26H-- IN ORDER  SUBROUTINE --)
      IV(1)=0
      IV(2)=0
      IV(3)=0
      DO 20 L=1,3
      IF (S(L).GT.0)IV(L)=IV(L)+2
      IF (A(L).GT.0)IV(L)=IV(L)+1
20    CONTINUE
      IF (IV(3).GT.IV(2))THEN
          CALL TRNSFR(3,2)
          IT=IV(3)
          IV(3)=IV(2)
          IV(2)=IT
          ENDIF
      IF (IV(2).GT.IV(1))THEN
          CALL TRNSFR(2,1)
          IT=IV(2)
          IV(2)=IV(1)
          IV(1)=IT
          ENDIF
      IF (IV(3).GT.IV(2))THEN
          CALL TRNSFR(3,2)
          IT=IV(3)
          IV(3)=IV(2)
          IV(2)=IT
          ENDIF
             RETURN
             END
      SUBROUTINE SINANG(S1,A1,S2,A2)
      WRITE(*,1)
      WRITE(6,1)
1     FORMAT(26H-- IN SINANG SUBROUTINE --)
      A2=ASIN(SIN(A1)*S2/S1)
             RETURN
             END
      SUBROUTINE ZROANG(I)
      COMMON /ATS/ S(3),A(3)
      WRITE(*,1)
      WRITE(6,1)
1     FORMAT(26H-- IN ZROANG SUBROUTINE --)
      DO 10 J=1,3
      IF (A(J).GT.0)GOTO 10
      I=J
      GOTO 20
10    CONTINUE
20           RETURN
             END
```

program. *(Continued)*

angle, or two real angles and one real side. If three real angles are entered, this is included in condition #1 (Figs. 9-11 and 9-12). A triangle has no solution when only three angles are given.

Condition #0 (Figs. 9-11 and 9-12) is the method used to terminate the program. When RETURN is pressed, or real zeros (0.) are placed in all six columns and RETURN is pressed, the program terminates.

Condition #1 (Figs. 9-11 and 9-12) is created by using the decision statement, IF (ISIDE + IANGLE .LT. 3 .OR. IANGLE .EQ. 3) GOTO 800 (Fig. 9-10). When the sum of the sides and angles is less than three, or the number of angles is equal to three, the program outputs the statement, INSUFFICIENT INFORMATION. A triangle cannot be solved when three angles are given.

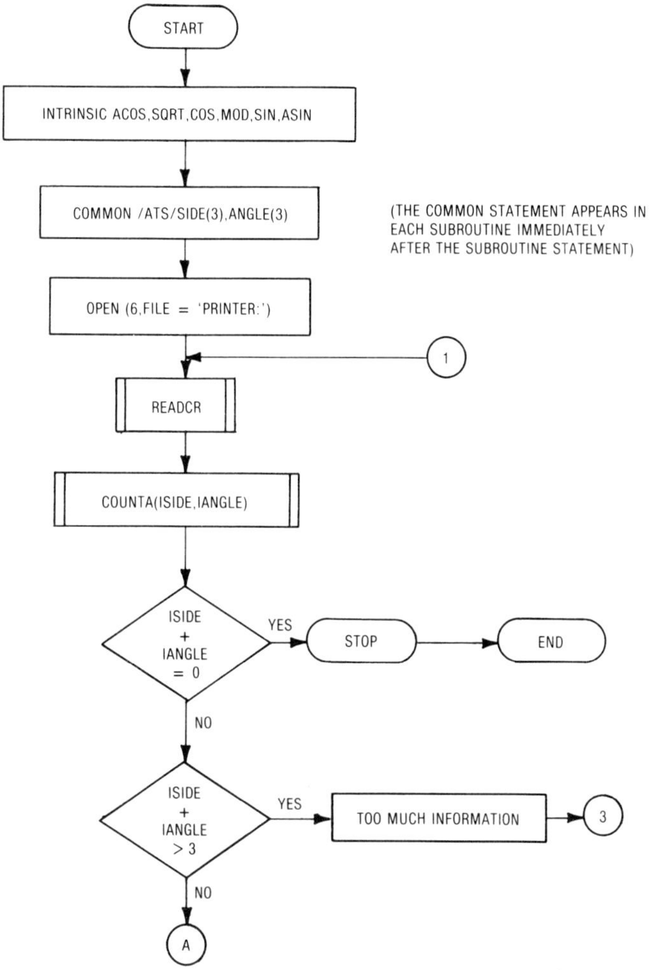

Fig. 9-11. Flowchart of the geometry program.

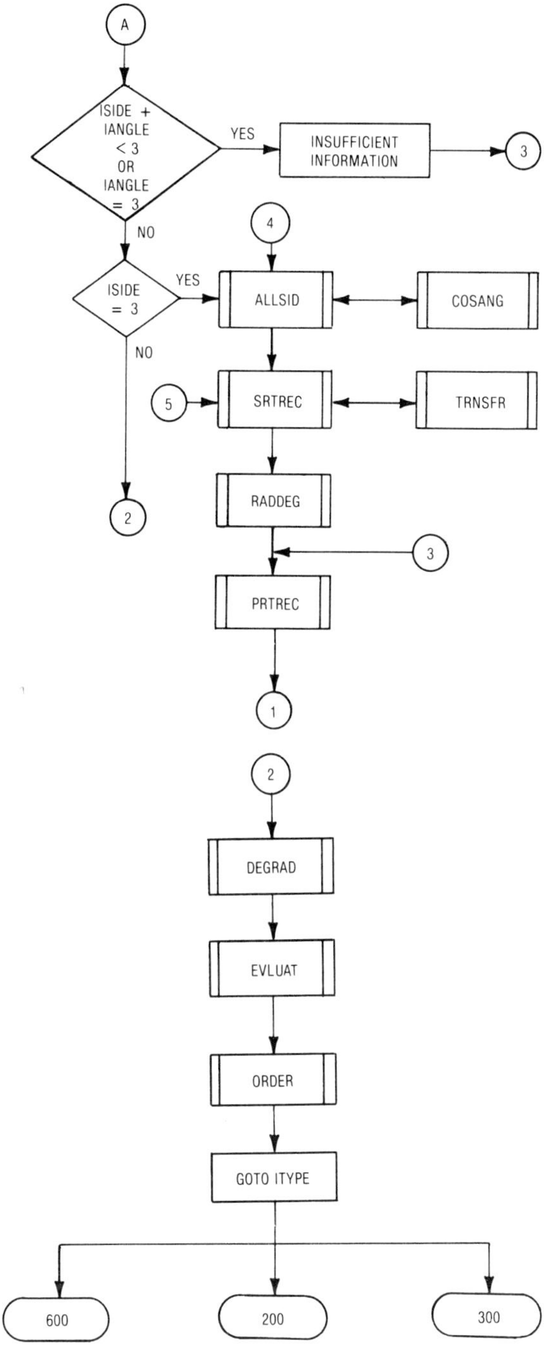

Fig. 9-11. Flowchart of the geometry program. *(Continued)*

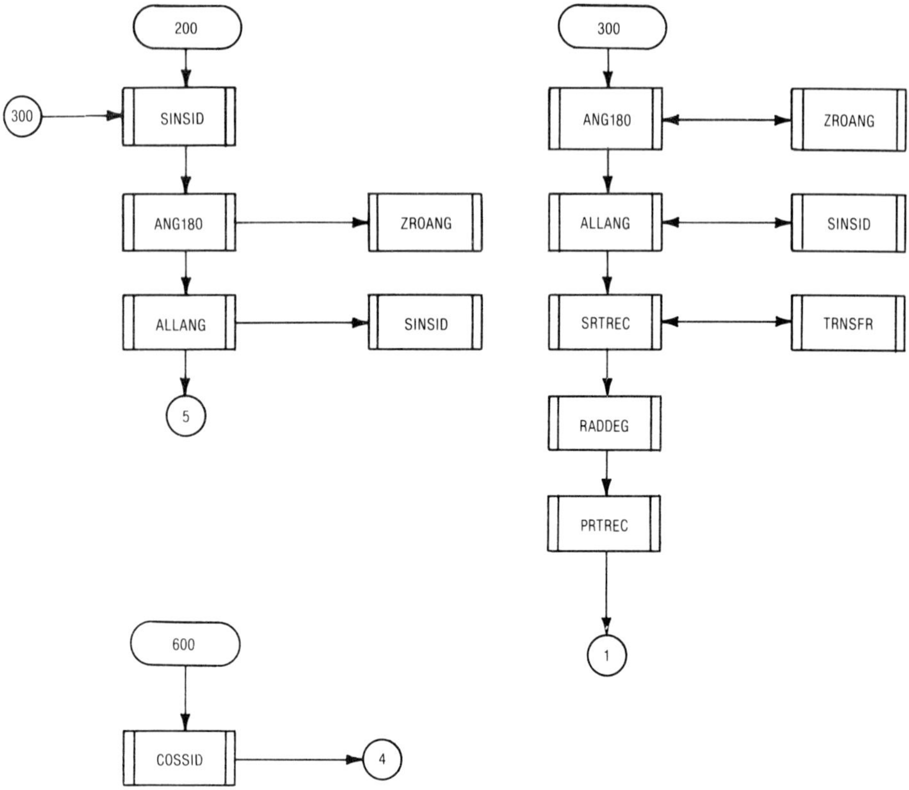

Fig. 9-11. Flowchart of the geometry program. *(Continued)*

Condition #2 (Figs. 9-11 and 9-12) is created by using a decision statement, IF (ISIDE + IANGLE .GT. 3) GOTO 780 (Fig. 9-10). When the sum of the side count and angle count is greater than three, the program outputs the statement, TOO MUCH INFORMATION.

When the input data passes the tests in the three conditions, #0, #1, and #2, the three real data values are used by the program to compute the sides and/or angles of the triangle. The computations are made using (1) the law of sines, (2) the law of cosines, or (3) the 180° rule.

1. Law of sines:

$$\frac{\text{side A}}{\sin A} = \frac{\text{side B}}{\sin B} = \frac{\text{side C}}{\sin C}$$

2. Law of cosines:

$$A^2 = B^2 + C^2 - 2BC \cos A$$
$$B^2 = A^2 + C^2 - 2AC \cos B$$
$$C^2 = A^2 + B^2 - 2AB \cos C$$

3. 180° rule:

$$A + B + C = 180°$$

In the main program the statement, INTRINSIC ACOS, SQRT, COS, MOD, SIN, ASIN (Figs. 9-10 and 9-11), sets up the trigonometric standard and inverse functions to compute the sine, cosine, arcsine, arccosine, remainder, and square root from the transcendental, or internal library functions within the language. MOD is the transcendental function to compute the remainder of a division problem, and SQRT is the transcendental function to compute the square root of a real value.

```
!--------*!--------*!--------*!--------*!--------*!--------*
       .00       .00       .00       .00       .00       .00

# OF SIDES=    0    # OF ANGLES=      0
```

(A) Condition #0: If RETURN is pressed, or real zeros are placed in all six columns, the program terminates.

```
!--------*!--------*!--------*!--------*!--------*!--------*
     20.00       .00       .00       .00       .00       .00

# OF SIDES=    1    # OF ANGLES=      0

INSUFFICIENT INFORMATION

     20.00       .00       .00       .00       .00       .00
```

(B) Condition #1: If fewer than three values are input, or three angles are input, the program outputs INSUFFICIENT INFORMATION and prints out the record as input.

```
!--------*!--------*!--------*!--------*!--------*!--------*
     30.00     40.00     50.00     20.00       .00       .00

# OF SIDES=    3    # OF ANGLES=      1

TOO MUCH INFORMATION

     30.00     40.00     50.00     20.00       .00       .00
```

(C) Condition #2: If more than three values are input, the program outputs TOO MUCH INFORMATION and prints out the record as input.

Fig. 9-12. Conditions that are provided for in the geometry program.

The statement, COMMON/ATS/ SIDE(3), ANGLE(3), reserves memory locations for the array SIDE and the array ANGLE. The main program and each subroutine use the same side and angle values, so the COMMON/ATS/ SIDE(3), ANGLE(3) statement appears in each part of the program. The keyword COMMON allows each part of the program to reference the same memory storage.

The first subroutine, READCR, sets up six contiguous fields, each of 10 places, to prompt the user where each value is input. This prompt is placed on the CRT and the printer. Each field represents a floating-point format of 10 places. Each field begins with an exclamation mark and ends with an asterisk. The values of the sides and/or angles are read from the keyboard and stored in memory. The values read from the keyboard are output to the CRT and the printer.

Subroutine COUNTA counts the sides and/or angles input and returns to the four decision statements (Fig. 9-10) in the main program, to make the

Table 9-2. Input Data and Output Information

INPUT DATA							
Entry #	Column						Condition or Case
	1–10	11–20	21–30	31–40	41–50	51–60	
1	0.	0.	0. or press RETURN	0.	0.	0.	Condition #0 Program Terminates
2	20.						Condition #1
3	30.	40.	50.	20.			Condition #2
4	30.	40.	50.				Case #0
5	25.	18.				45.	Case #1
6	30.	40.		37.			Case #2
7	25.			40.		38.	Case #3
8	25.			90.		90.	Case #4 — No Solution

OUTPUT INFORMATION							
1	.00	.00	.00	.00	.00	.00	Program Terminates
2	20.00	.00	.00	.00	.00	.00	Insufficient Information
3	30.00	40.00	50.00	20.00	.00	.00	Too Much Information
4	50.00	40.00	30.00	90.00	53.13	36.87	Case #0 — 3 Sides
5	25.00	21.07	18.00	79.14	55.86	45.00	Case #1 — 2 Sides and 1 Included Angle
6	49.85	40.00	30.00	89.64	53.36	37.00	Case #2 — 2 Sides and 1 Nonincluded Angle
7	38.04	25.00	23.94	102.00	40.00	38.00	Case #3 — 1 Side and 2 Angles
8	20.00	20.00	.00	90.00	90.00	.00	Case #4 — No Solution

decision as to the values input. If zeros are input and RETURN is pressed, the program terminates. If more than three values are input, the program outputs the statement, TOO MUCH INFORMATION. If less than three values are input, or three angles are input, the output statement is INSUFFICIENT INFORMATION.

The fourth decision statement (Fig. 9-10) is IF (ISIDE .EQ. 3) GOTO 700. If this statement is true, the program branches to line 700. When three sides of a triangle are input (case #0, Table 9-2), the ALLSID subroutine is called to use the law of cosines to compute the angles of the triangle (Figs. 9-10, 9-11, and 9-13). The subroutine ALLSID calls the subroutine COSANG three times (Fig. 9-10) to compute the three angles of the triangle. After the three angles have been computed, subroutines SRTREC and TRNSFR (Figs. 9-10 and 9-11) sort and transfer the records so the largest side is placed in columns 1–10 and the largest angle is placed in columns 31–40. The next largest side is placed in columns 11–20 and the next largest angle is placed in columns 41–50. The smallest side is placed in columns 21–30 and the smallest angle is placed in columns 51–60. This sorting procedure is used in each case so the sides and angles are output from largest to smallest.

Apple FORTRAN computes all angles in radians. The angles are input in degrees. The angles input must be converted from degrees to radians before the computer can correctly process them. After the angles are computed in relation to the triangle, they must be converted from radians to degrees before they are output. The subroutine DEGRAD converts the angles from degrees to radians, and the subroutine RADDEG converts the angles from radians to degrees. The formulas for converting degrees to radians and radians to degrees follow:

1. To convert degrees to radians:

$$\text{radians} = \text{degrees}\left(\frac{\pi}{180}\right)$$

   where,

$$\pi = 3.1416$$

2. To convert radians to degrees:

$$\text{degrees} = \text{radians}\left(\frac{180}{\pi}\right)$$

The constant, 57.2958 ($180/\pi$), is used so the value of $180/\pi$ does not have to be computed each time by the program.

The subroutine PRTREC is the last subroutine called in each case, and outputs the three sides and three angles of the triangle in descending order. The subroutine PRTREC returns to the main program at statement GOTO 10, which sets up the program for the next set of data to be input.

SOLVE BY:
1. LAW OF COSINES.

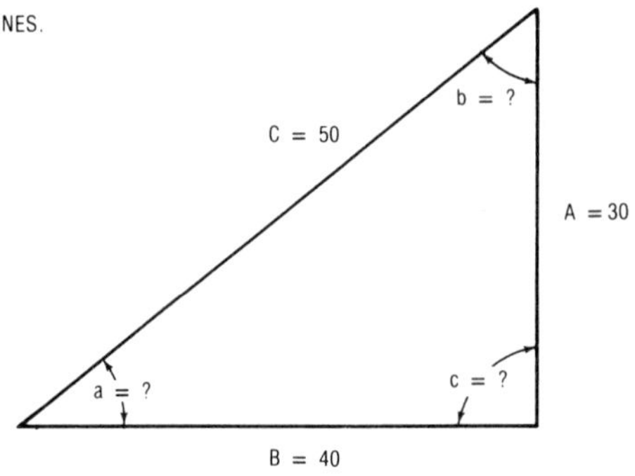

COS a = $(B^2 + C^2 - A^2) / (2BC)$ | COS a = $(40^2 + 50^2 - 30^2) / (2*40*50)$

COS a = 0.8 | ANGLE a = 36.87°

COS b = $(A^2 + C^2 - B^2) / (2AC)$ | COS b = $(30^2 + 50^2 - 40^2) / (2*30*50)$

COS b = 0.6 | ANGLE b = 53.13°

COS c = $(A^2 + B^2 - C^2) / (2AB)$ | COS c = $(30^2 + 40^2 - 50^2) / (2*30*40)$

COS c = 0 | ANGLE c = 90°

(A) Relationship of sides and angles.

```
!---------*!---------*!---------*!---------*!---------*!---------*
    30.00     40.00     50.00       .00       .00       .00


# OF SIDES=   3   # OF ANGLES=     0


-- IN ALLSID SUBROUTINE --
-- IN COSANG SUBROUTINE --
-- IN COSANG SUBROUTINE --
-- IN COSANG SUBROUTINE --
-- IN SRTREC SUBROUTINE --
-- IN TRNSFR SUBROUTINE --
-- IN RADDEG SUBROUTINE --

    50.00     40.00     30.00     90.00     53.13     36.87
```

(B) Printout of results for Case #0.

Fig. 9-13. Program GMETRY: Case #0 — three sides are input.

If the decision statement IF (ISIDE .EQ. 3) GOTO 700 is false, the program defaults to the next line, CALL DEGRAD. The angles input must be converted from degrees to radians for use by the transcendental functions of the FORTRAN language.

After the angles are converted from degrees to radians, the subroutine EVLUAT (Figs. 9-10 and 9-14) evaluates the input data. Case #1, ITYPE = 1

(Fig. 9-15) is input data that has two sides and one included angle. Case #2, ITYPE = 2 (Fig. 9-16) is input data that has two sides and one nonincluded angle. Case #3, ITYPE = 3 (Fig. 9-17) is input data that has one side and two angles. When the correct ITYPE is determined, the subroutine returns to the ARITHMETIC GOTO statement, GOTO (600,200,300), ITYPE, which causes the program to branch to the correct subroutines to compute the remaining sides and angles of the triangle.

Case #1, ITYPE = 1, two sides and one included angle (Figs. 9-10, 9-11, and 9-15) uses the following order to process the input data: subroutines DEGRAD, EVLUAT, ORDER, COSSID, ALLSID, COSANG, COSANG, COSANG, SRTREC, RADDEG, and PRTREC. These subroutines are used to process the input data, and output the three sides and the three angles of the triangle.

Case #2, ITYPE = 2, two sides and one nonincluded angle (Figs. 9-10, 9-11, and 9-16) uses the following order to process the input data and output information: subroutines DEGRAD, EVLUAT, ORDER, SINANG, ANG180, ZROANG, ALLANG, SINSID, SINSID, SRTREC, TRNSFR, RADDEG, and PRTREC.

Case #3, ITYPE = 3, one side and two angles (Figs. 9-10, 9-11, and 9-17)

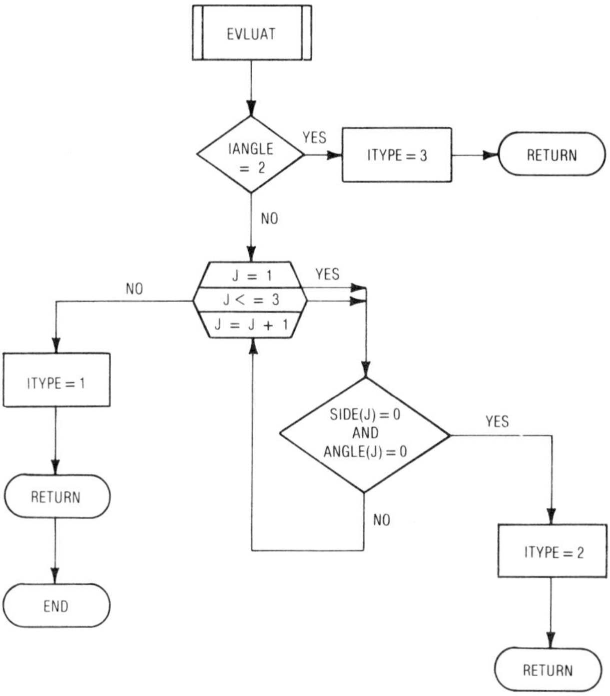

Fig. 9-14. Flowchart of subroutine EVLUAT.

uses subroutines DEGRAD, EVLUAT, ORDER, TRNSFR, ANG180, ZROANG, ALLANG, SINSID, SINSID, SRTREC, TRNSFR, TRNSFR, RADDEG, and PRTREC to process the input data and output the three sides and three angles of a triangle.

SOLVE BY:

1. LAW OF COSINES.
2. LAW OF SINES.
3. 180° RULE.

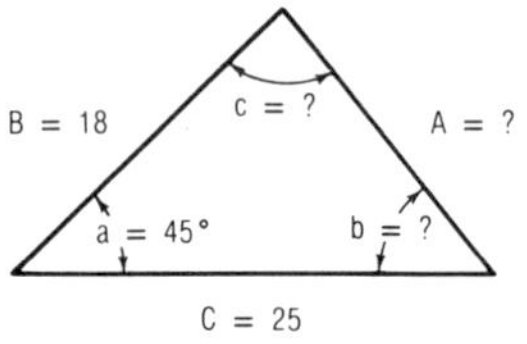

$A^2 = B^2 + C^2 - 2BC\ COS\ a$

$A^2 = 18^2 + 25^2 - 2*18*25*0.7071$

$A^2 = 949 - 636.39$

$A = 17.68$

A/SIN a = C/SIN c   17.68/0.7071 = 25/SIN c   ANGLE c = 88.96°

ANGLE b = 180 − (a + c)

ANGLE b = 180 − (45 + 88.96)

ANGLE b = 46.04°

(A) Relationship of sides and angles.

```
!---------*!---------*!---------*!---------*!---------*!---------*
      25.00      18.00        .00        .00        .00      45.00


# OF SIDES=   2    # OF ANGLES=       1


-- IN DEGRAD SUBROUTINE --
-- IN EVLUAT SUBROUTINE --
-- IN ORDER  SUBROUTINE --
-- IN COSSID SUBROUTINE --
-- IN ALLSID SUBROUTINE --
-- IN COSANG SUBROUTINE --
-- IN COSANG SUBROUTINE --
-- IN COSANG SUBROUTINE --
-- IN SRTREC SUBROUTINE --
-- IN RADDEG SUBROUTINE --

      25.00      18.00      17.68      88.96      46.04      45.00
```

(B) Printout of results for Case #1.

Fig. 9-15. Program GMETRY: Case #1, ITYPE = 1 — two sides and one included angle are input.

SOLVE BY:

1. LAW OF SINES.
2. 180° RULE.
3. LAW OF SINES

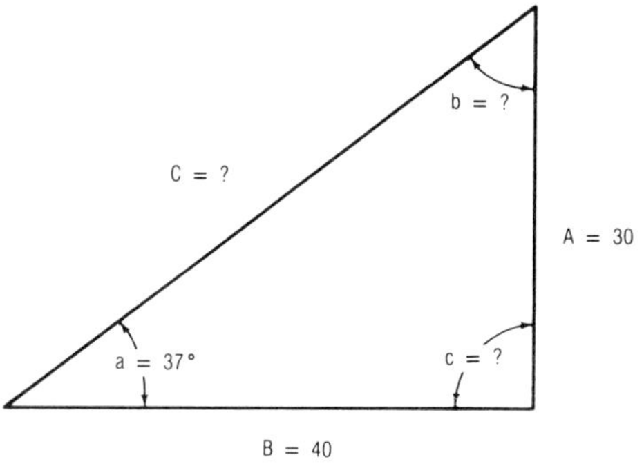

A/SIN a = B/SIN b — 30/0.6018 = 40/SIN b — SIN b = 0.8024

ANGLE b = 53.36°

ANGLE c = 180 − (a + b)
ANGLE c = 180 − (37. + 53.36)
ANGLE c = 180 − 90.36
ANGLE c = 89.64°

C/SIN c = A/SIN a — C/SIN c = 30/0.6018 — SIN c = 0.9999

SIDE c = 49.85

(A) Relationship of sides and angles.

```
!---------*!---------*!---------*!---------*!---------*!---------*
     30.00      40.00        .00      37.00        .00        .00


# OF SIDES=   2   # OF ANGLES=      1


-- IN DEGRAD SUBROUTINE --
-- IN EVLUAT SUBROUTINE --
-- IN ORDER  SUBROUTINE --
-- IN SINANG SUBROUTINE --
-- IN ANG180 SUBROUTINE --
-- IN ZROANG SUBROUTINE --
-- IN ALLANG SUBROUTINE --
-- IN SINSID SUBROUTINE --
-- IN SINSID SUBROUTINE --
-- IN SRTREC SUBROUTINE --
-- IN TRNSFR SUBROUTINE --
-- IN RADDEG SUBROUTINE --
     49.85      40.00      30.00      89.64      53.36      37.00
```

(B) Printout of results for Case #2.

Fig. 9-16. Program GMETRY: Case #2, ITYPE = 2 — two sides and one nonincluded angle are input.

SOLVE BY:

1. 180° RULE.
2. LAW OF SINES.
3. LAW OF SINES.

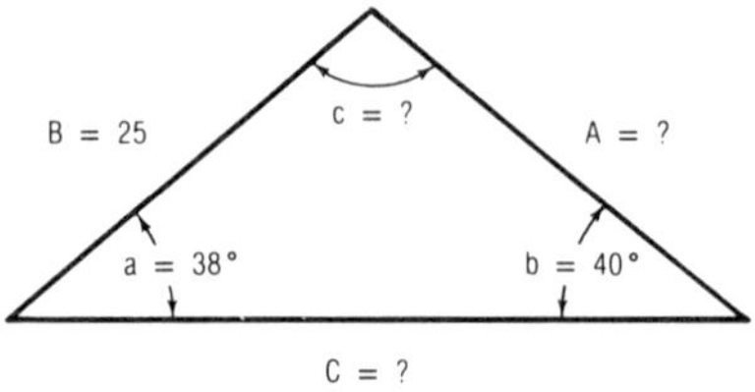

ANGLE c = 180 − (a + b)
ANGLE c = 180 − (38 + 40)
ANGLE c = 180 − 78
ANGLE c = 102°

B/SIN b = A/SIN a	25/0.6428 = A/0.6157	SIDE A = 23.94
C/SIN c = B/SIN b	C/0.9782 = 25/0.6428	SIDE C = 38.04

(A) Relationship of sides and angles.

```
!---------*!---------*!---------*!---------*!---------*!---------*
      25.00       .00        .00       40.00        .00       38.00


# OF SIDES=   1    # OF ANGLES=     2


--- IN DEGRAD SUBROUTINE --
--- IN EVLUAT SUBROUTINE --
--- IN ORDER  SUBROUTINE --
--- IN TRNSFR SUBROUTINE --
--- IN ANG180 SUBROUTINE --
--- IN ZROANG SUBROUTINE --
--- IN ALLANG SUBROUTINE --
--- IN SINSID SUBROUTINE --
--- IN SINSID SUBROUTINE --
--- IN SRTREC SUBROUTINE --
--- IN TRNSFR SUBROUTINE --
--- IN TRNSFR SUBROUTINE --
--- IN RADDEG SUBROUTINE --
      38.04      25.00      23.94     102.00      40.00       38.00
```

(B) Printout of results for Case #3.

Fig. 9-17. Program GMETRY: Case #3, ITYPE = 3 — one side and two angles are input.

Case #4 is not specifically programmed, but is a case in which the input data does not physically constitute a triangle (Fig. 9-18). The given data in Fig. 9-18 is that two of the angles of the triangle are each 90°. This condition causes two sides of the triangle to be parallel lines. The program solves the problem, but the answers are not correct solutions, since a triangle cannot contain parallel lines. Many other situations could be presented that would result in an incorrect solution. If a negative angle or angles were input, or if the side/angle relationship did not permit closure of the triangle, no solution would be possible.

SOLVE BY:

1. NO SOLUTION.

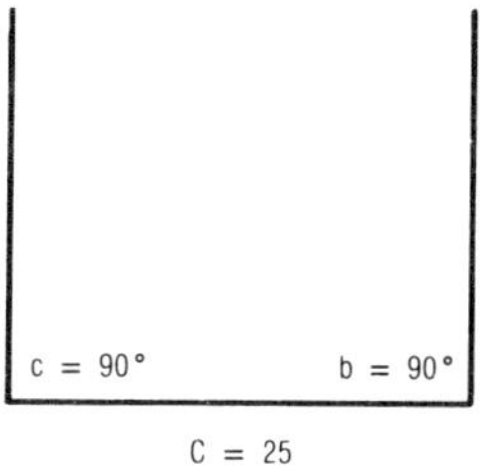

PROGRAM GOES THROUGH THE ROUTINE AND OUTPUTS THE FOLLOWING VALUES:

A = 0	a = 0°
B = 25	b = 90°
C = 25	c = 90°

(A) Relationship of sides and angles.

```
!---------*!---------*!---------*!---------*!---------*!---------*
    25.00        .00        .00      90.00        .00      90.00


# OF SIDES=    1   # OF ANGLES=      2


-- IN DEGRAD SUBROUTINE --
-- IN EVLUAT SUBROUTINE --
-- IN ORDER  SUBROUTINE --
-- IN TRNSFR SUBROUTINE --
-- IN ANG180 SUBROUTINE --
-- IN ZROANG SUBROUTINE --
-- IN ALLANG SUBROUTINE --
-- IN SINSID SUBROUTINE --
-- IN SINSID SUBROUTINE --
-- IN SRTREC SUBROUTINE --
-- IN RADDEG SUBROUTINE --

    25.00      25.00        .00      90.00      90.00        .00
```

(B) Printout of results for Case #4.

Fig. 9-18. Program GMETRY: Case #4 — one side and two 90° angles are input.

No possible solution (case #4) can also be caused when the computations of the INTRINSIC SIN or COS functions are greater than plus one (+ 1) or minus one (– 1). The sine of a positive angle 0° to 180° must be between plus one (+ 1) and minus one (– 1). The cosine of a positive angle must be between the ranges of zero (0), plus one (+ 1), and minus one (– 1). When the INTRINSIC SIN and COS functions are out of these ranges, WRITE CODE ERR #662 is produced, which causes the program to terminate. WRITE CODE ERR #662 is ARGUMENT TO ASIN OR ACOS OUT OF BOUNDS (ABS(X) .GT. 1.0).

A series of checks could be placed in the program to rule out any undesired effects.

CHAPTER 10
Function Subprograms

In mathematics, a function is a mathematical quantity whose value depends on, or varies with, the value given to one or more related quantities. The area of a circle is a function of the radius. The total interest on a savings account is a function of the interest rate, the amount of the deposit, and the time factor. The volume of a cube is a function of the side.

In programming, a function subprogram uses a mathematical or logical expression to return a single value. In Fig. 10-1, the function subprogram is of the real type. It adds two real numbers and passes the result to the main program.

Function subprograms closely follow the routine of mathematical functions by using expressions to calculate the solution to a problem. When the calculation is complete, a single value is passed in a function name from the

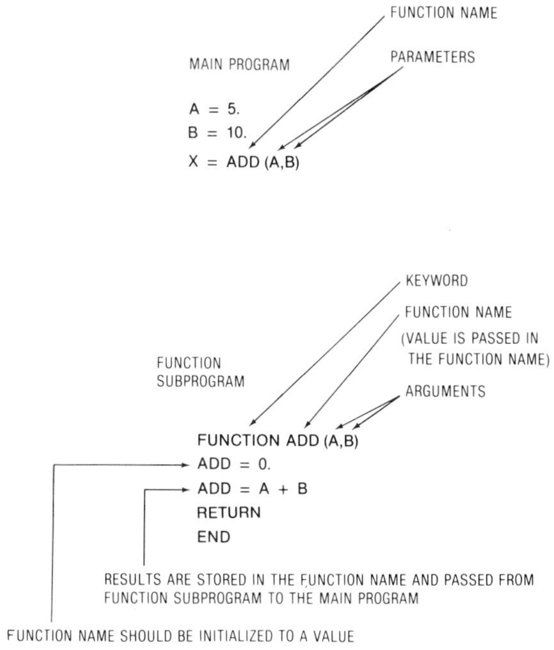

Fig. 10-1. A function subprogram must be a specific type — integer, real, or logical. This function subprogram is of the real type.

function subprogram to the function name in the main program. Fig. 10-2 shows that the parameters in the function expression in the main program are passed to the arguments in the function subprogram designator. The real values, A and B, are used in the expression, ADD = A + B, to compute the sum of the two values. After the computation is complete, the single value is assigned to the function name ADD, and the function subprogram returns the value stored in ADD to the function name ADD in the main program. The value stored in ADD in the main program is assigned to the variable X in the expression X = ADD(A,B). The function statement, X = ADD(A,B), sends the values of A and B to the function subprogram statement, and X = ADD(A,B) receives the value computed by the function subprogram. In function subprograms, the function statement in the main program is both the sending and receiving statement.

In the function subprogram, the statement, ADD = 0., initializes the function name to zero. In all computations, the memory location that holds the computation should be initialized to a specific known value before the computation is performed. If this initialization is not performed before the computation is performed, the results may be inaccurate since some unknown value may be stored in the memory location.

TYPES OF FUNCTIONS

Functions are designated as to type, and the values passed must agree as to the type of the function. In Apple FORTRAN there are three function types — integer, real, and logical.

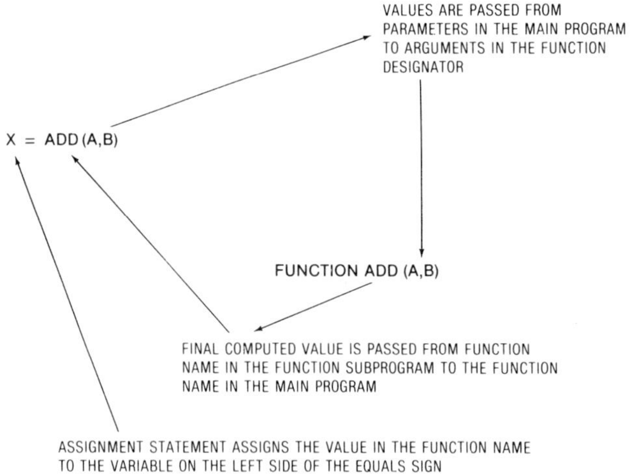

Fig. 10-2. Passing values from the main program to the function subprogram, and from the function subprogram to the main program.

Integer Function

Fig. 10-3 is an integer function to compute the factorial of the number 6. All variables and function names follow the integer rule (I–N).

Fig. 10-4 is a function subprogram written to demonstrate how the type can be changed using the type statements of external functions, INTEGER and REAL. Internal functions, IFIX and FLOAT, are used to change reals to integers and integers to reals. A second principle is demonstrated in how to overcome a deficiency of the Apple FORTRAN language: *Neither argument names nor function names can appear in COMMON, DATA, EQUIVALENCE, or INTRINSIC statements.*

```
C**** PROGRAM USING A FUNCTION TO COMPUTE
C**** THE FACTORIAL OF A NUMBER
C234567
      PROGRAM FUNCT1
      OPEN (6,FILE = 'PRINTER:' )
      NUMBER = 6
      N = IFACT(NUMBER)
      WRITE (0,20) NUMBER,N
      WRITE (6,20) NUMBER,N
   20 FORMAT (///,'THE FACTORIAL OF ',I3,
     *'    IS ',I9,///)
      STOP
      END
      FUNCTION IFACT(NUMBER)
      IFACT = 1
      DO 10 J = 1,NUMBER
      IFACT = IFACT * J
   10 CONTINUE
      RETURN
      END




 THE FACTORIAL OF   6    IS          720
```

Fig. 10-3. Program to compute the factorial of a number using an integer function subprogram.

In Fig. 10-4, the array GRADE(10) is the array name to be used in the main program and function subprogram. If GRADE is used in the DIMENSION statement as the primary array, and is the designated array in the DATA statement, the program will not compile. However, by using the array G(10) as the primary array in the DIMENSION statement and the DATA statement, the contents of G can be assigned to GRADE by using a standard DO loop, and the program will compile successfully.

```
DIMENSION G(10), GRADE(10)
DATA G(1),G(2),G(3), (etc.)
```

```
KOUNT = 10
DO 5 K = 1,KOUNT
GRADE(K) = G(K)
5 CONTINUE
```

Fig. 10-4 is a function subprogram to compute the average (mean) of a list of grades. The grades are initially stored in the array G, but are assigned to the array GRADE. The statement that references, or invokes, the function subprogram, IVAL = MEAN(GRADE,KOUNT), contains three integers, IVAL, MEAN, and KOUNT, and one real array, GRADE.

On entry into the function subprogram, the INTEGER FUNCTION MEAN(GRADE,KOUNT) statement reinforces that MEAN is an integer, and the array GRADE is not affected by the integer since it is a parameter.

Real Function

The REAL GRADE(KOUNT) statement emphasizes that at this point the

```
C**** PROGRAM TO COMPUTE THE MEAN OF A LIST
C**** OF NUMBERS - USING A FUNCTION SUBPROGRAM
C234567
      PROGRAM MEAN1
      DIMENSION G(10),GRADE(10)
      DATA G(1),G(2),G(3),G(4),G(5),G(6),
     *G(7),G(8),G(9),G(10)/90.,70.,85.,100.,100.,
     *79.,89.,95.,82.,99./
      OPEN (6,FILE = 'PRINTER:')
      KOUNT = 10
      DO 5 K = 1,KOUNT
      GRADE(K) = G(K)
    5 CONTINUE
      IVAL = MEAN(GRADE,KOUNT)
      WRITE (0,30) KOUNT, IVAL
      WRITE (6,30) KOUNT, IVAL
   30 FORMAT (///,'THE MEAN OF ',I3,4X,'GRADES
     * IS ',I8,///)
      STOP
      END
      INTEGER FUNCTION MEAN(GRADE,KOUNT)
      REAL GRADE(KOUNT)
      MEAN = 0
      SUM = 0.
      DO 10 J = 1,KOUNT
      SUM = SUM + GRADE(J)
   10 CONTINUE
      MEAN = IFIX(SUM/FLOAT(KOUNT))
      RETURN
      END

THE MEAN OF  10      GRADES IS          88
```

Fig. 10-4. Program to compute the mean of a list of numbers using a function subprogram in which the function type is changed.

array GRADE is a real type. The variable KOUNT is not affected by the real since it is a subscript.

Changing Functions from One Type to Another

The sum of the grades is computed as a real type using a standard DO loop and a summing statement. When the loop has completed execution and the real SUM is computed, the MEAN is computed.

MEAN = IFIX(SUM/FLOAT(KOUNT))

The intrinsic function FLOAT converts the integer KOUNT to a real type. The real SUM is divided by the converted real KOUNT. This produces a real value. The intrinsic function IFIX converts the real value to an integer. That integer value is assigned to the integer MEAN, and that integer value is returned to the main program to the referencing statement, IVAL = MEAN (GRADE,KOUNT). The integer value stored in MEAN is assigned to the integer variable IVAL.

Fig. 10-5 is a program written to demonstrate a logical function that determines if the three given values are the correct length to form a triangle. The statement, LOGICAL ANSWER, TEST, sets up ANSWER, the logical variable, and TEST, the logical function name.

```
C**** PROGRAM TO USE THE LOGICAL TYPE TO
C**** DETERMINE IF THREE GIVEN SIDES WILL
C**** FORM A TRIANGLE - USING A FUNCTION SUBPROGRAM
C234567
      PROGRAM LOGIC
      LOGICAL ANSWER, TEST
      OPEN (6,FILE = 'PRINTER:' )
      A = 7.
      B = 8.
      C = 12.
      ANSWER = TEST( A,B,C )
      WRITE (0,20) ANSWER
      WRITE (6,20) ANSWER
   20 FORMAT (///,'THE LOGICAL ANSWER IS: ',L3,///)
      STOP
      END
      LOGICAL FUNCTION TEST( A,B,C )
      TEST = .FALSE.
      IF (A + B .GT. C .AND.
     *B + C .GT. A .AND.
     *C + A .GT.B) TEST = .TRUE.
      RETURN
      END

 THE LOGICAL ANSWER IS:    T
```

Fig. 10-5. Program to determine if three given sides will form a triangle using a logical function subprogram.

Logical Function

The LOGICAL FUNCTION TEST(A,B,C) statement receives the three arguments, A, B, and C, the real values of the sides of the triangle. The TEST = .FALSE. statement sets up the initial logical value to FALSE. If the three given sides do not form a triangle, and the test fails, the logical value of FALSE will be returned to the invoking statement, ANSWER = TEST(A,B,C). It is preferable to set the initial value of the function name to FALSE, so if the test fails, the value of FALSE is returned to the invoking statement. For the given values to form a triangle, sides A plus B must be greater than C, AND B plus C must be greater than A, AND C plus A must be greater than B. When these three conditions are true, the logical value is set to TRUE. The function subprogram returns the logical value stored in TEST to the invoking statement in the main program, ANSWER = TEST(A,B,C). The value stored in TEST is assigned to the logical variable ANSWER. The logical ANSWER is output by using a WRITE statement.

The referencing, or invoking, statement in the main program may be either an expression or a WRITE statement.

In Fig. 10-1, the expression X = ADD(A,B) was used as the sending and receiving statement. The statement, WRITE (0,30) ADD(A,B), could also be used as the invoking statement. Fig. 10-6 shows examples of two methods to invoke a function subprogram.

SUBROUTINE SUBPROGRAMS PREFERRED OVER FUNCTION SUBPROGRAMS

In all cases, a subroutine subprogram can be used instead of a function subprogram, and subroutines are more frequently used than functions.

Fig. 10-1:	1. X = ADD(A,B) 2. WRITE (0,30) ADD(A,B)	FUNCTION ADD(A,B)
Fig. 10-3:	1. N = IFACT(NUMBER) 2. WRITE (0,50) IFACT(NUMBER)	FUNCTION IFACT(NUMBER)
Fig. 10-4:	1. IVAL = MEAN(GRADE,KOUNT) 2. WRITE (0,60) MEAN(GRADE,KOUNT)	INTEGER FUNCTION MEAN(GRADE,KOUNT)
Fig. 10-5:	1. ANSWER = TEST(A,B,C) 2. WRITE (0,100) TEST(A,B,C)	LOGICAL FUNCTION TEST(A,B,C)

Fig. 10-6. Methods to invoke or reference a function subprogram.

DIFFERENCES BETWEEN SUBROUTINE AND FUNCTION SUBPROGRAMS

The major differences between a function subprogram and a subroutine are: (1) a function is referenced or invoked, while a subroutine is called; (2) a function can return only one value, while a subroutine can return several values; and (3) a function uses the invoking statement as both the sending and receiving statement, while the subroutine uses the CALL statement as the sending statement, and the statement immediately below the CALL is used as the receiving statement.

CHAPTER 11
Internal Functions

Internal functions are functions built into the Apple FORTRAN language. External functions are functions developed by the programmer.

The internal functions are referenced, or invoked, by using the function name and the correct arguments within the function. Most of the functions are specific for type — integer or real.

CATEGORIES OF INTERNAL FUNCTIONS

The internal functions are divided into categories — (1) intrinsic functions and (2) transcendental functions.

Intrinsic Functions

A definition of intrinsic is that it belongs to a thing by its very nature — essential, inherent. In Apple FORTRAN, the intrinsic functions convert one type to another, select the minimum or maximum from a list, or produce remainder values. The intrinsic functions are nonmathematical functions, with the exception of the square root function, SQRT.

Transcendental Functions

A mathematical definition of transcendental is that the operation cannot be produced by algebraic operations of addition, subtraction, multiplication, division, and the extraction of roots, each repeated only a finite number of times.

The transcendental functions in Apple FORTRAN are exponential, common and natural logarithm, trigonometric, and hyperbolic. Trigonometric functions deal with functions of a circle, while hyperbolic functions deal with a hyperbola.

ACTIONS OF INTRINSIC FUNCTIONS

Most of the intrinsic functions are straightforward in their actions. ICHAR and CHAR need some explanation because the program must contain statements not required to process the other functions.

ICHAR converts alphabetic, numeric, and special characters to the ASCII integer value (Table 1-1).

```
      CHARACTER*1 Z
      DATA Z /'Z'/
      I = ICHAR(Z)
      WRITE (0,20) I,Z
   20 FORMAT (/,15,'IS = ',A1,/ )
      STOP
      END
```

When executed, this program outputs

```
90 IS = Z
```

CHAR takes the ASCII integer value and converts it into an alphabetic character.

```
      INTEGER C
      CHARACTER*1 Z
      DATA Z /'Z'/
      C = 90
      Z = CHAR(C)
      WRITE (0,30) Z,C
   30 FORMAT (/,A1,'IS = ',I3,/)
      STOP
      END
```

When executed, this program outputs

```
Z IS = 90
```

ASCII integer values of numeric characters are determined by using a similar program.

```
      CHARACTER Z
      DATA Z /'0'/
      N = ICHAR(Z)
      WRITE (0,20) N,Z
   20 FORMAT (I5,3X,A1)
      STOP
      END
```

When executed, this program outputs

```
48 0
```

Finally, the ASCII integer value of special characters is found by placing the special character in the DATA statement.

```
      CHARACTER Z
      DATA Z /'%'/
      N = ICHAR(Z)
      WRITE (0,20) N,Z
   20 FORMAT (I5,3X,A1)
      STOP
      END
```

When executed, this program outputs

```
37 %
```

Fig. 11-1 is a program to demonstrate the internal functions in Apple

FORTRAN. Fig. 11-2 contains an execution of the program in Fig. 11-1. In Fig. 11-2, the program statement that produced the line of execution is printed below each output statement. Fig. 11-1 can be referenced for variables and FORMAT statements for better understanding of the internal functions in Apple FORTRAN.

```
C**** PROGRAM TO DEMONSTRATE THE INTERNAL
C**** FUNCTIONS IN APPLE FORTRAN
C
C234567
C::::VARIABLES USED IN THE PROGRAM
C
      CHARACTER*1 CH1
      CHARACTER*1 Z
      DATA Z/'Z'/
      A = 9.
      ANG = 30.
      B = 9.237
      C = 12.
      CO2 = .8660
      D = -13.2
      E = 79.
      F = 12.345
      I = 6
      J = 8
      K = -12
      L = 9
      M = 4
      PI = 3.1416
      R1 = 4.0
      R2 = 3.0
      S = 0.5
      TA1 = .57735
C
C:::: FORMAT STATEMENTS
C
   10 FORMAT (/,'THE INTEGER VALUE IS: ',I3,' AND
     *WAS CONVERTED FROM THE REAL: ',F3.0,//)
   20 FORMAT ('THE REAL VALUE IS: ',F3.0,' AND
     *WAS CONVERTED FROM THE INTEGER: 'I3,///)
   30 FORMAT ('THE VALUE OF "Z" IS: ',I5,
     *' AND THE CHARACTER IS: ',A2,///)
   40 FORMAT ('THE NUMBER: ',F9.3,' WAS TRUNCATED
     *FROM: ',F9.3,///)
   50 FORMAT ('THE NEAREST INTEGER IS: ',I3,' FROM
     *THE REAL: ',F9.3,///)
   60 FORMAT ('THE ABSOLUTE VALUE OF THE INTEGER: ',I5,
     *' IS',I5,///)
   70 FORMAT ('THE ABSOLUTE VALUE OF THE REAL: ',F8.1,
     *' IS:',F8.1,///)
   80 FORMAT ('THE REMAINDER IS: ',I5,' WHEN: ',I5,
     *' IS DIVIDED BY: ',I5,///)
   90 FORMAT ('THE REMAINDER IS: ',F9.3,' WHEN: ',F5.0,
     *' IS DIVIDED BY: ',F5.0,///)
  100 FORMAT ('THE TRANSFERRED SIGN: ',I5,' FROM: ',I5,
     *' TO: ',I5,///)
  110 FORMAT ('THE TRANSFERRED SIGN: ',F7.3,' FROM: ',
     *F7.3,' TO:',F7.3,///)
  120 FORMAT ('THE POSITIVE DIFFERENCE BETWEEN: ',
     *I5,' AND:',I5,' IS:',I5,///)
  130 FORMAT ('THE POSITIVE DIFFERENCE BETWEEN: ',
     *F5.0,' AND:',F5.0,' IS:',F5.0,///)
```

Fig. 11-1. Program to demonstrate the internal functions in Apple FORTRAN.

```
 135 FORMAT ('IF THE DIFFERENCE IS NEGATIVE
    *THE RESULT IS ZERO (0)',///)
 140 FORMAT (I5,' IS THE LARGEST INTEGER IN A LIST OF
    *INTEGERS',///)
 150 FORMAT (I5,' IS THE GREATEST CONVERTED INTEGER
    *IN A LIST OF REALS',///)
 160 FORMAT (F7.3,' IS THE LARGEST REAL IN A LIST
    * OF REALS',///)
 170 FORMAT (F7.3,' IS THE LARGEST CONVERTED
    *REAL IN A LIST OF INTEGERS',///)
 180 FORMAT (I5,' IS THE SMALLEST INTEGER IN A LIST
    *OF INTEGERS',///)
 190 FORMAT (I5,' IS THE SMALLEST CONVERTED INTEGER
    *IN A LIST OF REALS',///)
 200 FORMAT (F7.2,' IS THE SMALLEST REAL IN A LIST
    *OF REALS',///)
 210 FORMAT (F7.3,' IS THE SMALLEST CONVERTED REAL
    *IN A LIST OF INTEGERS',///)
 220 FORMAT ('THE SQUARE ROOT OF: ',F7.3,2X,' IS:',F10.5,///)
 230 FORMAT ('THE EXPONENT OF: 'F10.2,2X,'IS:',E10.2,///)
 240 FORMAT ('THE NATURAL LOGARITHM OF: ',F10.5,2X,'IS:',
    *F10.5,///)
 250 FORMAT ('THE COMMON LOGARITHM OF: ',F10.5,2X,'IS:',
    *F10.5,///)
 260 FORMAT (F10.5,' IS THE SINE OF: 'F5.0,' DEGREES',
    *' AND:',F10.5,' RADIANS',///)
 270 FORMAT (F10.5,' IS THE COSINE OF: ',F5.0,' DEGREES
    *AND: ',F10.5,' RADIANS',///)
 280 FORMAT (F10.5,' IS THE TANGENT OF: ',F5.0,' DEGREES
    *AND: ',F10.5,' RADIANS',///)
 290 FORMAT ('THE ARCSINE OF: ',F8.6,3X,' IS:',F5.0,
    *2X,'DEGREES',///)
 300 FORMAT ('THE ARCCOSINE OF: ',F8.6,2X,' IS:',F5.0,
    *2X,'DEGREES',///)
 310 FORMAT ('THE ARCTAN OF: ',F8.6,2X,' IS:',F5.0,
    *2X,'DEGREES',///)
 320 FORMAT ('SIDE: ',F3.0,2X,'AND SIDE: ',2X,F3.0,
    *2X,'PRODUCE AN ANGLE OF: ',F7.2,2X,'DEGREES',///)
 330 FORMAT (F10.6,' IS THE HYPERBOLIC SINE OF: ',F5.0,
    *'DEGREES',///)
 340 FORMAT (F10.6,' IS THE HYPERBOLIC COSINE OF: ',F5.0,
    *' DEGREES',///)
 350 FORMAT (F10.6,' IS THE HYPERBOLIC TANGENT OF: ',
    *F5.0,' DEGREES',///)
C
C::::::INTRINSIC FUNCTIONS
C
C234567
      OPEN (6,FILE='PRINTER:')
      IR = INT(A)
      IR1 = INT(C)
      WRITE (6,10) IR, A
      WRITE (6,10) IR1,C
      RI = REAL(I)
      RI1 = REAL(J)
      WRITE (6,20) RI,I
      WRITE (6,20) RI1,J
      IH5 = ICHAR(Z)
      CH1 = CHAR(90)
      WRITE (6,30) IH5,CH1
      TR = AINT(B)
      WRITE (6,40) TR,B
      TR1 = ANINT(B)
      WRITE (6,40) TR1,B
```

Fig. 11-1. Program to demonstrate the

```
      IN1 = NINT(B)
      WRITE (6,50) IN1,B
C
C::::::THE ABSOLUTE VALUE IS ALWAYS NON-NEGATIVE
C
C234567
      IV = IABS(K)
      RV = ABS(D)
      WRITE (6,60) K,IV
      WRITE (6,70) D,RV
      IM = MOD(L,M)
      RM = AMOD(E,A)
      WRITE (6,80) IM,L,M
      WRITE (6,90) RM,E,A
      IS = ISIGN(J,K)
      RS = SIGN(C,D)
      WRITE (6,100) IS,K,J
      WRITE (6,110) RS,D,C
      ID = IDIM(J,M)
      RD = DIM(E,A)
      WRITE (6,120) J,M,ID
      WRITE (6,130) E,A,RD
      WRITE (6,135)
      IM = MAX0(I,J,K)
      WRITE (6,140) IM
      IM1 = MAX1(A,B,C)
      WRITE (6,150) IM1
      RA = AMAX1(A,B,C)
      WRITE (6,160) RA
      RA1 = AMAX0(I,J,K)
      WRITE (6,170) RA1
      IM2 = MIN0(K,L,M)
      WRITE (6,180) IM2
      IM3 = MIN1(C,D,E)
      WRITE (6,190) IM3
      RA2 = AMIN1(C,D,E)
      WRITE (6,200) RA2
      RA3 = AMIN0(I,J,K)
      WRITE (6,210) RA3
      S1 = SQRT(B)
      WRITE (6,220) B,S1
C
C**** TRANSCENDENTAL FUNCTIONS
C       1.  RETURN REAL RESULTS
C       2.  DEGREES ARE INPUT - CONVERTED
C           TO RADIANS
C       3.  RADIANS ARE CONVERTED TO DEGREES
C           AND OUTPUT AS DEGREES
C
C234567
      EX = EXP(F)
      WRITE (6,230) F,EX
      AL = ALOG(C)
      WRITE (6,240) C,AL
      AL1 = ALOG10(C)
      WRITE (6,250) C,AL1
      RAD = ANG*(PI/180)
      SI = SIN(RAD)
      WRITE (6,260) SI,ANG,RAD
      CO = COS(RAD)
      WRITE (6,270)CO,ANG,RAD
      TA = TAN(RAD)
      WRITE (6,280) TA,ANG,RAD
      SI1 = ASIN(S)
```

internal functions in Apple FORTRAN. *(Continued)*

```
      ANG1 = SI1*(180/PI)
      WRITE (6,290) SI1,ANG1
      AC = ACOS(CO2)
      ANG2 = AC*(180/PI)
      WRITE (6,300) AC,ANG2
      AT1 = ATAN(TA1)
      AT2 = AT1*(180/PI)
      WRITE (6,310) AT1,AT2
      ATAN1 = ATAN2(R1,R2)
      ATAN4 = ATAN1*(180/PI)
      WRITE (6,320) R1,R2,ATAN4
C
C**** HYPERBOLIC FUNCTIONS
C      THERE ARE SIX HYPERBOLIC FUNCTIONS
C      (THREE IN APPLE FORTRAN) THAT ARE
C      RELATED TO THE HYPERBOLA IN A MANNER
C      ANALOGOUS TO THE RELATIONSHIP OF
C      TRIGONOMETRIC FUNCTIONS TO THE CIRCLE.
C
C234567
      HS = SINH(RAD)
      HS1 = HS*(180/PI)
      WRITE (6,330) HS1,ANG
      HC = COSH(RAD)
      HC1 = HC*(180/PI)
      WRITE (6,340) HC1,ANG
      HT = TANH(RAD)
      HT1 = HT*(180/PI)
      WRITE (6,350) HT1,ANG
      STOP
      END
```

Fig. 11-1. Program to demonstrate the internal functions in Apple FORTRAN. *(Continued)*

```
THE INTEGER VALUE IS:   9 AND WAS CONVERTED FROM THE REAL:  9.
 IR = INT(A)

THE INTEGER VALUE IS:  12 AND WAS CONVERTED FROM THE REAL: 12.
 IR1 = INT(C)
THE REAL VALUE IS:  6. AND WAS CONVERTED FROM THE INTEGER:    6
 RI = REAL(I)

THE REAL VALUE IS:  8. AND WAS CONVERTED FROM THE INTEGER:    8
 RI1 = REAL(J)

THE VALUE OF "Z" IS:    90 AND THE CHARACTER IS:  Z
 IH5 = ICHAR(Z)                        CH1 = CHAR(90)

THE NUMBER:     9.000 WAS TRUNCATED FROM:     9.237
 TR = AINT(B)

THE NUMBER:     9.000 WAS TRUNCATED FROM:     9.237
 TR1 = ANINT(B)

THE NEAREST INTEGER IS:   9 FROM THE REAL:     9.237
 IN1 = NINT(B)
```

Fig. 11-2. Execution of

```
THE ABSOLUTE VALUE OF THE INTEGER:   -12 IS   12
 IV = IABS(K)

THE ABSOLUTE VALUE OF THE REAL:    -13.2 IS:    13.2
 RV = ABS(D)

THE REMAINDER IS:     1 WHEN:     9 IS DIVIDED BY:     4
 IM = MOD(L,M)

THE REMAINDER IS:     7.000 WHEN:   79. IS DIVIDED BY:    9.
 RM = AMOD(E,A)

THE TRANSFERRED SIGN:    -8 FROM:   -12 TO:     8
 IS = ISIGN(J,K)

THE TRANSFERRED SIGN: -12.000 FROM: -13.200 TO: 12.000
 RS = SIGN(C,D)

THE POSITIVE DIFFERENCE BETWEEN:     8 AND:    4 IS:    4
 ID = IDIM(J,M)

THE POSITIVE DIFFERENCE BETWEEN:   79. AND:   9. IS:  70.
 RD =  DIM(E,A)

IF THE DIFFERENCE IS NEGATIVE THE RESULT IS ZERO ( 0 )
 RD =  DIM (A,E)

    8 IS THE LARGEST INTEGER IN A LIST OF INTEGERS
 IM =  MAX0(I,J,K)  0 = ZERO

   12 IS THE GREATEST CONVERTED INTEGER IN A LIST OF REALS
 IM1 = MAX1 (A,B,C)

 12.000 IS THE LARGEST REAL IN A LIST  OF REALS
 RA  = AMAX1 (A,B,C)

  8.000 IS THE LARGEST CONVERTED REAL IN A LIST OF INTEGERS
 RA1 = AMAX0 (I,J,K)  0 = ZERO

  -12 IS THE SMALLEST INTEGER IN A LIST  OF INTEGERS
 IM2 = MIN0 (K,L,M)  0 = ZERO

  -13 IS THE SMALLEST CONVERTED INTEGER IN A LIST OF REALS
 IM3 = MIN1 (C,D,E)

 -13.20 IS THE SMALLEST REAL IN A LIST OF REALS
 RA2 = AMIN1 (C,D,E)
```

the program in Fig. 11-1.

```
-12.000 IS THE SMALLEST CONVERTED REAL IN A LIST OF INTEGERS
 RA3 = AMINO (I,J,K)  0 = ZERO

THE SQUARE ROOT OF:    9.237    IS:    3.03924
 S1 = SQRT (B)

THE EXPONENT OF:        12.34  IS:    .23E+06
 EX = EXP (F)

THE NATURAL LOGARITHM OF:    12.00000  IS:    2.48491
 AL = ALOG (C)

THE COMMON LOGARITHM OF:    12.00000  IS:    1.07918
 AL1 = ALOG10 (C)

    .50000 IS THE SINE OF:    30. DEGREES AND:     .52360 RADIANS
 SI = SIN (RAD)    RAD = ANG*(PI/180)  ANG = 30.

    .86602 IS THE COSINE OF:    30. DEGREES AND:      .52360 RADIANS
 CO = COS (RAD)    RAD = ANG*(PI/180)   ANG = 30.

    .57735 IS THE TANGENT OF:    30. DEGREES AND:      .52360 RADIANS
 TA = TAN (RAD)    RAD = ANG*(PI/180)   ANG = 30.


THE ARCSINE OF:  .523599     IS:  30.   DEGREES
 SI1 = ASIN(S)    S = .5    ANG1 = SI1*(180/PI)

THE ARCCOSINE OF:   .523650    IS:  30.   DEGREES
 AC = ACOS(CO2)    CO2 = .8660    ANG2 = AC*(180/PI)

THE ARCTAN OF:  .523599    IS:  30.   DEGREES
 AT1 = ATAN(TA1)   TA1 = .57735    AT2 = AT1*(180/PI)

SIDE:  4.   AND SIDE:     3.   PRODUCE AN ANGLE OF:    53.13   DEGREES
 ATAN1 = ATAN2(R1,R2)    ATAN4 = ATAN1*(180/PI)

 31.389700 IS THE HYPERBOLIC SINE OF:    30.DEGREES
 HS = SINH(RAD)   RAD = .52359    HS1 = HS*(180/PI)

 65.330700 IS THE HYPERBOLIC COSINE OF:   30. DEGREES
 HC = COSH(RAD)   RAD = .52359    HC1 = HC*(180/PI)

 27.529100 IS THE HYPERBOLIC TANGENT OF:   30. DEGREES
 HT = TANH(RAD)   RAD = .52359    HT1 = HT*(180/PI)
```

Fig. 11-2. Execution of the program in Fig. 11-1. *(Continued)*

CHAPTER 12
BLOCK IF

The BLOCK IF and companion statements are new to FORTRAN 77, and are an adaptation from the Pascal language structure. They were designed to produce a specific structure to programming, and increase the efficiency of writing correct programs. Experts estimate that approximately 50% of a programmer's time is spent debugging programs. The structured approach reduces the number of errors built into the program, and reduces debugging time.

STRUCTURED PROGRAMMING

Structured programming techniques are reported to have produced four beneficial effects for the professional programmer. Those benefits are (1) a reduction in the number of logic errors, (2) an improvement in the readability and comprehension of programs, (3) a reduction in program maintenance and updating time, and (4) an increase in programmer productivity.

The structured program consists of blocks of program statements that are executed when the initial block statement is true. This is a departure from the normal logic. Normal logic causes the program to branch when the decision statement is true (or one thing is done). When the statement is false, the program defaults to the statement below the decision statement. In structured programming the opposite happens. When the BLOCK IF is true, the statements immediately below the BLOCK IF are executed. When the BLOCK IF is false, the program continues execution with the first statement following the end of the block.

Structured programming can build large complex blocks of program statements from the basic building blocks. The advantage of the BLOCK IF is that the true statements act as one statement from the IF (expression) THEN to the ENDIF statement. The disadvantage is that in large complex blocks, the program logic can be difficult to follow.

The programs in Figs. 12-1 through 12-8 were written to demonstrate the simplest structures using all options available with the BLOCK IF. A FORTRAN program was written to show how the program would look without using the BLOCK IF structure. The BLOCK IF programs are Figs. 12-1, 12-3, 12-5, and 12-7. The non–BLOCK IF programs are Figs. 12-2, 12-4, 12-6, and 12-8.

In all programs the input is read from the keyboard, so the program can be followed to determine the execution sequence when the IF (expression) THEN is true, and when it is false. Each program terminates when the A input is zero (0).

BLOCK IF STRUCTURE

The simplest BLOCK IF structure is Fig. 12-1, and its corollary program is in Fig. 12-2.

```
IF (A .LT. B) THEN
   C = C/D
   B = B + C
   WRITE (0,10) (true condition)
   ENDIF
   GOTO 5
```

```
 C**** ENDIF EXPLAINER (KNOWN AS THE BLOCK IF
C**** STATEMENT)
C234567
        PROGRAM BLOCKS
        OPEN (6,FILE='PRINTER:')
      5 WRITE (0,200)
        WRITE (6,200)
        READ (0,100)A,B,C,D
        IF (A.EQ.0) GOTO999
        WRITE (6,100)A,B,C,D
C****   !!!
        IF (A.LT.B) THEN
           C=C/D
           B=B+C
           WRITE (0,10)
           WRITE (6,10)
           ENDIF
C****   !!!
        WRITE (0,100)A,B,C,D
        WRITE (6,100)A,B,C,D
        GOTO 5
    999 STOP
     10 FORMAT (/,'TRUE CONDITION -- ')
    100 FORMAT(4(F5.2))
    200 FORMAT (2X,'A',4X,'B',4X,'C',
       *4X,'D',/,4('!---*'))
        END



   A     B     C     D
!---*!---*!---*!---*
12.3010.0015.2080.00
12.3010.0015.2080.00
   A     B     C     D
!---*!---*!---*!---*
10.0012.5020.00 5.00

TRUE CONDITION --
10.0016.50 4.00 5.00
   A     B     C     D
!---*!---*!---*!---*
```

Fig. 12-1. Program to demonstrate the basic BLOCK IF structure (program execution shown below program).

```
C**** PROGRAM EQUIVALENT TO THE IF-BLOCK
C**** PROGRAM USING TRANSFER OF CONTROL
C**** STATEMENTS RATHER THAN BLOCK
C**** STRUCTURES.
C234567
      PROGRAM BLOCKS
      OPEN (6,FILE='PRINTER:')
    5 WRITE (0,200)
      WRITE (6,200)
      READ (0,100)A,B,C,D
      IF (A.EQ.0) GOTO999
      WRITE (6,100)A,B,C,D
C**** !!!
      IF (A.LT.B) GOTO 500
      GOTO 600
  500    C=C/D
         B=B+C
         WRITE (0,10)
         WRITE (6,10)
C**** !!!
  600 WRITE (0,100)A,B,C,D
      WRITE (6,100)A,B,C,D
      GOTO 5
  999 STOP
   10 FORMAT (/,'TRUE CONDITION -- ')
  100 FORMAT(4(F5.2))
  200 FORMAT (2X,'A',4X,'B',4X,'C',
     *4X,'D',/,4('!---*'))
      END


  A    B    C    D
!---*!---*!---*!---*
12.3010.0015.2080.00
12.3010.0015.2080.00
  A    B    C    D
!---*!---*!---*!---*
10.0012.3020.00 5.00

TRUE CONDITION --
10.0016.30 4.00 5.00
  A    B    C    D
!---*!---*!---*!---*
```

Fig. 12-2. FORTRAN equivalent to the program of Fig. 12-1 (program execution shown below program).

IF (A .LT. B) THEN is the beginning decision statement in the block. If A is less than B, the statements below IF (A .LT. B) THEN are executed. When IF (A .LT. B) THEN is true, the program is structured so that TRUE CONDITION is printed out with the data (A, B, C, and D). When IF (A .LT. B) THEN is false, the program branches to the statement immediately below the ENDIF statement. In this case, the statement is GOTO 5, to allow the user to input more data.

NESTED BLOCK IF'S

Fig. 12-3 is a BLOCK IF program with nested blocks.

```
IF (A .LT. B) THEN
   C = C/D
```

```
C**** ENDIF EXPLAINER (KNOWN AS THE BLOCK IF
C**** STATEMENT WITH A MULTIPLE BLOCK
C**** STRUCTURE)
C234567
      PROGRAM BLOCKS
      OPEN(6,FILE='PRINTER:')
    5 WRITE (0,200)
      WRITE (6,200)
      READ (0,100)A,B,C,D
      IF (A.EQ.0) GOTO999
      WRITE (6,100)A,B,C,D
C**** !!!
      IF (A.LT.B) THEN
         C=C/D
         WRITE (0,110)
         WRITE (6,110)
         WRITE (0,100)A,B,C,D
         WRITE (6,100)A,B,C,D
         IF (D.GT.B)THEN
            WRITE (0,120)
            WRITE (6,120)
            B=B+C
            D=D-B
            WRITE (0,100)A,B,C,D
            WRITE (6,100)A,B,C,D
            ENDIF
         ENDIF
C**** !!!
      GOTO 5
  999 STOP
  100 FORMAT(4(F5.2))
  110 FORMAT ('CONDITION # 1 IS TRUE')
  120 FORMAT ('CONDITION # 2 IS TRUE')
  200 FORMAT (2X,'A',4X,'B',4X,'C',
     *4X,'D',/,4('!---*'))
      END

  A     B     C     D
!---*!---*!---*!---*
12.3010.0020.00 5.00
  A     B     C     D
!---*!---*!---*!---*
10.0012.3020.00 5.00
CONDITION # 1 IS TRUE
10.0012.30 4.00 5.00
  A     B     C     D
!---*!---*!---*!---*
10.0012.3020.0015.00
CONDITION # 1 IS TRUE
10.0012.30 1.3315.00
CONDITION # 2 IS TRUE
10.0013.63 1.33 1.37
  A     B     C     D
!---*!---*!---*!---*
```

Fig. 12-3. Program to demonstrate the BLOCK IF with nested blocks (program execution shown below program).

```
   WRITE (0,110) (condition #1 is true)
   WRITE (0,100) A,B,C,D
IF (D .GT. B) THEN
   WRITE (0,120) (condition #2 is true)
   B = B + C
   D = D - B
   WRITE (0,100)A,B,C,D
```

```
    ENDIF
ENDIF
GOTO 5
```

When IF (A .LT. B) THEN is true, all statements below the initial block statement are executed until the IF (D .GT. B) THEN is reached. When IF (D .GT. B) THEN is true, the statements that follow are executed through ENDIF, and GOTO 5 causes the program to jump to the statement whose label number is five (5).

```
C**** PROGRAM EQUIVALENT TO ENDIF EXPLAINER
C**** (KNOWN AS THE BLOCK IF STATEMENT WITH
C**** A MULTIPLE BLOCK STRUCTURE)
C234567
      PROGRAM BLOCKS
      OPEN(6,FILE='PRINTER:')
    5 WRITE (0,200)
      WRITE (6,200)
      READ (0,100)A,B,C,D
      IF (A.EQ.0) GOTO999
      WRITE (6,100)A,B,C,D
C**** !!!
      IF (A.LT.B) GOTO 500
         GOTO 600
  500    C=C/D
         WRITE (0,110)
         WRITE (6,110)
         WRITE (0,100)A,B,C,D
         WRITE (6,100)A,B,C,D
         IF (D.GT.B)GOTO 700
            GOTO 600
  700       WRITE (0,120)
            WRITE (6,120)
            B=B+C
            D=D-B
            WRITE (0,100)A,B,C,D
            WRITE (6,100)A,B,C,D
C**** !!!
  600 GOTO 5
  999 STOP
  100 FORMAT(4(F5.2))
  110 FORMAT ('CONDITION # 1 IS TRUE')
  120 FORMAT ('CONDITION # 2 IS TRUE')
  200 FORMAT (2X,'A',4X,'B',4X,'C',
     *4X,'D',/,4('!----*'))
      END

  A    B    C    D
!----*!----*!----*!----*
10.0012.3020.00 5.00
CONDITION # 1 IS TRUE
10.0012.30 4.00 5.00
  A    B    C    D
!----*!----*!----*!----*
10.0012.3020.0015.00
CONDITION # 1 IS TRUE
10.0012.30 1.3315.00
CONDITION # 2 IS TRUE
10.0013.63 1.33 1.37
  A    B    C    D
!----*!----*!----*!----*
```

Fig. 12-4. FORTRAN equivalent to the program of Fig. 12-3 (program execution shown below program).

When IF(A .LT. B) THEN is false, the program branches to the statement below the ENDIF. GOTO 5 causes the program to jump to the statement whose label is five (5).

IF — THEN — ELSE

The next level of block statements is IF (expression) THEN, ELSE, and ENDIF (Fig. 12-5).

```
C**** IF THEN/ELSE EXPLAINER (KNOWN AS THE
C**** BLOCK IF STATEMENT WITH FALSE CONDITION
C**** DEFAULTS)
C234567
      PROGRAM BLOCKS
      OPEN (6,FILE='PRINTER:')
    5 WRITE (0,200)
      WRITE (6,200)
      READ (0,100)A,B,C,D
      IF (A.EQ.0) GOTO999
      WRITE (6,100)A,B,C,D
C**** !!!
      IF (A.LT.B) THEN
         WRITE (0,110)
         WRITE (6,110)
         C=C/D
         B=B+C
            ELSE
         WRITE (0,120)
         WRITE (6,120)
         A=A+D
         C=B/D
         ENDIF
         WRITE(0,100)A,B,C,D
         WRITE(6,100)A,B,C,D
C**** !!!
      GOTO 5
  999 STOP
  100 FORMAT(4(F5.2))
  110 FORMAT('THE CONDITION IS TRUE')
  120 FORMAT('THE CONDITION IS FALSE')
  200 FORMAT (2X,'A',4X,'B',4X,'C',
     *4X,'D',/,4('!----*'))
      END


  A    B    C    D
!----*!----*!----*!----*
10.0012.3020.00 5.00
THE CONDITION IS TRUE
10.0016.30 4.00 5.00
  A    B    C    D
!----*!----*!----*!----*
12.3010.0020.00 5.00
THE CONDITION IS FALSE
17.3010.00 2.00 5.00
  A    B    C    D
!----*!----*!----*!----*
```

Fig. 12-5. Program to demonstrate the BLOCK IF with false condition defaults (program execution shown below program).

```
IF A .LT. B) THEN
   WRITE (0,110) (the condition is true)
   C = C/D
   D = B + C
         ELSE
   WRITE (0,120) (the condition is false)
   A = A + D
   C = B/D
   ENDIF
GOTO 5
```

When IF (A .LT. B) THEN is true, the statements following IF (A .LT. B)

```
&C**** EQUIVALENT PROGRAM TO THE IF THEN/ELSE EXPLAINER
C**** (KNOWN AS THE BLOCK IF STATEMENT WITH FALSE
C**** CONDITION DEFAULTS USING GOTO'S )
C234567
      PROGRAM BLOCKS
      OPEN (6,FILE='PRINTER:')
    5 WRITE (0,200)
      WRITE (6,200)
      READ (0,100)A,B,C,D
      IF (A.EQ.0) GOTO999
      WRITE (6,100)A,B,C,D
C**** !!!
      IF (A.LT.B) GOTO 500
         GOTO 600
  500    WRITE (0,110)
         WRITE (6,110)
         C=C/D
         B=B+C
         GOTO 700
  600    WRITE (0,120)
         WRITE (6,120)
         A=A+D
         C=B/D
  700    WRITE(0,100)A,B,C,D
         WRITE(6,100)A,B,C,D
C**** !!!
      GOTO 5
  999 STOP
  100 FORMAT(4(F5.2))
  110 FORMAT('THE CONDITION IS TRUE')
  120 FORMAT('THE CONDITION IS FALSE')
  200 FORMAT (2X,'A',4X,'B',4X,'C',
     *4X,'D',/,4('!---*'))
      END


  A    B    C    D
!---*!---*!---*!---*
10.0012.3020.00 5.00
THE CONDITION IS TRUE
10.0016.30 4.00 5.00
  A    B    C    D
!---*!---*!---*!---*
12.3010.0020.00 5.00
THE CONDITION IS FALSE
17.3010.00 2.00 5.00
  A    B    C    D
!---*!---*!---*!---*
```

Fig. 12-6. FORTRAN equivalent to the program of Fig. 12-5 (program execution shown below program).

```
C**** IF THEN/ELSE EXPLAINER (KNOWN AS THE
C**** BLOCK IF STATEMENT WITH A QUALIFIED
C**** FALSE CONDITION )
C234567
      PROGRAM BLOCKS
      OPEN (6,FILE='PRINTER:')
    5 WRITE (0,200)
      WRITE (6,200)
      READ (0,100)A,B,C,D
      IF (A.EQ.0) GOTO999
      WRITE (6,100)A,B,C,D
C**** !!!
      IF (A.LT.B) THEN
          WRITE (0,110)
          WRITE (6,110)
          C=C/D
          B=B+C
          ELSEIF (A+B.GT.C+D) THEN
              WRITE (0,120)
              WRITE (6,120)
              A=A+D
              C=B/D
          ENDIF
          WRITE(0,100)A,B,C,D
          WRITE(6,100)A,B,C,D
C**** !!!
      GOTO 5
  999 STOP
  100 FORMAT(4(F5.2))
  110 FORMAT('IF TEST IS TRUE')
  120 FORMAT('ELSEIF TEST IS TRUE')
  200 FORMAT (2X,'A',4X,'B',4X,'C',
     *4X,'D',/,4('!---*'),/)
      END
  A    B    C    D
!---*!---*!---*!---*

10.0012.3025.0020.00
IF TEST IS TRUE
10.0013.55 1.2520.00
  A    B    C    D
!---*!---*!---*!---*

12.3010.0025.0020.00
12.3010.0025.0020.00
  A    B    C    D
!---*!---*!---*!---*

12.3010.0025.0080.00
12.3010.0025.0080.00
  A    B    C    D
!---*!---*!---*!---*

12.3060.0010.00 5.00
IF TEST IS TRUE
12.3062.00 2.00 5.00
  A    B    C    D
!---*!---*!---*!---*

60.0012.0010.00 5.00
ELSEIF TEST IS TRUE
65.0012.00 2.40 5.00
  A    B    C    D
!---*!---*!---*!---*
```

Fig. 12-7. Program to demonstrate the BLOCK IF with a qualified false condition (program execution shown below program).

```
C**** IF THEN/ELSE EXPLAINER (KNOWN AS THE
C**** BLOCK IF STATEMENT WITH A QUALIFIED
C**** FALSE CONDITION USING 'GOTO' COMMANDS)
C234567
      PROGRAM BLOCKS
      OPEN (6,FILE='PRINTER:')
    5 WRITE (0,200)
      WRITE (6,200)
      READ (0,100)A,B,C,D
      IF (A.EQ.0) GOTO999
      WRITE (6,100)A,B,C,D
C**** !!!
      IF (A.LT.B) GOTO 500
          GOTO 600
  500     WRITE (0,110)
          WRITE (6,110)
          C=C/D
          B=B+C
          GOTO 800
  600     IF (A+B.GT.C+D) GOTO 700
              GOTO 800
  700         WRITE (0,120)
              WRITE (6,120)
              A=A+D
              C=B/D
  800     WRITE(0,100)A,B,C,D
          WRITE(6,100)A,B,C,D
C**** !!!
      GOTO 5
  999 STOP
  100 FORMAT(4(F5.2))
  110 FORMAT('IF TEST IS TRUE')
  120 FORMAT('ELSEIF TEST IS TRUE')
  200 FORMAT (2X,'A',4X,'B',4X,'C',
     *4X,'D',/,4('!----*'),/)
      END


  A    B    C    D
!----*!----*!----*!----*

10.0012.3025.0020.00
IF TEST IS TRUE
10.0013.55 1.2520.00
  A    B    C    D
!----*!----*!----*!----*

12.3010.0025.0020.00
12.3010.0025.0020.00
  A    B    C    D
!----*!----*!----*!----*

12.3060.0010.00 5.00
IF TEST IS TRUE
12.3062.00 2.00 5.00
  A    B    C    D
!----*!----*!----*!----*

60.0012.0010.00 5.00
ELSEIF TEST IS TRUE
65.0012.00 2.40 5.00
  A    B    C    D
!----*!----*!----*!----*
```

Fig. 12-8. FORTRAN equivalent to the program of Fig. 12-7 (program execution shown below program).

THEN are executed until ELSE is reached. The ELSE causes the program to jump to the statement following ENDIF, which is GOTO 5.

When IF (A .LT. B) THEN is false, the program branches to the ELSE statement. The statements following ELSE are executed to the statement following the ENDIF, which is GOTO 5.

The IF (expression) THEN, ELSE, ENDIF gives the programmer the option to process data when the beginning BLOCK IF is false. In Fig. 12-1, there is no option to process data when the BLOCK IF statement is false.

IF — THEN — ELSEIF

The highest level of BLOCK IF is the IF (expression) THEN, ELSEIF (expression) THEN, and ENDIF (Fig. 12-7).

```
IF (A .LT. B) THEN
   WRITE (0,110) (the test is true)
   C = C/D
   B = B + C
   ELSEIF (A+B .GT. C+D) THEN
   WRITE (0,120) (ELSEIF test is true)
   A = A + D
   C = B/D
   ENDIF
GOTO 5
```

When IF (A .LT. B) THEN is true, the statements to ELSEIF (A + B .GT. C + D) THEN are executed, and the program branches to the statement immediately following the ENDIF, which is GOTO 5.

When IF (A .LT. B) THEN is false, the program branches to ELSEIF (A + B .GT. C + D) THEN, and tests the ELSEIF condition. If false, it branches to the ENDIF.

When IF (A .LT.B) THEN is false, the program branches to ELSEIF (A + B .GT. C + D) THEN. When IF (A .LT. B) THEN is false, and IF (A + B .GT. C + D) THEN is true, the statements from ELSEIF to ENDIF are executed, and the program executes the GOTO 5 statement.

CHAPTER 13
Using the Operating System

APPLE PASCAL OPERATING SYSTEM

The Apple Pascal operating system is used to manipulate the Apple FORTRAN language. The Pascal operating system has several command levels that create and change text files, handle disk selection and disk files, and execute or run the program.

Before the beginning programmer attempts to use FORTRAN, the intricacies of the Pascal operating system should be mastered. The Pascal operating system is a powerful and complex system that does an excellent job for the user. The APPLE I Pascal Operating System Reference Manual, 1980, by Apple Computer, Inc., is the source of information for the Pascal operating system. The manual should be studied so the user has control of the system. When the features of the operating system are known and understood, then the study of the FORTRAN language can begin.

FORTRAN DISK CONFIGURATION

The Apple FORTRAN language skeleton is on two disks — FORT1 and FORT2. The FORT1 disk comes with one program on it — FORTLIB.CODE. All other programs must be transferred from APPLE1 and APPLE2. When FORT1 is properly configured (Fig. 13-1), there are 93 unused blocks on the disk. For information on FORTRAN disk configuration, see the Apple FORTRAN Language Reference Manual, 1980, by Apple Computer, Inc.

FORT2 comes with two programs on the disk — SYSTEM.COMPILER and

```
FORT1:
FORTLIB.CODE          9  19-Jun-80       6  Code
SYSTEM.APPLE         32  26-Jul-79      15  Data
SYSTEM.PASCAL        36   4-May-79      47  Data
SYSTEM.MISCINFO       1   4-May-79      83  Data
SYSTEM.EDITOR        45  29-Jan-79      84  Code
SYSTEM.FILER         28  24-May-79     129  Code
SYSTEM.CHARSET        2  14-Jun-79     157  Data
SYSTEM.LINKER        24   3-May-79     159  Code
IF-BLOCK.TEXT         4  15-May-81     183  Text
< UNUSED >           93                187
9/9 files, 93 unused, 93 in largest
```

Fig. 13-1. FORT1 configuration.

SYSTEM.LIBRARY. All other programs must be transferred from APPLE1 to FORT2. The SYSTEM.COMPILER *cannot be copied.* When properly configured (Fig. 13-2), FORT2 has 47 blocks of unused space.

The FORTRAN language is *very* difficult to use on a one-disk drive system. The FORTRAN language is difficult to use on a two-disk drive system because of space limitations on FORT1 and FORT2, and the frequency of exchanging disks. The FORTRAN language is a pleasure to use on a system with more than two disk drives.

FORT2 should be configured as in Fig. 13-2. The 47 unused blocks are reserved for SYSTEM.WRK.TEXT and SYSTEM.WRK.CODE programs. If the SYSTEM programs use more than 47 blocks, there will be a WRITE CODE ERROR. If FORT2 is not properly configured, the directory can be destroyed. If the directory on FORT2 is destroyed, the disk is useless as it cannot be read and no files or programs can be accessed. On a two-disk drive system, the space limitations on FORT1 and FORT2 are a serious deficiency. This deficiency is relieved on a system that has more than two disk drives.

```
FORT2:
SYSTEM.COMPILER     92   4-Jun-80     6 Code
SYSTEM.LIBRARY      64  26-Jul-79    98 Data
SYSTEM.APPLE        32  26-Jul-79   162 Data
SYSTEM.PASCAL       36   4-May-79   194 Data
SYSTEM.MISCINFO      1   4-May-79   230 Data
SYSTEM.CHARSET       2  14-Jun-79   231 Data
< UNUSED >          47              233
6/6 files, 47 unused, 47 in largest
```

Fig. 13-2. FORT2 configuration.

FORTRAN COMPILER CANNOT BE COPIED

The FORTRAN compiler (SYSTEM.COMPILER on FORT2) cannot be copied. When FORT2 is tested for bad blocks (B under FILER), blocks 30, 31, and 32 are identified as bad. The bad blocks are produced by the feature that prevents the compiler from being copied.

BOOT UP WITH DISKS IN THE PROPER DISK DRIVE

The FORTRAN disks must be placed in the proper disk drive to boot up the system. On a two-disk drive system, FORT2 is placed in disk drive #1 (boot drive) and FORT1 is placed in disk drive #2. When the system is properly booted, a prompt line appears in the first row of the CRT.

COMMAND LEVELS

The commands E(ditor), R(un), F(iler), C(ompile), and L(ink) can be viewed on the Apple 40-column screen. By pressing CONTROL A on a

40-column screen, the remaining commands, X(execute), R(un), D(ebug), U(ser), and H(alt), are placed on the screen.

By pressing the first letter of the command E (for editor), the operating system selects the correct command level.

Command R (for run), is a special command that is used to run a text program stored in the workfile on FORT2, or a file specified by the user. The R(un) command causes the text file to be compiled to a code file. The listing option of the compile step can be answered in four ways — (1) by pressing RETURN for an abbreviated compile to the CRT, (2) by typing in #2: to view the compiled code on the CRT, (3) by typing in #6: the compiled code will be sent to the printer, and (4) by typing #5:COMPILE.TEXT the file can be put to disk. The R(un) command takes the compiled code file, links it to the necessary library programs, produces a linked code file, and then runs the program. The linked code file is stored on FORT2 as the SYSTEM.WRK.CODE. When the run is completed, there will be two files stored in the workspace — SYSTEM.WRK.TEXT and SYSTEM.WRK.CODE (linked). The compiled work code file is removed after it is used in the linking program.

Command F (for filer) is the section of the operating system that operates disk drives and disk files. For details, see the Apple Pascal Operating System Reference Manual, 1980, by Apple Computer, Inc.

Command C (for compile) causes a text file to be compiled into a code file. The compiler cannot be copied, and can be accessed indirectly by the R(un) command, or accessed directly by the C(ompile) command.

Command L (for link) links the compiled code file to the necessary library programs to produce a linked code file. The linker can be accessed indirectly through the R(un) command, or directly through the L(ink) command.

Command X (for execute) is the first operating system command not viewed on the Apple 40-column screen. To view X(execute), press CONTROL A. CONTROL A causes the second half of the 80 columns to be placed on the screen. Command X(execute) causes a linked code program to run. The X(execute) command must be differentiated from R(un). R(un) can be used only in relation to the SYSTEM.WRK.TEXT or (linked) SYSTEM.WRK.CODE files stored in the workfile on FORT2. X(execute) can be used to execute the linked SYSTEM.WRK.CODE file on FORT2, or a linked code file on any other disk.

There are other commands at the command level, but they are not especially pertinent to FORTRAN.

SIZE OF THE FORTRAN PROGRAM IS SIGNIFICANT

The size of a FORTRAN program is of significant importance as to where it should be stored. The FORT2 disk has 47 unused blocks for program storage. The FORT1 disk has 93 unused blocks for program storage. A small FORTRAN program that has 6 blocks for a text file, 6 blocks for a compiled code file, and 27 blocks for a linked code file occupies 39 blocks. When the compiled code file is not saved, total disk space used is reduced to 33 blocks.

The text file and the linked code file take up 33 blocks. This size program can easily be stored on the FORT2 disk. A 6-block text program will contain from 50 to 100 lines of code, depending on how many lines of comment the program contains.

A medium-sized program that has 30 blocks for text and 51 blocks for the linked code cannot be placed on FORT2 because of the size. The 51-block program could be stored on FORT1. Large programs that use more than 93 blocks for the text and linked code files must be placed on storage disks.

New FORTRAN programs are written, or previously written programs are edited, in a scratchpad file. This scratchpad is in the E(ditor) command level. At the command level, when E (for editor) is pressed, the Pascal operating system sets up the workfile to receive a previously written program. This program can be read in by typing #5:MEAN1. If a new program is to be written, RETURN is pressed to set up the scratchpad. The edit prompt is displayed in row one of the CRT. The edit prompt line contains those commands that insert the text, manipulate the text, set the margins, and search for specific strings or tokens.

WRITING PROGRAMS — EDITOR THEN EDIT

At the edit level (not editor), to insert text into the scratchpad, press I (for insert). The insert mode allows the user to type in the program statements so they can be stored in memory. When the statements are to be stored in memory, press CONTROL C. Any time an insertion or change is made to the text, that insertion or change must be verified by pressing CONTROL C. When CONTROL C is pressed, the change is verified and the edit prompt line is placed in row one of the CRT. The routine is to change the text, press CONTROL C, and return to the edit command. All changes are made from the edit level, and CONTROL C verifies the change and returns to the edit level. If CONTROL C is pressed at the edit level, the computer beeps to let you know that the operating system is at the edit level.

Other commands that are frequently used from the edit level are D(elete), X(exchange), P(age), J(ump), and A(djust).

Command D (for delete) from the edit level causes a character or line to be deleted. To delete a character, place the cursor over the character, press D, press the space bar once, or the forward arrow key, and press CONTROL C. The character is then deleted. To delete an entire line of text, place the cursor at the beginning of the line, press D, press the RETURN key, and then press CONTROL C. The line is then deleted. Multiple characters or multiple lines can be deleted by holding the repeat key down, then using the space bar, forward arrow key, or the RETURN key.

In the edit mode the cursor can be moved upward by pressing CONTROL O. The cursor can be moved down by pressing CONTROL L. The cursor can be moved to the right by pressing the forward arrow key, and the cursor can be moved to the left by pressing the back arrow key. These actions can be repeated by holding the specific keys down and pressing the repeat key. In the edit mode, the cursor can be moved up or down by changing the direction of the less-than (<) or greater-than (>) indicator, and pressing the RETURN key. The less-than indicator and RETURN key move the cursor toward the top of the screen. The greater-than indicator and the RETURN key move the cursor toward the bottom of the screen. If the cursor is at the last line of text, it cannot be moved downward except in the insert mode.

A character, or characters, can be exchanged by placing the cursor over the character to be exchanged, pressing X (for exchange), then changing the character, or characters. After the characters have been exchanged, CONTROL C must be pressed to verify the change, and return to the edit level.

Command P (for page) at the edit level causes the text to move forward or back the full length of the screen. If the less-than designator is placed before the edit and P is pressed, the text jumps one screen length backward. If the greater-than designator is placed before the edit and P is pressed, the text jumps one screen length forward.

Commands J (for jump) and B (for beginning) cause the cursor to jump to the beginning line. Commands J (for jump) and E (for end) cause the cursor to jump to the ending line.

Command A (for adjust) is used to adjust a line of text toward the right screen margin or toward the left screen margin. In FORTRAN, the column position of the program statements on the screen is of extreme importance. A program statement in an incorrect column will cause a fatal compile error. Pressing A (for adjust) and the back arrow key will adjust the program statement toward the left side of the screen. CONTROL C is pressed to record the change. Pressing A and the forward arrow key moves the program statement toward the right side of the screen.

WRITING THE COMPLETED PROGRAM TO DISK

When all program statements have been entered, and CONTROL C is pressed for the last time to verify the changes, it is time to leave the edit mode. To leave the edit mode, press Q (for quit). The FORTRAN program is stored in memory and the computer prints four lines to the CRT:

```
> QUIT:
    U(PDATE THE WORKFILE AND LEAVE
    E(XIT WITHOUT UPDATING
```

R(ETURN TO THE EDITOR WITHOUT UPDATING
W(RITE TO A FILE NAME AND RETURN

U(PDATE THE WORKFILE AND LEAVE causes the FORTRAN text program to be placed on the workfile in the unused sectors on FORT2. The new text file or updated text file is written to the workfile.

E(XIT WITHOUT UPDATING causes a return to the outer Pascal operating system command level. The text file remains the same as it was when read into the editor, and all corrections are lost.

R(ETURN TO THE EDITOR WITHOUT UPDATING causes a return to the edit level, where the text program is written. There are no changes to the program.

W(RITE TO A FILE NAME AND RETURN. Typing #5:MEAN1 and pressing RETURN causes the text file to be written to the disk in disk drive #5.

If U(PDATE or W(RITE TO FILE NAME is selected, the operating system displays on the CRT that the file is being written (WRITING . . .), and YOUR FILE IS XXX bytes long.

When the W(RITE TO FILE NAME has been completed, the computer writes two options to the screen.

DO YOU WANT TO E(XIT OR R(ETURN TO THE EDITOR?

Pressing E (for exit) causes the outer level of the operating system to be displayed on row one of the CRT. Pressing R (for return) causes a return to the edit mode, and the text file is written on the CRT.

COMPILING THE TEXT FILE

The text file is ready to be compiled and converted to a compiled code file. The compiled code file (Fig. 13-3) can be accessed by either of two means — (1) R (for run) or (2) C (for compile) if the text file is on FORT2, or FORT1, or a storage disk.

Pressing R (for run) takes the SYSTEM.WRK.TEXT, if there is one, else it asks for a file name, compiles it to create a compiled code file, links it to produce a linked code file, and runs the program.

This is the quick and easy way to handle a short program stored as the SYSTEM.WRK.TEXT on FORT2. If there are compile errors in the text file, the errors are shown by the listing, and the operating system returns to the outer command level. Pressing E (for editor) causes the text file to be read into the scratchpad for the compile errors to be corrected. The corrected text file is written to the SYSTEM.WRK.TEXT, or to a text file, and R (for run) is again pressed.

Pressing C (for compile) permits the user to compile either the SYSTEM.WRK.TEXT on FORT2, or a text file on FORT1, or a text file on a storage disk. If there are compile errors under the C (for compile) option, the operating system returns to the outer command level. When E (for

```
'FORTRAN Compiler II.1   [1.1]
     0.        0 C**** PROGRAM TO COMPUTE THE MEAN OF A LIST
     1.        0 C**** OF NUMBERS - USING A FUNCTION SUBPROGRAM
     2.        0 C234567
     3.        0       PROGRAM MEAN1
     4.        0       DIMENSION G( 10 ),GRADE( 10 )
     5.        0       DATA G( 1 ),G( 2 ),G( 3 ),G( 4 ),G( 5 ),G( 6 ),
     6.        0      *G( 7 ),G( 8 ),G( 9 ),G( 10 )/90.,70.,85.,100.,100.,
     7.        0      *79.,89.,95.,82.,99./
     8.      100       OPEN (6,FILE = 'PRINTER:')
     9.      120       KOUNT = 10
    10.      123       DO 5 K = 1,KOUNT
    11.      132       GRADE( K ) = G( K )
    12.      152     5 CONTINUE
    13.      167       IVAL = MEAN( GRADE,KOUNT )
    14.      177       WRITE (0,30) KOUNT, IVAL
    15.      207       WRITE (6,30) KOUNT, IVAL
    16.      237    30 FORMAT (///,'THE MEAN OF ',I3,4X,'GRADES
    17.      237      * IS ',I8,///)
    18.      237       STOP
    19.      244       END

G       REAL              3
GRADE   REAL             23
IVAL    INTEGER          46
K       INTEGER          45
KOUNT   INTEGER          43
MEAN    INTEGER   FUNCTION      2,FWD
MEAN1   PROGRAM

    20.        0       INTEGER FUNCTION MEAN( GRADE,KOUNT )
    21.        0       REAL GRADE( KOUNT )
    22.        0       MEAN = 0
    23.        7       SUM = 0
    24.       13       DO 10 J = 1,KOUNT
    25.       22       SUM = SUM + GRADE( J )
    26.       39    10 CONTINUE
    27.       51       MEAN = IFIX( SUM/FLOAT( KOUNT ))
    28.       63       RETURN
    29.       65       END

FLOAT   INTRINSIC
GRADE   REAL             4*
IFIX    INTRINSIC
J       INTEGER          9
KOUNT   INTEGER          3*
MEAN    INTEGER   FUNCTION      2
SUM     REAL             6
MEAN    INTEGER   FUNCTION      2,7
MEAN1   PROGRAM

30 lines.    0 errors.
Smallest available space = 4853 words.
```

Fig. 13-3. Compiled code file of the MEAN1.TEXT program.

editor) is pressed, the disk drive number and file name must be written to retrieve the text file and edit it.

The C (for compile) option asks for the text file to be compiled.

COMPILE WHAT TEXT? #4:SYSTEM.WRK

or

COMPILE WHAT TEXT? #5:MEAN1

On either option, run or compile, the computer asks where the compilation is to be listed. There are four options — (1) to the CRT in an abbreviated form, (2) to the CRT in a complete form, (3) to the printer, and (4) to a disk.

LISTING THE COMPILATION TO THE CRT

LISTING FILE? (press RETURN)

Pressing RETURN to the question, LISTING FILE?, puts an abbreviated version of the compilation to the CRT. This listing is completely unsatisfactory because it does not show where the compile errors are located.

LISTING FILE? #2:

Typing #2: places the compilation and symbol table on the CRT. When compile errors are discovered, pressing CONTROL S can freeze the compilation on the CRT so the line in which the error occurred can be viewed and the error number and line number can be recorded. Again pressing CONTROL S causes the compile to continue.

Listing #2: to the CRT is a very satisfactory way to view the compile as it is taking place. CONTROL S enables the user to stop and start the compile. When the compile is stopped, the errors can be viewed and/or written down so the program can be corrected.

LISTING COMPILATION TO PRINTER

LISTING FILE? #6:

Typing #6: to the listing file question causes the compilation to be output to the printer. If there are errors in the program, the line number and error number are placed below the incorrect line of code. When syntax errors are difficult to detect, seeing the hard copy of the compile is of great benefit. Except for the waste of paper, putting the compilation to the printer is a very satisfactory way to debug syntax errors in the program.

LISTING COMPILATION TO DISK

LISTING FILE? #5:COMPILE.TEXT

Typing #5:COMPILE.TEXT causes the compilation to be placed on the disk in disk drive #5. This compilation can be viewed by using the editor and reading in #5:COMPILE.TEXT.

After asking for the listing option desired, LISTING FILE?, the question, WHAT CODE FILE?, is asked. The compiled code can be stored in either of two places — (1) as the compiled SYSTEM.WRK.CODE on FORT2 (the compiled code file is overwritten with the linked code file in the R(un) option), or (2) as #5:MEAN1 compiled code file on FORT1 or a storage disk. The only use for the compiled code file is to link to the system library to create the linked code file.

WHAT CODE FILE? (press RETURN)

Pressing RETURN in response to the WHAT CODE FILE? question causes the compiled code file to be stored on FORT2.

WHAT CODE FILE? #5:MEAN1

Typing #5:MEAN1 in response to the WHAT CODE FILE? question causes the compiled code file to be stored on FORT1 or on a storage disk in disk drive #5. There is no reason to save a compiled code file after the linked code file is created.

An efficient way to handle a large program on a two-disk system is to transfer the text file from a storage disk to FORT1. The text file is compiled and is placed on FORT2 as the SYSTEM.WRK.CODE. When the compiled code file is linked, it can be stored as #5:MEAN1.CODE file, and it can be executed.

LINKING CODE FILE USING FORT2 DISK

COMPILE WHAT TEXT? #5:MEAN1
LISTING FILE? #2:
WHAT CODE FILE? (press RETURN)

places compiled code on FORT2.

When the linking routine is accessed, it asks for the host file.

LINKING . . . (ROUTINE)
HOST FILE? (press RETURN)

accesses SYSTEM.WRK.CODE.

OUTPUT FILE? #5:MEAN1.CODE

After the compile step is error free, the compiled code file can be linked to the system library. This linking adds 21 sectors to the compiled code file.

Command L (for link) is pressed from the outer command level.

LINKING . . .
HOST FILE?

Again there are two options — (1) if the compiled code is on FORT2 as the SYSTEM.WRK.CODE and (2) if the compiled code file is on FORT1 or on a storage disk.

HOST FILE? (press RETURN)

Pressing RETURN to the question, HOST FILE?, causes the operating system to access the compiled SYSTEM.WRK.CODE on FORT2.

LINKING CODE FILE USING DISK OTHER THAN FORT2

HOST FILE? #5:MEAN1

Typing #5:MEAN1 to the question, HOST FILE?, causes the operating system to access the compiled code file stored on FORT1 or a storage disk.

After the linker opens the compiled code file, it asks the question:

LIB FILE? * (RETURN)

To access the library file, an asterisk (*) is typed and RETURN is pressed. This causes the necessary programs in the library file to be linked to the compiled code file.

The linker asks for LIB FILE? again, and then MAP FILE?. To both questions, RETURN is pressed.

LIB FILE? (press RETURN if there are no other files necessary)
MAP FILE? (press RETURN)

The next question that requires a user response is OUTPUT FILE?.

OUTPUT FILE? (press RETURN)

If RETURN is pressed in response to the question, OUTPUT FILE?, the linked code file is stored on FORT2 as SYSTEM.WRK.CODE.

.CODE SUFFIX IS MANDATORY

If #5:MEAN1.CODE is typed in response to the question, OUTPUT FILE?, the linked code file is stored on FORT1 or a storage disk in disk drive #5. The suffix, .CODE, must be attached to #5:MEAN1 for the file to be legal. If the suffix, .CODE, is not attached to #5:MEAN1, the system recognizes this as a data file.

If the option to run a SYSTEM.WRK.TEXT on FORT2 was originally selected, and there were no compile errors or write code errors, the program runs. If the initial option was to compile and link a file on FORT1 or a storage disk, the last link in the chain is to execute the linked code file.

EXECUTE A LINKED FILE

Command X (for execute) is pressed at the outer command level of the operating system.

EXECUTE WHAT FILE? #5:MEAN1

When #5:MEAN1 is typed in response to the question, EXECUTE WHAT FILE?, the operating system selects the linked code file and executes it.

Even at this point there can be write code errors in the program. An integer value printed in a floating-point field causes a write code error.

After the program executes, it must be debugged for logic errors and input data errors.

CHAPTER 14
FORTRAN Using Multidisk Drives

The Apple FORTRAN language has programs on two disks. FORT2 has 47 unused blocks and FORT1 has 93 unused blocks. Using FORTRAN on a single-disk drive system is very difficult due to space limitations and numerous disk exchanges.

USING A TWO-DISK DRIVE SYSTEM

FORTRAN on a two-disk drive system is difficult to use. Even with small programs, there are numerous disk exchanges. When a small program is placed in the 47 unused blocks on FORT2, there is always the question, "What do you do with it after the program has run?" The same question has to be asked when a program is placed on FORT1. The completed program has to be stored somewhere, and this is one thing that causes the disk exchanges. This is not the fault of Apple Computer, Inc., which has done a superior job providing FORTRAN for the Apple. The problem is due to space limitations of a single- or dual-disk drive system.

Fig. 14-1 is an outline with a minimal number of commands to manipulate the FORTRAN language, using the Pascal operating system, to write and save a small program.

After a small new program has been typed using the editor mode, the easiest way to handle the program is to write it to the workfile (U(PDATE THE WORKFILE AND RETURN) and run it. This is an extremely efficient way to get the program from text file to the linked code file and run it. If there are no compile errors or write code errors, the operation is performed quickly and the program results can be viewed in a very short time. This method is a real pleasure to use.

Edit a Previously Written Program

Fig. 14-2 is an outline to edit a previously written program named MEAN1.TEXT that is on a storage disk. The FORTRAN language is booted with FORT2 in disk drive #1 (boot drive) and FORT1 in disk drive #2. If MEAN1.TEXT is to be transferred to the unused space on FORT2, the operating system must be in the FILER command level, FORT1 must be removed, and the storage disk placed in disk drive #2. Command T (for transfer) is pressed, and TRANSFER? is written on the CRT. Typing in

#5:MEAN1.TEXT in response to the question, TRANSFER?, and also typing in #4:SYSTEM.WRK.TEXT in answer to the question, TO WHERE?, causes #5:MEAN1.TEXT to be placed on FORT2 as the SYSTEM.WRK.TEXT.

```
TRANSFER? #5:MEAN1.TEXT
TO WHERE? #4:SYSTEM.WRK.TEXT
```

If there are logic or data changes to be made, the editor command level is used to make the changes. After the changes are completed, the program is written to the workfile. SYSTEM.WRK.TEXT (MEAN1) requires 6 blocks of disk space. When SYSTEM.WRK.TEXT is rewritten to the workfile, it is not returned to the 6 blocks it previously occupied. The 6 blocks below the original 6 are used to write SYSTEM.WRK.TEXT. Consequently, the original disk space is broken into two usable parts of 6 and 35 blocks each. If the SYSTEM.WRK.TEXT (MEAN1) is edited three more times, the space is broken into an 18-block space and a 23-block space. When the SYSTEM.WRK.TEXT and the linked code files use more than 47 blocks on FORT2, a write code error is produced and the file cannot be written to the disk.

Krunch the Files on Disk

After the SYSTEM.WRK.TEXT has been edited several times, and before the R(un) command is given, the SYSTEM.WRK.TEXT should be moved so maximum space is available for future programs when the R(un) command is given. The disk should be krunched.

To get to K(runch), F (for filer) is pressed from the outer command level of the operating system. When the filer level is displayed in row one of the CRT, K (for Krunch) is pressed. The system responds and the user types in either of the following commands:

CRUNCH? * (press RETURN for boot drive)

or

CRUNCH? #4: (press RETURN for disk drive #1)

A. Boot the system.
   1. FORT2 is in disk drive #1 (boot drive).
   2. FORT1 is in disk drive #2.
   3. Turn the power switch to the ON position.
B. To write a new program.
   1. Press E (for editor) from the outer command level.
   2. Press RETURN to set up the workfile.
   3. Press I (for insert) to begin writing.
      a. Comply with FORTRAN language rules in writing the program.
   4. CONTROL C accepts the program and returns to Edit.
   5. Edit commands to change the program.
      a. D(elete)—from Edit press D.
         1. Press RETURN to delete a line.
         2. Press space bar, back or forward arrow, to delete a character.
         3. Press CONTROL C to complete the deletion.

Fig. 14-1. Minimal commands to manipulate the FORTRAN language,

b. I(nsert).
   1. Place cursor over the character where insertion is to be made. Press I (for insert).
   2. Insert text.
   3. CONTROL C to accept the insertion.
c. X(exchange).
   1. Place cursor over the character at the beginning of the exchange. Press X (for exchange).
   2. Type in the new characters.
   3. CONTROL C to accept the exchanges.
d. A(djust).
   1. Place the cursor on the character to be adjusted.
   2. Use the forward or back arrow key to make the adjustment.
   3. CONTROL C to accept the adjustment.
e. For other commands refer to the Apple Pascal Operating System Reference Manual, 1980, by Apple Computer, Inc.

C. To leave the Editor.
   1. Press Q (for quit).
   2. Four options are printed on the screen—UPDATE, EXIT, RETURN, and WRITE.
   3. Press U (for UPDATE THE WORKFILE AND LEAVE).

D. To run the program.
   1. Press R (for run).
      a. COMPILING... appears on the screen.
   2. Asks for LISTING FILE?
      a. Press RETURN for an abbreviated listing on the screen.
      b. #2: then RETURN for a line-by-line listing on the screen.
      c. #6: then RETURN for a listing on the printer.
      d. #5:COMPILE.TEXT then RETURN for a listing on the disk in disk drive #5.

E. If there are no compile errors, the program automatically links.
   1. If there are compile errors, press E (for editor) to correct the errors.
      a. Errors corrected.
         1. Q (for quit).
         2. U (for UPDATE THE WORKFILE AND LEAVE).
         3. R (for run).

F. The linker is referenced by pressing L (for link).
   1. Linker asks for HOST FILE?
      a. Press RETURN — this causes the linker to access the compiled code file stored on FORT2.
   2. Linker asks for LIB FILE?
      a. Asterisk (*) then RETURN accesses the library file.
   3. Linker asks for LIB FILE again.
      a. Press RETURN, unless there are other files to linl. to the program.
   4. Linker asks for MAP FILE.
      a. Press RETURN.
   5. The linker completes the linking process.

G. RUNNING... appears on the screen.
   1. If there are no write code errors, the program runs, and when the run is completed, the outer command prompt line appears on the screen.

H. To save the text and code files.
   1. Press F (for filer).
   2. Press S (for save).
      a. SAVE AS? appears on the screen.
         1. To save on FORT1, leave FORT1 in disk drive #2 and type #5:MEAN1—both the text and code files will be saved on FORT1.
         2. To save on a storage disk.
            a. Take FORT1 out of disk drive #2.
            b. Place formatted storage disk in disk drive #2—type #5:MEAN1. The text and code files will be saved on the storage disk.

using the Pascal operating system, to write and save a small program.

The operating system responds:

FROM END OF DISK BLOCK 280? (Y/N) Y

The user response is Y (for yes), and the SYSTEM.WRK.TEXT is moved to the space next to the last program on FORT2. The maximum usable space is now available for the programs created when the R(un) command is given. When K(runch) is completed, Q (for quit) is given, and the operating system returns to the outer command level.

Run the Program

Command R (for run) is pressed, the SYSTEM.WRK.TEXT is compiled, the user selects the place to list the compiled code, and the program is linked and run.

Programs that the user is through running can be saved to a storage disk, the workfile can be cleared, or the workfile left intact.

Save Text and Linked Code Files

To save the text file and the linked code file versions of the program, F (for filer) is pressed. When the filer level is reached, FORT1 is removed from disk drive #2, and the storage disk is placed in disk drive #2. Command S (for save) is pressed, and the system responds as follows:

SAVE AS? #5:MEAN1 (press RETURN)

A. Boot the system.
   1. FORT2 is in disk drive #1 (boot drive).
   2. FORT1 is in disk drive #2.
   3. Turn the power switch to the ON position.
B. From the outer level command prompt.
   1. Press F (for filer).
   2. Remove FORT2 from disk drive #1.
   3. Place disk on which MEAN1.TEXT is stored in disk drive #1.
   4. Press T (for transfer).
      a. TRANSFER? #4:MEAN1.TEXT
      b. TO WHERE? #5:MEAN1.TEXT
   5. MEAN1.TEXT is now stored in the 97 unused sectors on FORT1.
   6. Remove the storage disk from disk drive #1.
   7. Place FORT2 in disk drive #1.
   8. Press Q (for quit the filer).
C. Press C (for compile) from the outer command level.
   1. COMPILING... appears on the screen.
      a. COMPILE WHAT TEXT? #5:MEAN1
         1. Typing in TEXT is not necessary.
         2. If TEXT is typed in, it must be #5:MEAN1.TEXT.
      b. LISTING FILE?
         1. Press RETURN for an abbreviated listing on the screen.
         2. #2: for a complete listing to the screen.
         3. #6: for a listing to the printer.
         4. #5:COMPILE.TEXT for a listing to the disk in disk drive #5.
      c. TO WHAT CODEFILE?
         1. Press RETURN to place the compiled code file on FORT2, as the SYSTEM.WRK.CODE.
         2. #5:MEAN1 to place the compiled code file on FORT1.

Fig. 14-2. Outline to edit a previously written program

D. If there are no compile errors, the MEAN1.CODE or SYSTEM .WRK.CODE is ready to be linked.
   1. If there are compile errors, return to the editor to correct the errors and write the text file back to FORT1 — #5:MEAN1.
   2. See Fig. 14-1 or the Apple Pascal Operating System Reference Manual, 1980, Apple Computer, Inc., for editor details.

E. Press L (for link), from the outer command level.
   1. Linker responds with HOST FILE?
      a. Type in #5:MEAN1 if the compiled code file is on FORT1.
      b. Press RETURN if the SYSTEM.WRK.CODE is on FORT2.
   2. Linker responds with LIB FILE?
      a. Asterisk (*) then RETURN to access the library file.
   3. Linker responds with LIB FILE.
      a. Press RETURN if there are no other library files to be accessed by the program.
   4. Linker responds with MAP FILE.
      a. Press RETURN.
   5. Linker responds with OUTPUT FILE?
      a. Press RETURN if the linked code file is to be placed on FORT2 as SYSTEM.WRK.CODE.
      b. #5:MEAN1.CODE if the linked code is to be placed on FORT1.
         1. .CODE is mandatory for a linked code file to be placed on FORT1 or a storage disk. Without .CODE, the system thinks the linked code is a data file, and the file will not execute.

F. Execute from the command level.
   1. Press X (for execute). Computer responds:
      a. EXECUTE WHAT FILE? #5:MEAN1
      b. The program executes.
      c. The command level prompt returns to row one of the screen.

G. MEAN1.TEXT and MEAN1.CODE have been saved to FORT1.
   1. To save the files on a storage disk.
      a. Press F (for filer).
      b. Remove FORT2 from disk drive #1.
      c. Place storage disk in disk drive #1.
      d. Press T (for transfer).
         1. TRANSFER? #5:MEAN1.TEXT
         2. TO WHERE? #4:MEAN1.TEXT
         3. MEAN1.TEXT is transferred from the disk in drive #2 to the disk in drive #1.
      e. Press T (for transfer).
         1. TRANSFER? #5:MEAN1.CODE
         2. TO WHERE? #4:MEAN1.CODE
         3. MEAN1.CODE is transferred from the disk in drive #2 to the disk in drive #1.
      f. Press Q (for quit the filer).

H. If the linked code file is on FORT2 as the SYSTEM.WRK.CODE.
   1. Press F (for filer) at the outer command level.
      a. Take FORT2 out of disk drive #1.
      b. Place the storage disk in disk drive #1.
      c. Press T (for transfer).
         1. TRANSFER? #5:MEAN1.TEXT
         2. TO WHERE? #4:MEAN1.TEXT
      d. Press T (for transfer).
         1. Take the storage disk out of disk drive #1.
         2. Place FORT2 in disk drive #1.
         3. Take FORT1 out of disk drive #2.
         4. Place the storage disk in disk drive #2.
         5. TRANSFER? #4:SYSTEM.WRK.CODE
         6. TO WHERE? #5:MEAN1.CODE
         7. Press Q (for quit the filer).

I. The command prompt returns to row one of the screen.

named MEAN1.TEXT that is on a storage disk.

This causes the SYSTEM.WRK.TEXT to be saved as MEAN1.TEXT, and SYSTEM.WRK.CODE to be saved as MEAN1.CODE.

Clear the Workfile on FORT2

If the workfile is to be cleared, press N (for new). Pressing N (for new) causes the system to respond:

```
THROW AWAY CURRENT WORKFILE? Y
```

Pressing Y (for yes) clears the workfile space on FORT2. Pressing Q (for quit) returns the system to the outer command level.

Transfer a Program from One Disk to Another

If a previously written program on a storage disk is to be transferred to FORT1, the filer is entered, FORT2 is removed from disk drive #1, and the storage disk is placed in disk drive #1. Command T (for transfer) is pressed, and the system responds as follows:

```
TRANSFER? #4:MEAN1.TEXT
TO WHERE? #5:MEAN1.TEXT
```

This causes MEAN1.TEXT to be transferred from the storage disk in disk drive #1 to FORT1 in disk drive #2. When the transfer is complete, the storage disk in disk drive #1 is removed and FORT2 is placed in disk drive #1. Command Q (for quit the filer) is pressed and the system is returned to the outer command level.

Compile and Link a Code File

One point to emphasize is how the compiled code file is handled for maximum efficiency. The compiled code file has no use except as the intermediary step between the text file and the linked code file.

The text file, MEAN1.TEXT, is on FORT1 and ready to be compiled. When C (for compile) is pressed, the system responds:

```
COMPILE WHAT TEXT? #5:MEAN1
LISTING FILE? #2:
WHAT CODE FILE? (press RETURN)
```

When RETURN is pressed in response to the question, WHAT CODE FILE?, the system places the compiled code file on FORT2 as the SYSTEM.WRK.CODE. After the text file is successfully compiled, the compiled code file must be linked.

Pressing L (for link) from the outer command level causes the system to respond:

```
HOST FILE? (press RETURN)
```

Pressing RETURN in response to the question, HOST FILE?, causes the system to access the compiled code file (SYSTEM.WRK.CODE) placed on FORT2. The system continues:

```
LIB FILE *   (RETURN)
```

```
LIB FILE     (RETURN)
MAP FILE     (RETURN)
        —
        —
        —
        —
OUTPUT FILE? #5:MEAN1.CODE
```

When #5:MEAN1.CODE is typed in response to the question, OUTPUT FILE?, the linked code is placed on FORT1. It is mandatory that the suffix .CODE be attached to MEAN1, or the system does not recognize it as a linked code file but creates a data file. When the linking is complete, the system returns to the outer command level.

Execute a Linked Code File

Pressing X (for execute) causes the system to respond:

```
EXECUTE WHAT FILE? #5:MEAN1
```

Typing #5:MEAN1 in response to the question, EXECUTE WHAT FILE?, causes the system to access the linked code file and run it.

Transfer a Program to a Storage Disk

After the user is through using the program and is ready to store it, the filer is entered. FORT2 is removed from disk drive #1, and the storage disk is placed in disk drive #1.

Command T (for transfer) is pressed, and the text and linked code files on FORT1 must be transferred to a storage disk. The files are transferred in two operations:

```
TRANSFER? #5:MEAN1.TEXT
TO WHERE? #4:MEAN1.TEXT
```

After this transfer is completed, the system returns to the filer. Press T (for transfer).

```
TRANSFER? #5:MEAN1.CODE
TO WHERE? #4:MEAN1.CODE
```

When these two transfers are successfully made, the files are saved on the storage disk in disk drive #1. The system returns to the filer level. If other programs are to be written or used, the storage disk is removed from disk drive #1, and FORT2 is placed in disk drive #1.

USING A THREE-DISK (OR MORE) DRIVE SYSTEM

FORTRAN using a three-disk (or more) drive system is a real pleasure to use. FORT2 is placed in disk drive #1, FORT1 is placed in disk drive #2, and the storage disk is placed in the third disk drive.

If a large program of over 100 lines and using more than 15 blocks is to be written, the text file can be placed directly on the storage disk. The compiled code file can be placed on FORT2 as the SYSTEM.WRK.CODE, and the linked code file can go directly back to the storage disk.

If a small program is written, it can be placed on FORT2 as the SYSTEM.WRK.TEXT. When it is run, the program is compiled, linked, and run. The SYSTEM.WRK.TEXT and SYSTEM.WRK.CODE can be saved directly to the storage disk.

A three-disk (or more) system allows the user to get a text file from a storage disk. Command G (for get), under filer, loads the text file (and, if available, the code file) into memory. The text file is compiled. If the text file has a compile error, pressing E (for editor) causes the text file to be read back into the editor automatically.

After the text file has been edited, it must be written back to the storage disk. After CONTROL C is pressed from edit, Q (for quit) is pressed. The system responds with four options:

```
>QUIT:
   U(PDATE THE WORKFILE AND LEAVE
   E(XIT WITHOUT UPDATING
   R(ETURN TO THE EDITOR WITHOUT UPDATING
   W(RITE TO A FILE NAME AND RETURN
```

In this case, the option selected is W, WRITE TO A FILE NAME AND RETURN. Command W (for write) causes the system to respond:

```
>QUIT:
NAME OF OUTPUT FILE (<CR> TO RETURN-->
```

The cursor is accessed by pressing CONTROL A, to shift the screen to the 40–80 character view.

```
>#9:MEAN1 (press RETURN)
```

This causes MEAN1.TEXT to be written to the disk in disk drive #9. After MEAN1 is written to the storage disk, the system asks the user to make one of two selections:

```
>QUIT:
WRITING . . .
YOUR FILE IS XXXX BYTES LONG.
DO YOU WISH TO E(XIT OR R(ETURN TO THE EDITOR?
```

Command E (for exit) causes the operating system to return to the outer command level.

After #9:MEAN1.TEXT has been written to the storage disk, pressing R (for return) causes the system to write #9:MEAN1.TEXT back into the editor scratchpad. This is a very convenient feature when writing a long program. The text file can be updated without having to go through several command levels to get the program back into the editor.

With minimal change, the outlines in Figs. 14-1 and 14-2 can be used to write short and long programs using a three-disk (or more) system. One of the differences is that programs can be transferred directly from the storage disk, and transferred or saved to the storage disk.

Index

G

H

I

K

L

M

TO THE READER

Sams Computer books cover Fundamentals — Programming — Interfacing — Technology written to meet the needs of computer engineers, professionals, scientists, technicians, students, educators, business owners, personal computerists and home hobbyists.

Our Tradition is to meet your needs and in so doing we invite you to tell us what your needs and interests are by completing the following:

1. I need books on the following topics:

____

____

____

____

____

____

2. I have the following Sams titles:

____

____

____

____

____

____

3. My occupation is:

______ Scientist, Engineer

______ Personal computerist

______ Technician, Serviceman

______ Educator

______ Student

______ D P Professional

______ Business owner

______ Computer store owner

______ Home hobbyist

Other ______________________

____

Name (print) ______________________________________

Address ______________________________________

City ______________________ State ______________ Zip ______________

Mail to: **Howard W. Sams & Co., Inc.**
Marketing Dept. #CBS1/80
4300 W. 62nd St., P.O. Box 7092
Indianapolis, Indiana 46206

21911